This book is the result of a project I began writing in 2003, when my fledgling magazine Don Diva, my first ever, legitimate endeavor, was still gaining ground. After many years of tweaking and tinkering it is finally ready to be received. I trust you will all be informed as well as entertained.

–Cavario H. AKA "BoPp The Hustler"

Written By Cavario H.

Edited By Cavario H. & Zada Atun

Production Assistance from Kevin "KT" Thomas

Consulting By Mr. Richard Jole of PMG

This book is dedicated to my mother, Vivian, without whom I would be nothing, and to my children and theirs through whom I have everything. Shout out to my little brother J. "Monsta" Holder. Come home soon!

"The twin towers of struggle and failure are laziness and ignorance." —Bopp

Cavario H.

Body of Power publishing PRESENTS:

Old Gangsters & Young Guns-The True Tales of Two Worlds

Introduction

From as early as the 1930s the Fedora has been a trademark worn in every city by gangsters of all backgrounds and distinctions. Whether worn low over the eyes, casting a shadow over the mirrors into their motives, or cocked "ace-deuce" (to one side) leaving one eye spying from beneath a razor-edged brim, the Fedora G's power was understated but certain. To this day, one can still see some Old Gangsters or "OGs," now almost undetectable, having turned their negatives into positives, as they move quietly but distinguished, through society's backdrop…their Fedoras worn just so.

The Young Guns often called "YGs" of today are a great deal less illustrious and care nothing about discretion, and their undaunted flash and brutal approach to the paper chase is often violent and unrelenting. As a result of such practices few YGs ever see OG status. The average life expectancy of today's self-proclaimed "gangstas" is twenty years -give or take a few. During that very short existence they attempt to squeeze in a lifetime of excess and no rest, believing that they will inevitably meet an early demise or trade their government names for government numbers, and therefore caution has no point or purpose in their narrow minds.

A gangster is considered "old" at a relatively young age, the reason being that our lives are measured by a scale similar to that of 'man's best friend'. If, as was my case, an individual embarks upon his career just as he enters his teenage years, and he manages to remain continuously and progressively ensconced in that existence, by the time he's 25 he is regarded as *old*, after all, 12 X 7 is 84.

Although a well experienced 'G', who has managed to survive a dozen years within the moral paradox that is gangsterism, may have existed in the world for a mere quarter of a century, his time in the underworld where time is expedited exponentially, will, if he pays close attention, afford him the knowledge, wisdom and overstanding of the worst of human nature. This, by the way, is what gives us our distinct glare; we know what lurks in the hearts of men. But the true trick is not simply coming out of it alive, healthy and free, but coming out of it at all.

Coming out of it or not, those of us who have lived to hear mainstream folk utilizing the expression "O.G." (which by my qualified account, initially pertained only to the Original Gangsters of the late 1800s on up to approximately the mid 1900s) in their common vernacular, accept that the majority of them do not know what its real meaning is. Nonetheless, we recognize that the reverence attached to the tag is kin to its origins. In other words, it's close enough to be appreciated by those very few of Us to whom it applies. To Us, however its contemporary application is perceived almost automatically. We know we are not *original gangsters*–we accept that. But regardless of how youthful we may appear, we are by virtue of our being, Old Gangsters.

Balancing the burden…

Each time an issue of Don Diva would hit the streets, an awkward silence often loomed throughout our offices. We worked tirelessly to grind out each issue, digging into the delicate past, checking facts against extraordinary claims and the ever expanding urban legend of ghetto celebs', and then, with almost bated breath, we awaited the reaction from the streets. Neither the subjects themselves nor people on the periphery could truly gauge the explosive potential that the resurfacing or revelation of this information might bring about.

Within the Don Diva hierarchy, we were left to wonder whether what was forthcoming would be something the streets would respect as the gospel on the particular situation or would they rebel against the righteous light of fact versus their fantasies. Sometimes in allowing the primaries in some of the broadest criminal conspiracies of the 80s and 90s to speak with their own voices, it was revealed that someone who may have been revered as a stand-up gangster, was, in light of the worse case scenario coming to full fruition, nothing more than an expensively dressed, high-profile punk.

In some cases the subjects of our stories may have wondered if they had done the right thing for the right reasons or had they placed their comrades–some of which who were still on the street, some even still in the struggle—in potential jeopardy, often leaving their people to ponder the same as they rushed to the newsstands to see what was said.

The calmest quiet came before what always had the potential to become a shit storm of rekindled beef, and a new string of violent retribution killings stemming from the impending reopening of old but far from forgotten wounds. The homies, relatives and even spouses of individuals betrayed or slain in the culmination of these urban epics sometimes are reminded of who did what to whom. In some cases the off-spring of one time comrades, turned mortal enemies, were living in the same neighborhood; as in the case of Pete "The Pistol" Rollack, leader of the notorious murder-for-hire gang, Sex, Money & Murder Incorporated and his former friend Yaro Pack whose adolescent sons once found themselves face to face while riding in the same elevator in the Soundview projects in the Bronx that their fathers grew up in.

Although there is merit in the subsequent education that results from sharing their stories, particularly for the youth, there is still a precarious balance between informing and inciting a new generation of street soldiers. This was Don Diva's charge, we wore it with honor and we executed it with care. WELCOME TO THE HOOD.

The accidental birth of a brand called Don Diva

The Don Diva brand was first introduced on the streets of Harlem, New York in the winter of 1999 and in just a few short years it spread across hood, city and state lines. Even the Atlantic Ocean wasn't a great enough barrier to impede its growth or deter its destiny to become the voice of the entire urban community the world over.

The creation of Don Diva itself was an accident, meaning it wasn't the deliberate intent of any of us to create a magazine. It started out as a nameless entertainment endeavor with film and music aspirations (as the first logo clearly indicated). The seed was planted when Tiffany Maughn, my by then ex-long-term-live-in girlfriend, began working for an older Jamaican gentleman named Tyrone whom she'd met through a lieutenant of his named Paul. Tiffany and Paul had gotten close and it was during this time she managed to convince Paul that she was the mastermind behind the then brand new label Ruff Ryders. She was operating under Darren Dean as, among other things, a road manager for the LOX. Having been impressed by Tiffany's apparent competence, Paul asked her if, after Darren was done with her, she'd be interested in helping him get his boss's independent record label in running order. Shortly afterwards she moved on and was introduced to the clandestine Tyrone, after which she cut Paul loose and shucked and jived her way into the boss's good graces.

Almost immediately she found herself running Tyrone's Harp Promotions out of a comfortable but modest office on North Avenue in New Rochelle. The rap faction, Git Down Records, seemed to be run more like a sideline than a main business and as it turned out, it was. According to the Federal Government, Tyrone's main interest and source of income was large-scale marijuana importation and distribution.

Prior to Tyrone's arrest Tiffany had become a Den mother of sorts to the various acts he had signed to his label—Martin actress Tischa Campbell's younger brother was one of those acts. Tiffany often complained about how undisciplined and irresponsible the artists were and although she didn't particularly believe that any of them were going anywhere in terms of industry success, she did see there was a need for management. She began to plot her next move, as it was her nature to do.

When she started considering names for her new company, which she intended to operate as an extension of Harp, she wanted to create a name that would stand out. When she called me from the North Avenue office I suggested that she adapt the nickname that had been given to her by the Ruff Ryders, "How about Tiflon?" I suggested. "Nah, I want something less personal," she said. The Tiflon Don was the entire moniker so I continued to pull from that, "What about The Don?" I said next. As we were having this conversation over the phone's speaker box, in walks a sexy young African girl who was signed to Tyrone's label, her stage name was Bonnie-Clyde and she interjected, "What about the divas you gotta include the ladies." I responded to Bonnie's suggestion, "Okay, what about using both, Don and Diva?" Tiffany seemed to like the idea. So with the name of her new company established, Don Diva Entertainment, she now had to come up with a way to introduce it to the world.

Meanwhile, I contacted a young man named Wayne who lived in Washington, D.C. and worked for B.E.T. in the graphics department for their news division. Wayne had been sidelining as a graphic artist and was already assisting in getting my S.O.B.E.R. clothing brand developed.

When I got well into my autobiographical manuscript (Raised By Wolves: Inside the Life & Mind of A Guerrilla Hustler) I hired Wayne to help me create the first draft of my cover. Wayne was the only graphic artist that I knew so when Tiffany told me that we needed a logo I immediately called him. Tiffany and I talked about what Don Diva Entertainment would do and what services it would provide– which were artist management and development as well as music and film production. I mentioned these details to Wayne and he sent me back an image that included these elements: the 'D' in Don was half of a CD while the 'D' in Diva was half of a film reel. The word "entertainment" was placed going upward along the bottom of the film reel. Finally there was a strip of film that flowed from the bottom of the second 'D' and the very first logo for Don Diva Entertainment was born. The thought of a magazine had still not formed.

Tiffany called me late one evening when it was time to promote the existence of Don Diva Entertainment. She said that her boyfriend Kevin, who was then a little more than halfway through a ten-year prison sentence, had suggested that we create something a little more outstanding than mere fliers. The two had a little known 'history' prior to his incarceration and through her visiting another old fling who was being held at the same federal farm as Kevin, the two became reacquainted. "KC says that we should create an album and make it look like a magazine," she stated. I agreed it was a good idea as well. What I was unaware of at the time was that Tiffany was using funds essentially siphoned off from monies allocated to her by Tyrone to run *his* business.

Tiffany continued, "He [Kevin] said I should reach out to Jewels to help me get some pictures to put in it so people will be interested." Jewels was known by some to be Kevin's younger cousin, but in actuality he was the younger brother of former cohorts of Kevin's and he and Kevin had scarcely (if ever) met because (as Kevin explained to me) he was but a boy when Kevin was initially incarcerated.

Jewels reached out to the exclusive photographer to the gangsters and hustlers of Harlem, (my family and me among them) the Haitian born Alix "Alley Cat" Dejean. For thirty years Alix has shot everyone from a young Stevie Wonder and Diana Ross to infamous narcotic traffickers like Frank Lucas and Nicky Barnes. It was Barnes in fact that hired Alley Cat as the single photographer to shoot his secreted and exclusive "(Drug) Council" events.

Alix reluctantly agreed to provide the images for the promotional album which included never before seen shots of Harlem notables such as Wayne "Dick" Davis, and the murderous "Black Hand" leader Clarence "Preacher" Heatley, as well as a young Sean "Puffy" Combs and his "Same Gang" cronies, and not to mention the scores of young men and women whose names never made it out of their Harlem neighborhoods due to their premature deaths or indefinite incarcerations.

When the product was finally put together, the result was five hundred shoddy magazine'esque photo albums consisting of several washed looking black and white pictures of people, places and events from Harlem's crack renaissance era circa 1984 to 1994. I later learned that Kevin suggested the idea of the album to Tiffany as a way of recouping some of her boss's money, which he was noticing the absence of.

Tiffany hit me on my Motorola Two-Way, early one morning, texting excitedly, "Call me!"

"Where are you? They're here! You gotta see 'em, they look crazy!" I clumsily read the message and then called. "I'm at Gwen's," I croaked out.

"Okay, I'm gonna have somebody bring you a coupl'a boxes. We gotta move these things, I spent a lot'a money! Whoo!" she finished.

"A'ight, I'm here." I murmured before my hand found the receiver.

I went from barbershop to beauty salon, from Amsterdam to Lenox Avenue, from 155th Street to across 110th and I introduced all patrons present to Don Diva Entertainment, selling at least three copies in each establishment after talking it up and showing the pictures, which in most instances at least two patrons recognized someone in. The shop owners or one of the more popular barbers or stylist took notice of the response I got and I was then able to arrange having them take ten copies on consignment at an 80/20 split (I began to do what I knew).

I went to every block and corner in every neighborhood I knew, which left few Harlem hoods untouched. By the end of the second day I had run through nearly one hundred copies of Don Diva Entertainment's promotional photo album, which was titled, "Reflections." I re'd up and began hitting all the clubs that Uptowners frequented and managed to get people to buy a slip-shod product that they'd never heard of for $20.00 a pop. I knew then that we were onto something.

The real confirmation for me came when I was standing in a local corner store on 145th Street on the downtown corner of 8th Avenue when a long time friend of mine who we call 40 walked up to me and said, "When y'all gon' do another issue?"

I responded quizzically, "An issue of what?"

To which he responded, "That Don Diva magazine." It was the very first time I'd heard those three words together but it was as though they'd been around forever.

I responded to 40's question, "Oh... yeah... we gon' drop another one next month." Then I called Tiffany and told her what was happening on the street.

"They think it's a magazine! They askin' me when we gon' do another one!" I exclaimed.

"They sayin' the same shit to Kev' [in jail]!"

Susan Hampstead (Tiffany's assistant/friend who wrote a great deal of the first few issues) explained how when she and Tiffany returned from Florida attending the How Can I Be Down convention that, "The office answering machine was full of messages, people were asking where they could get a subscription to the magazine, Tiffany was upset. She felt that the promo project had failed." That was October of 1999.

Prior to his arrest, Tyrone was not as enthused about the idea of the magazine since he'd become apprised of its proposed direction and its content. "What's the purpose of this magazine? What does it have to do with music?" He'd asked and then he'd grumble, "The government's gwon come ofter me if you do this t'ing, Tiff'." He may have been feeling heat from his other activities by then and therefore felt it better not to antagonize the authorities.

A short time after we released the first official magazine Tyrone was picked up by Immigration and Naturalization who were backed by DEA and FBI agents. In addition to not being a naturalized citizen of the United States and thus an illegal immigrant, he was charged with being the Kingpin of a nationwide marijuana conspiracy.

These events helped to accelerate the production of the magazine because without Tyrone around to dole out the cash needed to support his artists (he was extremely beneficent) another way to maintain had to be established quickly. Tiffany hadn't completely given up on the idea of managing the careers of the artists but as she would often state during that time, "It'd easier to manage a magazine than it would these crazy muthafuckas he got signed, they think he they father!" It was then that she decided that in Tyrone's absence, the length of which was indeterminable at that point, she would use his money to get the equipment and maintain the office to run Don Diva Magazine. Little by little she alienated the artists who then funneled their complaints to Tyrone but what could he do she had his money and her freedom, plus she likely was the most competent person he had around him in the legitimate capacity. Tyrone relented and Don Diva Magazine was up and jogging.

I hit the streets, Tiffany manned the office assisted by Susan, and Kevin represented the brand from the inside, assuring those around him that Don Diva Magazine, unlike other urban magazines in the market at that time, represented only the honorable players. By sheer virtue of his involvement Kevin was able to establish that Don Diva Magazine was not about the exploitation of the fallen soldiers of the war against poverty, but that we were real people who overstood the plight and even too, (in my case) had played the game with honor and respect. We vowed to never give a Snitch a voice in Don Diva and with that we were accepted and that is the fantasy-free truth about the accidental birth of Don Diva Magazine. Time tells all things.

Table of Contents

Preface

First widely publicized in 1970s Blaxploitation films, accounts of the extravagant lifestyles and deadly impact of Black and Hispanic gangsters have been chronicled time and again on screen, on records as well as in the press. Often the accounts are given by authors or journalists who have neither close ties to the street community nor a genuine interest in enlightening the populace as to the causes of the extreme conditions and ensuing choices of street people, thereby facilitating an understanding of our particular struggles.

For the most part it seems they (authors or journalists) just take advantage of an opportunity to exploit the desperate behavior and destruction of a nation of people, for their own gain–but such is the way of the world. Most books dealing with street-life, excluding the small minority that have been autobiographical, have been poured out from the perspective of the DEA, ATF, FBI or other law enforcement agencies and filtered through the minds of mainstream media–which comes down to little more than a mass theatrical production.

Few books on the subject of Blacks' and Latinos' roles within America's drug and organized crime culture have been from the actual person's lips to the mind's ear of the reader. This, finally, is that book.

This unique perspective was created by the real life experiences of the executive staff at Don Diva magazine, we brought it all together to shed new light on devastating stories that so many across our nation have seen in the headlines of their local newspapers or heard rumored on the streets of their cities. Having survived the game; coming out with my life, my health and freedom, afforded me the qualifications necessary to respectfully and responsibly unveil this collection of pain and destruction, and to share the often obscured but nonetheless valuable lessons to be learned. These lessons are frequently desperate and usually devastating, stemming from choices made by gifted individuals spawned by the "ghetto," under circumstances that are perpetuated largely through political policy in America. These are our trials and tribulations–walk with us, share our pain and hopefully grow in your understanding.

The Dope "Game," as it is commonly referred to is anything but a game. Actual games eventually yield winners; the game of dealing drugs has only losers–some more delayed than others. So play if you believe that you must but if you do not correlate your knowledge of managing wealth with your acquisition of it then you've resolved to lose it.

–Cavario "The Consigliere"

While developing our 3rd issue of Don Diva we chose to focus on the children, particularly those adolescents involved with dealing narcotics before they were old enough to attend an R-rated movie un-chaperoned.

The two stories that follow were the main features in that issue.

This first story is all but common, coming out of the urban coil of America's big cities. It was the summer of 1987; Georgie was on Webster Avenue sitting on the roof of his black Lamborghini Countach, casually twirling his car keys while staring into the red faces of frustrated federal agents who were known to follow him about the city... whenever they could keep up.

George Rivera aka "Boy George": THE PUERTO-RICAN JAMES BOND

Boy George and Son 1988

At the end of the 80s while America concerned itself with the crack epidemic, George Rivera was running one of the most lucrative and aggressive heroin organizations in the Bronx. Having begun his career as a preteen, George rose to the pinnacle of his power at the young age of 21, earning himself the nickname "Boy George." Government sources say Boy George was employing over 50 people and grossing a quarter of a million dollars a week.

1

According to these sources, Boy George bought heroin wholesale from a Chinese supplier, referred to privately as "Fried Rice," and passed it along to his lieutenant "Six-O," a Jamaican hustler. Six-O was George's first lieutenant and later on became the prosecution's primary cooperating witness when the Obsession operation fell. Six-O passed the heroin off to the girlfriends and friends of their associates who acted as $10-an-hour workers, cutting the heroin in drug "mills" that were set up in South Bronx walk-ups and project apartments as well as some Manhattan and New Jersey hotels. Cutting the heroin consisted of adding quinine, which provided a "rush" sensation and another substance called lactose, an innocuous ingredient found in milk, it has no narcotic characteristics–as its sole purpose is to double and most often triple the weight of the heroin packaged for retail. The processed heroin was then spooned into thousands of glassine (semi-transparent, waxy finished) bags that were pre-stamped with Boy George's brand name "Obsession" and his logo, a red crown. The bags were packaged into bundles containing ten bags each, each bag priced at $10. The bundles were given to street level dealers for sale at George's spots: 22nd Street on 2nd Avenue, the block long building on 139th Street and Brook Avenue, 153rd - 156th Streets along Cortlandt Avenue, 651 Southern Boulevard, and 166th Street on Washington Avenue.

Obsession was an organizational pyramid with several levels of authority; spot managers generally made 10-20% of the profit and were responsible for paying the pitchers, who represented the base of the structure. Pitchers handled the hand-to-hand transactions with customers and were expected to combat with the cops and robbers. Steerers (usually used at the beginning stages of building a "spot") were responsible for bringing in new customers and directing customer traffic to pitchers. Their commission or "tops" (meaning "off-of-the-top" once the sale was made) was typically $1.00 a bag and that responsibility also fell on the pitcher. Lookouts were probably the least compensated although they were the first line of defense between the pitchers and the police. The reason for this is probably due to the fact that a lookout need not be especially smart or tough; they need only have at least one good eye and a loud mouth and were therefore easily replaced. Lookouts were typically paid $50-$100 a day. Lieutenants represent a rung much higher up than all the others previously mentioned, they made $2,500 per week and the top-lieutenant of the Obsession crew, Six-O, made $12,000 a week. Boy George, Obsession's capstone, made $45,000 a week.

2

George Rivera, barely out of his teens, built an organization so lucrative that he registered a fleet of Mercedes Benzes, BMWs and customized Porsches to one of his corporate fronts, Tuxedo Enterprises. George customized one of his favorite cars with a $12,000 Ostrich-skin interior, 630-watt stereo, 10-track CD player, multiple televisions, a VCR, and cell phones. Keep in mind we're talking about the mid-eighties. Several of his cars were something straight out of a James Bond movie. Some had rear license plates that slid into compartments to expose blinding "ZAP" lights, a feature used to throw off would be "trailers," be they cops or robbers. All of his cars had hidden safes, which George used to conceal money, guns and drugs. One Mercedes 190E released oil from its tail, another spat out large razor-like tacks to burst the tires of pursuers and enable the driver to escape in a car chase.

In 1989 Boy George bought real estate in Puerto Rico, and with the help of a financial consultant, began preparing to open a fast-food mall with a McDonald's, Church's Fried Chicken, and Pizza Hut inside. He also started to renovate and convert the Puerto Rican Estate that he purchased for $140,000 in cash into a permanent home. George had "Obsession" inscribed in tile on the bottom of his Mediterranean-blue swimming pool.

Boy George who has been described as charismatic and hardhearted, was extremely generous to his crew. He kept loyalty and admiration strong among his people with cash bonuses, gifts, and paid vacations. Lieutenants and managers received 18k gold belt buckles with their names encrusted in diamonds. Top dealers received red and white leather baseball jackets with "CCCP" written on the back. On Christmas Eve, 1988 Boy George rented the Riveranda at World Yacht's 23rd St. dock. He and about 150 others in black tie attire set out to party while cruising around the New York Harbor. George paid $30,000 in cash to rent the Riveranda, which included dinner for 120 and a disc jockey. Boy George spent $12,000 in small bills to have Big Daddy Kane perform for 15 minutes. The menu included steak tartar, skewered lamb, prime rib, and $12,000 in champagne alone. There were raffles- a fully loaded Mitsubishi was the grand prize, $20,000 cash was the first prize, a Rolex watch was second prize, a week in Hawaii was third prize and a trip to Disney was fourth prize. George gave one of his lieutenants a BMW 750, with gold and diamond "Obsession" belt buckles going to his top four men, each appraised at over $8,000.00. Six-O received a gold Rolex and $50,000 in cash.

Unbeknownst to George and his guests, there were three off-duty New York City detectives aboard as part of the yacht security. However when it came time to talk to the DEA, these detectives were uncooperative and during George's trial they remained steadfast in their refusal to testify to what they had witnessed.

Despite those officers lack of cooperation, in April of 1988, the government had enough information from a confidential informant, to seek a court order to set up a monitoring device known as a PEN Register. The PEN, an early form of caller ID, was attached to telephones widely used by members of the Obsession organization. When the devices were removed over 40% of the calls were to beeper numbers, a large number of these to the government's CI (confidential informant). The government then went before a federal judge to request a wiretap to be placed on the telephones of Boy George's network. On April 4, 1989 the wiretaps were in place and Spanish translators and agents were busy listening to the dealers transact business. Within a month the federal agents realized that their wiretaps were being circumvented by the use of beepers, pay phones and cellular phones.

The next step in the government's plan to bring down the "Spanish Prince" was a rash of raids. One raid resulted in 13 arrests, seven pounds of heroin, seven guns, $60,000 in cash and a set of the famed gold and diamond Obsession belt buckles. A photo album was also seized that displayed pictures of the 1988 Christmas Eve boat ride. All would pay dearly for posing for those pictures. These pictures led the government to subpoena the World Yacht Club's books. The yacht crew kept meticulous records. The government now had evidence of all the cash that was spent, documents of the drug use on board and all the luxurious gifts and prizes that were given away that night. In an attempt to show the lavish lifestyles of the co-defendants, the same Christmas Eve photos were enlarged and pinned up on the courtroom bulletin boards for the Judge and jury to see during George and his co-defendants trials. In the second phase of the government raids, George and his top lieutenants were dragged in. From the mouths of George's lieutenants' came the first hint that cooperation was going to follow. These top lieutenants gave the government the last pieces of evidence they needed to prove the conspiracy charges they were alleging. By June 1989, the government was planning their last set of raids. The Feds needed to get every available shred of evidence and every possible cooperating witness. Agents began to raid the homes of the lower level workers in the organization. They knew that the top dealers viewed the lower level, ten-dollar an hour, mill-workers as expendable. The government knew that they wouldn't be receiving warning calls from any bosses that may have escaped the earlier round of raids. More than forty people were arrested in the Boy George case. Almost all waived their right for trial and pleaded guilty to a variety of minor narcotics charges. In September 1990 Boy George and several of his top co-conspirators opted to stand trial in federal court. Boy George was charged with 14 counts, among them were conspiring to run a continuing criminal enterprise (the Kingpin charge), drug possession and distribution and ownership of multiple firearms. George and his co-defendants got to witness several of their crewmembers reveal themselves as government witnesses. One of the most incriminating pieces of evidence was a conversation in which the government taped George and one of his lieutenants using pig Latin in an attempt to covertly communicate their intentions of opening crack dealing locations. The informants' testimony and the evidence gathered by the government were enough to convince a jury of their guilt. George was only found guilty of 2 of the 14 charges: attempted tax evasion and conspiracy to distribute heroin. Although the prosecution didn't get the victory they had strived for, George would still pay heavily. On Wednesday, April 23, 1991, George Rivera, at the age of 23, was sentenced to life in federal prison without the possibility of parole.

The information you have just read was compiled from mainstream mediums. When Don Diva talked to Boy George, he made it clear that there were many untruths in the information that was printed in the media. Since there are two sides to every story, we now introduce you to Boy George and afford you the opportunity to read his story, in his own words.

My full name is George Rivera. I was born on January 10, 1968. I was arrested on May 1, 1989 after the DEA concluded a 2½-year investigation. I was charged with various counts consisting of both drugs and weapons charges along with a $5 million tax evasion charge. I was the youngest criminal co-defendant ever to have a federal 848(a) and 848(b) charge (Kingpin charge).

My case originally started with the number of codefendants ranging from 32 to 125, Puerto Ricans and African Americans. I also have some Asian codefendants that are alleged members of the "Flying Dragons" from New York. Since the number of codefendants was so great, the case was broken down with a main case against the lieutenants and managers and high-seated members. The other trials were for mill workers and alleged hit men.

My trial lasted three months; it started in August and ended in November. The jury deliberated for two weeks on me before they finally convicted me on two of the 36 counts: conspiracy to distribute 100 kilos of heroin and tax evasion for $5,000,000. On February 27, 1991 I was sentenced to natural life without parole. My main informant was an individual named Joey Novado a.k.a. Joey White. He introduced me to an undercover cop who Joey called Compai (a family member). I did two sales to this undercover, which I beat thanks to Les Wolf, my investigator. Joey White took his story to the grand jury and with that came the beginning of the end. But Joey White's a witness to the saying that God don't like ugly. He was found in someone's trunk in an airport parking lot. No one was charged but I assume theories passed through the minds of the Feds.

Aside from Joey White, the Feds used an under-boss of mine named Ward Johnson, a delivery boy named Luis Gautier and his sidekick Ralph Hernandez. These individuals who played the role of die-hard gangsters, met with the Feds, the 'real gangsters' and turned out to be true pranksters... 'females' in disguise.

I am not alone when I make this statement: consider the 'Federalēs' the true gangsters for many reasons consistent with the authority and manipulations they're mastered in: 1. The apprehension of felons and 2. The manner in which they take the so-called rock hard hustlers or shot callers and convert them into a heap of clay for their designing.

True there exists an elite group of men who did their thing and laughed in the face of adversity (the Feds) but they are few and far between. And to those men and women I say it is a great honor to know that despite our dying numbers, we are still a force that needs to be dealt with, with respect and admiration for we have lived lives others failed to visualize.

I grew up in the Bronx; I lived in many areas within the Bronx. At one time I was in a group home in New Rochelle. There I learned to fend for myself. I lived with Five Percenters (a group that operates largely under Islamic doctrine) and learned their various aspects of living and beliefs.

Did I floss a lot? Yeah, I did. While I was in high school in the tenth grade I was driving to school in a Mercedes Benz of that year. I guess my ambitions got the best of me at the early age of seventeen. To believe that I was already in the seven digit bracket at that young age would be unbelievable but when you have an imagination and ambition that knows no limits, why go half ass when you can go full steam ahead.

Why did I become hot? Well how many black Bentley Turbos or Lamborghinis did you see in the South Bronx? The heat, I brought to myself—just as my ambitions got the best of me, so did my ignorance. When I'd get stopped by the police, and that's if I wanted to stop, I'd present legitimate information showing the vehicle as one owned by a corporation and I was a representative of the said corporation. The prosecutors went to every car dealer I ever dealt with or real estate agent I dealt with both here in the US and overseas to prove I wasn't a representative of any company other than the illegal one I allegedly ran.

During the course of my trial the jurors were shown sales receipts, which amounted in the excess of one million dollars just in vehicles, a mall in development overseas, and countless pieces of jewelry. Now try to figure how one could win a trial alleging a drug conspiracy when your assets are worth more than a few neighborhoods in New York and you're only 21 years old.

George Rivera 2000
USP Beaumont

This experience is not one that I'd say caused me any regret. But I am sorry for the pain I've caused my family because I am still living although I am in prison. My mother, especially, is doing this with me, day for day and it's killing her slowly. Just recently my partner Ice lost his mother and I was fucked up 'cause he was so close to her. My mom is everything to me. Despite my sentence and the trials and tribulations I've encountered I have no regrets. Not one!

To the youngsters and the old heads doing their thing, I am sure you've heard the saying, "You learn from your mistakes." Well those words weren't spoken in vain, but it is much better to learn from the mistakes of others because their mistakes are free to you. I'm not gonna attempt to portray myself as some saint coming to preach against hustling. Nah, get yours man, but use your head and study your moves like a chess master. And it may sound funny but take a day out of your week and watch the following movies: Godfather I, II, III, Scarface, Bone Collector and Seven. I've been in prison for eleven years, so I am sure there are other good movies, but don't watch these movies for the same reason we all saw them when they came out. These movies and others like them are learning tools. They can teach you obvious steps, which are rarely taken, thus always overlooked. Study other's mistakes, study investigative procedures and always scrutinize everyone. No one should be above suspicion... no one!

8

I'd never say or agree to the statement one old head made that the game is dead! To the contrary I believe that computers, real estate and drugs are the biggest generators of money in this country so how could the game be dead? The press called me the, "Puerto Rican James Bond" because of the gadgets in my cars. I'd have oil slicks, changing license plates, steel tacks, zapping lights and other toys, which I would use to get away from a scene or police. I was on foot when I was arrested. If I could have gotten to my car, they'd still be chasing me.

P.S.

I'd like to send my love and respect to the following comrades: Walter "Ice" Cook, Anthony Cruz, Danny Delgado, Juan "Cann" Diaz, Manny Concepcion, Tommy "Tony Montana" Mickens, The Supreme Team, Group 27, and Rich Porter—may you Rest in Peace along with your little brother. Big Pun—Rest in Peace, Snail, Lil Will and John Gotti and Fat Joe for putting me in his record "Sique Para Lante Boriqua"!

Interview conducted by Tiffany Chiles
Edited by Cavario H.

Don Diva's Susan Hampstead, out of New Jersey, researched this story and ended up not only with an incredible piece but also a relationship with one of the subjects who resides in a maximum security prison. A lot of letters and phone calls–not to mention a hell of a plane ride–went into this chapter but the finished product is undeniable.

In 2000 Susan went into the streets of Elizabeth, New Jersey, commonly referred to as "Eastwick," to hand distribute copies of Don Diva's Issue #2, which featured Akbar Pray. Susan was approached by several people, working class and street dwellers alike, who inquired when they could expect to read about the "E'port Posse," headed by Bilal Pretlow. "The one that caught the first federal death penalty case for drugs in New Jersey," "The one that isn't really dead," "The one who was murdered by the correction officers in the Union County Jail," or "The one whose death was staged to look like a suicide." These were just a few of the intriguing comments Susan heard about the young man who had reached icon status before he was twenty-one.

Susan immediately delved into this controversial story, which would prove to be more challenging than she had ever expected.

Although the streets wanted this story, no one was willing to give their assistance. Some were too afraid to speak on the subject without permission or feared being labeled an informant. Apparently, E'port Posse's reputation for dealing with those kinds of individuals preceded itself. In the mid 80s, they played a major part in raising the crime rate by terrorizing the town at large; this ominous air was still taking a toll on the streets more than a decade later.

Susan was warned that her persistent inquiries and constant snooping could put her in jeopardy of losing her life and that this was already true for one young lady who "snooped around where she didn't belong."

When it was all said and done, major breakthroughs were made, and Susan ended up with an incredible piece, and a genuine relationship with the surviving key members of this organization. Through this article, Susan provided the reader exclusive insight into the rise and fall of Bilal Pretlow and the E'Port Posse, as told to her by three individuals who played major roles both in the E'Port Posse's organization and in Bilal's life; his chief lieutenant and under-boss, Shawn Hartwell, another lieutenant, and first cousin, Vincent Jackson, and the enforcer of the organization, Corey Grant.

"After uncovering the chain of events surrounding this tragic tale, my career, and even more so my life, were forever changed." –Susan Hampstead.

E'PORT POSSE: "TEENAGE TERRORS"

Bilal Pretlow
age 15

Wakil at 18

Since the early 1960s the Pretlow/Graham family was known to cause havoc in Elizabeth as well as surrounding New Jersey communities. This family that carries two last names was known to be large in both number and physique. The relatives that bare an intimidating signature wide-bodied frame are infamously noted for their involvement in numerous beat downs and shootouts. It was an established fact that they were not to be trifled with, but in the '80s when this clan's third generation took advantage of their familial reputation and hit the drug scene, it was then assured that their brood would forever become a part of criminal history.

At the ages of 12 and 15, Bilal "EZ" Pretlow and Robert "Wakil" Pretlow were two of five siblings that were abandoned by their mother Catherine Jackson, who at the time was struggling with drug addiction. The children, originally from Newark, New Jersey were split up, sent to different foster homes and shifted around regularly. At the ages of 15 and 18 Bilal and Wakil, along with their older brother Thomas "Shamar" Pretlow, went to live with their grandmother Elenora "Sister" Graham in a subsidized apartment complex in Elizabeth, New Jersey.

While living with Sister, the three brothers got into several violent altercations at school, parties and throughout the projects as any member of their ill-famed family were expected to. After establishing their dominance largely through intimidation, Bilal and Wakil started a drug trafficking network in Elizabeth, Newark, Linden and Rahway, New

11

Jersey. The youths' enterprise was purported to be responsible for at least five attempted murders and seven execution style murders.

Named the E'Port Posse because the majority of its members resided in the Elizabeth Port section of Elizabeth, New Jersey, the brothers' organization consisted of two drug distribution teams. The group was eventually divided into two groups under the name E'Port Posse/ Faze II, with Bilal Pretlow as the leader.

Some of the original Faze II members that had been under the direction of Bilal Pretlow were Shawn Hartwell, Vincent "Vinnie" Jackson, Andre "Ondi" Williams, Robert "Raboo" Figuoroa, Irving "Irvin/Amir" Bethea, Wendell and Karnell Wilson, Quadir Lee, Duquan "Duke" Lee, Kip Kornegay, Jermaine "XL" Hartwell, Jamil "Oob" Hartwell, Jeffrey "Huck-a-Buck" Calone, Black Johnny, Reesie McNair, James Washington, Glenn "Stack Money" Jones, along with others such as Hussamiddi "Hussam" Williams, Onay Kinman, Calvin and Jamil "Lover J" Dean.

The E'Port Posse under the direction of Wakil Pretlow consisted of Antonio "Malik" Jones, Keith Cashwell, Mutah Sessoms, Keith Griggs, Corey Grant, June Moore, Cashous Pough, and Jamil "Lover J" Jordan.

Shawn Hartwell

Shawn Hartwell, then 15 years of age and impressionable, looked up to Bilal, and Shawn was considered his chief lieutenant. Bilal knew that he would always have Shawn's loyalty and in return, he took him on as his protégé and was hardly ever seen without him. Their genuine bond and the love that the two had for one another was similar to that of a

12

father and son. At some point the streets started referring to the two as the "King" and his "Prince."

Vincent Jackson, the Pretlow brothers' first cousin also became one of Bilal's lieutenants. He too was raised in one of the roughest areas of Newark, New Jersey, only to later migrate to Elizabeth and join forces with his other family members, thus making the E'Port Posse even stronger in notorious number. More like a brother than a cousin, Vincent shared the "Black Sheep of the family" title along with Bilal and Wakil causing them to bond just as their mothers Catherine and Brenda Jackson had done as they struggled together in the city of Newark years earlier.

Corey Grant was inducted into the organization at the rebellious age of 12. He befriended the brothers when they all lived in Newark and was yet another member who strayed off into the street life because there was no direction or parental supervision at home. Corey was eventually considered by the authorities to be the enforcer for this Afro-lineal organization known as the E'Port Posse.

Although they were thought to be a gang of ruthless individuals who defied all rules, there were still rules to the game, which they observed. As a condition of participation, the members were told not to indulge in any type of narcotics. Even though the majority of the participants were bonded in that they were all from the inner city and they were all products of broken homes, they vowed the rules would not be. These rules were erected and strictly enforced to keep the "family" on point.

Wakil was a college student at Drew University in Madison, New Jersey and stressed education to the members of the organization. Both Shawn and Vincent were told and encouraged to stay in school on numerous occasions and Bilal would often ask to see their homework. One day when they were found cutting school, Wakil took the teenagers' gold jewelry and cars away from them, causing them to maintain nearly perfect attendance thereafter.

Both the E'Port Posse and Faze II worked equally hard to build what became a multimillion dollar empire, bringing in hundreds of thousands of dollars a week, sometimes literally spending days in the street out of love and loyalty for the organization.

The group's illegal activities are estimated to have grossed between 3.5 and 5 million dollars during their reign.

13

With their sudden burst of wealth, Bilal in particular became very generous with his money. Of course, he bought himself the usual sort of jewelry one acquires to confirm status in the hood, and quickly became known for always having the prettiest women by his side whenever he was seen in one of his many cars. But more importantly, he looked out for others. Bilal gave sneakers and clothes to several children in his neighborhood, for no other reason than that it may have appeared they did not have any. He gave anything to anyone that seemed to need.

Bilal could have kept his wealth to himself but he took pride in building and bringing up others with him. That included his notorious crew who worked to get their own but were often spoiled by Bilal as well. Bilal would take his crew on shopping sprees once a month, buying 30 outfits and 30 pairs of sneakers for each of them.

By then, Bilal had acquired a taste for expensive customized vehicles. Although he once owned a canary yellow Eldorado Baritz, with matching yellow leather interior and chrome piping, an emerald green Peugeot 505, with tan leather interior and other fashionable whips, he was most often spotted around town in his "kitted-up" (aftermarket aerodynamic ground effects) candy-apple red Mercedes Benz 190E, with butter soft, tan leather interior. This very high profile carriage included the then exclusive gold package, which featured gold colored emblems and model numbers. The attention-grabbing whip was also accented with gold BBS rims. He may have even been seen in his legendary beige and green Sahara Desert Jeep, with the bikini door and soft top which housed one of the most thunderous and disturbing sound systems in the state of New Jersey. This state of the art system, complete with 25 15-inch woofers and top-of-the-line Zeus and Thor amplifiers, could be heard throughout the town from blocks away. Bilal could often be heard banging House music tapes with his name being chanted in the chorus.

Buying the latest cars was a hobby for Bilal and he purchased five of the most popular cars during that era, all in under a week. Bilal bought Vincent Jackson a white Maxima, John Brown a black Regal, twin brothers Wendell and Karnell Wilson matching Audi 5000 (one grey and silver and one blue and gold), Quadir Lee a blue and silver Mercedes Benz 190E, and Andre Williams a red and silver Mercedes Benz 190E.

Wakil was also known for his many vehicles as well. He upgraded from a Cadillac Seville to a fully equipped black 325i BMW with a gold package, then to a gold BMW 7 series with black leather interior. The latter purchases quickly caused him to become known as the "BMW Man" on the streets. Like Bilal, Wakil treated his team to their own cars. He bought Corey Grant a yellow on yellow Thunderbird, Mutah Sessoms a Samurai Suzuki, and Keith Cashwell a lime green and gold Jetta and later an aqua green Jaguar.

These youths certainly played hard but they were by no means, playing with the game. On July 24, 1988, Bilal, Wakil and Keith Griggs were said to have made threats to kill nine people with machine guns at the Pioneer Homes Projects. They were also said to have beat up and robbed Alfonso Byrd, a rival "clocker" who ended up having to be rushed to the hospital for a three day stay.

These tactics were customary for the organization. In fact, prior to the July 24th incident, this type of fear and intimidation kept the E'Port Posse and Faze II on top of the game and in charge of the streets. However, the same strategy would eventually become the cause of their demise. Jealousy and envy from their competitors and vengeance from their victims and victims' families led this crime family straight into the hands of the law. Initially authorities were unaware that many of the individuals they specifically sought were part of an African American organized crime group led by teenager Bilal Pretlow. A heavy amount of undercover buys in the Pioneer Homes along with tip-offs from complaining tenants of the drug infested housing project gave authorities a jump on what became a nine month investigation into the workings of the organization.

The Union County Narcotics Strike Force, the State Police and the Elizabeth Police Detective Division dubbed the investigation "Operation Pioneer." They alleged, "the majority of distributors of cocaine in the area were controlled by the Graham and Pretlow family." They set up a raid to bring down the family on November 9, 1988. On that date at 6:00 am, the Pioneer Homes and Loomis street addresses in Elizabeth were raided. In that raid, Wakil, Shamar, Corey, Mutah, Keith Griggs and Keith Cashwell were arrested along with 29 others. Items seized at the two locations included an Audi sports car, Suzuki Jeep, Nissan Pathfinder, $67,000 worth of cocaine, $31,000 in cash, a loaded .22 caliber revolver and a loaded double-barreled shotgun. Seven members of the Graham family including Bilal and Wakil's grandmother "Sister", 57, and their aunt Marva, 26, were brought in during the haul.

Once arrested, Mutah Sessoms would have had to do about five years on drug possession charges. Although intimidated, Mutah decided to become a confidential informant. "I sat down and thought, I'm ready to stop and get out of it and face what I have to face and come out and do what's best for me," Mutah said in a sworn statement. He confirmed the authorities' suspicion of the drug business being run by the family. He revealed that several of those arrested in the "Operation Pioneer" raid were in fact part of a big organization and more specifically named Bilal and Wakil as the masterminds. Mutah drew a perfect picture for the state and implicated others as well. With that, "Operation Pioneer" became bigger than expected. Phones were tapped and warrants were issued. Stings were set up and more houses were raided. A raid at the Swan Motel was conducted on November 25, 1988, bringing down six teenagers including Bilal, Corey, Duquan, and Jermaine Hartwell (Shawn's cousin). On the way to Elizabeth from the motel, Vincent, then 16, was stopped in a cab carrying a suitcase containing about 2 kilograms of cocaine worth about $16,000 a piece. Bilal had moved his packaging operation to Linden to avoid the authorities in Elizabeth. The Police seized $133,000 worth of cocaine and $72,000 in cash, which was found in a dresser drawer. They also discovered photographs of Shawn and Vincent posing with a banner that read "E'Port Posse".

Bilal was charged with being the leader of a drug trafficking network, maintaining and operating a drug manufacturing facility, possessing more than five ounces of cocaine with intent to distribute, employing juveniles in a drug distribution scheme and cocaine distribution within 1000 feet of a school. Bilal was told that if convicted, he could face life imprisonment

On December 22, 1988, five days after Bilal was released from the Union County Jail in Elizabeth on $250,000 bail, he and Wakil were again apprehended in a raid of their Fulton Street home. There they received more drug and gun charges including possessing a defaced firearm, which is a federal offense. The raid was based on one of the many tips given to law enforcement agents by one of Wakil's men, Mutah Sessoms.

On January 8, 1989, an attempt on Ricky William's life was carried out by members of the E'Port Posse (Keith Cashwell and Andre Williams), which was ordered by Bilal while being detained in the Union County Jail. The order was given via Shawn Hartwell, second in command conveyed the order.

In the hallway of the Pioneer Homes, Keith approached Ricky and shot him once in the abdomen, wounding him. When Andre realized that Williams wasn't dead, he instructed Cashwell to shoot him in the head. Following orders, Cashwell made another attempt to finish Williams off but the gun jammed, forcing them to have to flee the scene. Williams was later rushed to the hospital where he informed the local authorities that Cashwell was the shooter. A warrant was issued for Cashwell's arrest. After being apprehended, Andre was implicated. It was said that Bilal had allegedly threatened to kill Cashwell's mother if the hit wasn't carried out.

On January 20, 1989, three apartments at the Pioneer Homes and Miglore Manor housing projects were raided. Narcotics detectives seized cocaine worth $36,000, marijuana, drug paraphernalia, a handgun and several rounds of ammunition. Officers said that they arrested seven people that were part of the Pretlow-Graham organization. Their statement to the press was, "We've continually struck at the same organization trying to break its back. We can't say we've cured the problem, but we've struck at the heart of the organization." Ironically, none of those arrested at the stash houses were members of EPP.

In March of 1989, during the discovery phase in the criminal case stemming from "Operation Pioneer," the local authorities were able to obtain a statement, which had been provided by Mutah Sessoms. Soon after, Sessoms was severely beaten by individuals whom he identified as E'Port Posse members. Shawn Hartwell and Wendel Wilson were two of the attackers identified. Information was sent to Bilal and Wakil containing the statement Sessoms had made, confirming the fact that he was cooperating with authorities to bring Bilal and Wakil down.

While on furlough from Union County Jail, it is said that Mutah Sessoms was confronted by Bilal, Wakil, Corey and other members of the organization who took him at gunpoint to an apartment in East Orange. It is said that Sessoms pleaded for them not to do anything to him and claimed he didn't do anything. Bilal, Wakil, and others sat Sessoms on the couch while they taunted and scolded him and then proceeded to smash Sessoms several times in the head with a hammer. It is said that when Sessoms fell he screamed, "Don't kill me!" It is further alleged that Wakil then grabbed a machete and chopped at Mutah's neck. After Sessoms died, they allegedly carried him into the bathroom, plugged in an electric saw and cut his body up. It was said that Bilal walked around the apartment with Mutah's head in his hand.

17

The mutilated body was found in Newark, New Jersey, a day later in two separate suitcases. Ambulance workers found one suitcase on 9th Street, between 11th and 12th Avenue, while the other suitcase was found five blocks away on 14th Street, by children that took the suitcase home to their parents, thinking that the contents were food. Neither suitcase contained Mutah's head, feet, or hands.

On April 23, 1989, the body of Marvin Buckman was found tied to a pole on 18th Street near a park in Newark. The cause of death was 18 bullets to the body. The death would later be linked to Bilal and Wakil's organization.

In May of 1989, Bilal, released on $500,000 bail and Wakil, released on $250,000 bail, held a meeting at a Chinese restaurant in Linden with about 50 drug dealers. It was an enjoyable event for all present. A magician even performed. During the meeting, the brothers spoke of their intentions to monopolize the drug trafficking in Elizabeth. Bilal threatened that those who didn't go along with his plans would face consequences.

On June 14, 1989, the body of Melanie Baker was found in Newark. Law enforcement officials believed that Baker was killed by Corey Grant, Wakil Pretlow, Irving Bethea and Bilal. Melanie was shot four times in the head at point blank range.

Don Diva was told several different stories regarding the death of Melanie Baker. According to the streets, one story is that Melanie had dealings with one of the E'Port Posse members and stumbled across a substantial amount of money in one of their many "stash houses," and took the money, spending it on an elaborate shopping spree. Others say that she was given $60,000 in drug money that belonged to the organization to hold onto but shortly after receiving the money, she splurged with it. One of the E'Port Posse members told us, "She had just been in the wrong place at the wrong time, simple as that." Whatever the truth is behind the death of Melanie, only she and her attackers know.

Another Elizabeth native, Bobby Ray Davis, (who was also a known negative force in the community and throughout the prison system) had just reemerged on the scene after serving a lengthy prison sentence. He was considered to be the "Heroin King" in the Elizabeth area prior to his incarceration.

After a meeting, Bilal and Wakil agreed to allow Davis and his crew to distribute heroin in their area peacefully, provided none of their

18

crewmembers try to sell cocaine, which the E'Port Posse controlled exclusively.

Shortly after that agreement, members of the E'Port Posse came across some of Davis' crew hustling coke at the Pioneer Homes. The members of Davis' crew were confronted and a beef erupted causing the E'Port Posse to make examples of Davis' workers, using extreme measures to establish their point.

Early on July 9, 1989, Jeanette Griggs was severely beaten by Bilal, Shawn and others for selling cocaine in the vicinity of the Pioneer Homes for someone other than the Pretlow organization.

On that same day, at approximately 10:45 pm, Bobby Ray Davis, Walter "Rajohn" Griggs (Jeanette's brother) and Maurice Crowley (Jeanette's boyfriend at the time) caught up with Wakil on First Street in front of the Pioneer Homes. There, they shot him several times, leaving him to die in the arms of Shawn Hartwell.

Shortly after, on that same evening, Shawn, Irvin and Bilal armed themselves with heavy artillery and began an intense search. Regretfully, they did not heed to Wakil's prophecy. Police found Shawn, Irvin and Bilal a few blocks away from the spot where Wakil's shooting had taken place and they were arrested on gun possession charges.

Initially, the police thought Hartwell was the one who had killed Wakil since he had Wakil's blood all over him, but that was the furthest from the truth. Wakil was his comrade, associate and friend. On the very next day, July 10, 1989, Wendell Wilson and Thomas "Shamar" Pretlow, the eldest of the Pretlow brothers, sought out and found Bobby Ray Davis stepping out of his car in front of his home. Shamar shot Davis who fell to the ground from the blow. When he fell, Shamar walked over to Davis' injured body and stood over him, emptying the remaining three shots from the 357 revolver into his head.

The other two, Rajohn Griggs and Maurice Crowley, both of whom were identified as participants in the death of Wakil Pretlow, were said to have fled the state, not only to escape prosecution from the authorities, but also to escape retaliation from the E'Port Posse.

The funerals for Wakil Pretlow and Bobby Ray Davis were held a day apart. Hundreds came out to show their love and support for the highly respected individual icons. The media swarmed the occasion and the police stood heavily armed outside for fear that there would be retaliation from the rival crews.

Before Wakil's funeral, Bilal, not being able to attend, sent a gold medallion of a king's crown, to be placed around Wakil's neck. The word on the street is that Bilal also paid a substantial amount of money to have Wakil buried in a 14 karat gold casket, although this claim was unsubstantiated.

On July 26, 1989, Bilal Pretlow pleaded guilty to three narcotics charges in exchange for the dismissal of seventeen others. The most serious charge of being leader of a narcotics network was dismissed. The sentence in return was 20 years with eligibility for parole after 7 ½ years. Subsequently, Shawn Hartwell became the official underboss. Bilal continued to give orders via his lieutenants while imprisoned. He was reported to have purchased between 40 and 50 pairs of sneakers in one week as well as clothes for his fellow inmates in exchange for uninterrupted use of the phone.

On August 20, 1989, Corey Grant pistol-whipped Dion Lee, a drug dealer at the Pierce Manor housing project. Allegedly, Corey was supposed to have then fired shots at the running Lee. Nine days later, Dion's brother, another known drug dealer, was shot and killed. Police reported the incident as another murder done by the E'Port Posse over a territorial dispute. Corey, along with James "Raheem" Holman, is alleged to have done the shooting.

On September 6th, 1989, after a warrant was issued in connection to the murder of Mario Lee, Corey Grant voluntarily turned himself in to the local authorities while he was still under the age of 18 in an effort to avoid being prosecuted as an adult.

On October 23, 1989, surveillance was conducted as a result of telephone conversations that had been intercepted through wiretap at the Union County Jail. Information was obtained that approximately $100,000 would be taken to a bail bondsman's office in Montclair, New Jersey, for Thomas "Shamar" Pretlow's bail.

At 1:06 pm, Vincent Jackson, Samad Pretlow (Bilal's youngest brother) and a great-uncle arrived at the bails bondsman's office. When Jackson, his uncle and the younger brother exited the vehicle, a surveillance team surrounded them and ordered them to place their hands on their car. A pat down search revealed that Jackson possessed $2,054, cash in his pocket and his uncle possessed a similar amount.

Authorities observed one of the occupants taking a "goldish" vinyl bag out of the trunk of the car. The bag was secured until a search warrant could be obtained. While waiting for the warrant, a drug detection K-9 had a positive reaction to the bag. Jackson was subsequently given a DEA receipt for the contents of the bag later revealed to be a total of $104,047.00 in U.S. currency.

On November 13, 1989, Federal DEA agents joined both city and county narcotics officers in a series of raids called "Operation Glass Slipper." The name derived from statements Bilal's lawyer made regarding Bilal feeling like Cinderella. The raid brought down 31 people associated with the E'Port Posse, including Wendell and Karnell Wilson, Antonio "Malik" Jones, and it further implicated an already incarcerated Bilal Pretlow. This time Bilal was charged with running the organization while still incarcerated in the Union County Jail. His phone calls had been monitored through phone taps. Shortly thereafter, authorities began a massive manhunt for Bilal's chief lieutenants, Shawn Hartwell and Vincent Jackson, and the remainder of the E'Port Posse members. The murders of Bobby Ray Davis, Mario Lee, Melanie Baker, Mutah Sessoms and the attempted murders of Dion Lee and Ricky Williams were being linked to the organization.

On November 14, 1989, after outstanding warrants were issued for his arrest for his involvement with the E'Port Posse, Vincent Jackson voluntarily turned himself in to local authorities while he was still under the age of 18, also in an effort to avoid being prosecuted as an adult.

On December 19, 1989, Shawn Hartwell was captured after being on the run for over a month. Elizabeth Detective Thomas Swan then commented to the press, "Now the E'Port Posse is completely finished." Hartwell was charged as a Kingpin by the state of New Jersey.

On July 27, 1990, a federal grand jury in the District of New Jersey returned an indictment charging seven defendants including Bilal Pretlow, Shawn Hartwell, and Irving Bethea with over thirty-five counts of drug trafficking, violent crimes, and racketeering.

On August 23, 1990, Corey Grant, then 15 and Vincent Jackson, then 16, were slated, under the Federal Juvenile Delinquent Act, to be transferred and prosecuted as adults, pursuant to 18 U.S.C. 5032.

On January 25, 1991, a federal grand jury in the District of New Jersey handed down yet another indictment, which was a superseding indictment, charging nine defendants, including Bilal, Shawn, Vincent, Irving and

21

Corey with over thirty-five counts of drug trafficking, violent crimes, and racketeering.

In addition, Bilal, Shawn, and Vincent were charged with engaging in Continuing Criminal Enterprise under U.S.C. 848. Bilal was charged specifically with 848(e), which carried the death penalty, bringing some closure to one chapter of the E'Port Posse.

In July 1991, a judge granted a joint defense motion for severance of all defendants from the capital punishment trial of co-defendant Bilal Pretlow.

Bilal's controversial 848(e) case became the first death penalty case to be tried in New Jersey and second in the nation under the new death penalty law for those convicted of drug related murders. Bilal's attorney charged that federal authorities had systematically attempted to eliminate black jurors from the trial. He pointed out that they (the government) only investigated the backgrounds of potential black jurors eligible to sit on the final jury panel. It's likely that they feared the Pretlow/ Graham family's extended family tree and were concerned that they might inadvertently get a distant relative on the jury. In addition, they knew the E'Port Posse was too popular and feared in the black community for any black citizen to deliver a guilty verdict.

During the death penalty phase, it was reported in the Daily Journal that during a wire tapped conversation, Bilal, after being asked by Latiesha Drakes (his girlfriend at the time) if he had to get the most time [what would he do?], he said "I'll take the death deal, and before I die I'll say, stick me!"

Bilal's trial began on November 12, 1991, however it was halted on January 3, 1992 following his alleged suicide. Jury selection for the trial of Vincent Jackson, Corey Grant and Irvin Bethea began on February 28, 1992.

Corey Grant 1988   Corey Grant 2000
                    FCI- Leavenworth

Corey Grant serving LIFE in a Federal
Prison for Murder.

On May 13, 1992, after several federal and state convictions of both the E'Port Posse and family members, the jurors returned a guilty verdict for Vincent Jackson, Corey Grant, and Irvin Bethea on a RICO conspiracy and of substantive RICO violation. In addition, Jackson was found guilty in the

22

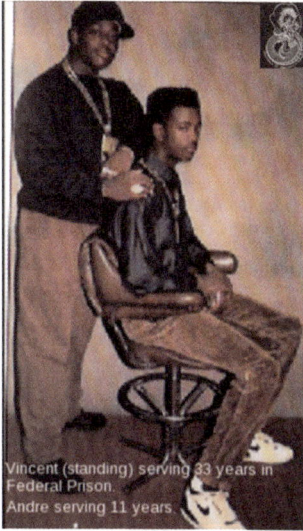
Vincent (standing) serving 33 years in Federal Prison.
Andre serving 11 years.

federal court system of engaging in Continuing Criminal Enterprise, as a Kingpin.

Prior to that year, in December 1991, 18-year-old Shawn Hartwell, was sentenced to 23 and one-third years on a federal Kingpin charge that superseded the state. When questioned by reporters outside the courthouse as to why he didn't accept the five years offered to him by the state, Shawn's response was, "I would never tell on my brothers."

Shawn Hartwell serving 23 years.
Convicted on 848 (drug kingpin charge)

On November 9, 1992, both Vincent and Corey were sentenced. Vincent received 33 and one-third years while Corey received a "Life" sentence in federal prison. Along with the drug and racketeering charges, Vincent was convicted of conspiracy to murder Anthony "Hasim" Martin, while Corey was convicted of murdering Mario Lee and the attempted murder of Dion Lee.

During sentencing, the newspapers said that both Vincent and Corey were cursing at the judge. Vincent was reported as saying, "C'mon man, give me what you're gonna give me," and Corey was later to have said, "I have

23

no respect for a man in a dress," referring to the judge's robe. At a later date, Irvin Bethea was also sentenced to a "Life" imprisonment term by the federal government for the role that he played in the organization.

Many other cases directly involved in the E'Port Posse takedown resulted in both lengthy state and federal sentences. Law enforcement officials believed that at least 20-30 additional members of the group, mostly juveniles, escaped detection and arrests. Members such as Antonio "Malik" Jones, Hussamiddi "Hussam" Williams, Andre "Ondi" Williams and Keith Cashwell, along with family members Terrance "Tareem-Terry" Graham (one of Bilal's uncles), James "Sonny" Jackson (one of Bilal's great-uncles), Marva Graham (Bilal's aunt), and Bilal's maternal grandmother, Mrs. Eleanor "Sister" Graham, were included in the state and federal sentences.

Both Marva and Mrs. Graham who plead "not guilty" on charges stemming from the "Operation Pioneer" raid, were brought to trial and found guilty. The fact that Raymond Graham Jr. testified that the drugs found were his and that his mother and sister had no knowledge of them did not spare their punishment. Mrs. Graham's attorney pleaded with the judge to show leniency and offer her probation since she was a mother and grandmother who had no prior convictions and was on medication. Marva's attorney asked for probation as well and explained that his client had a very limited involvement and no prior convictions.

As a result, on December 15, 1989, the judge sentenced them both to eight and seven years. The judge commented on how it was unfortunate for Mrs. Graham and that what the jury found was that she produced and nurtured two drug dealers, in the person of her son, Raymond Graham Jr., and her grandson, Bilal Pretlow. He also commented on how Marva Graham had an income without the assistance of welfare or gainful employment.

During that mysterious time, when Bilal Pretlow was found hanging in his cell, which was under 24-hour surveillance, Mrs. Graham, who had spoken to him the Saturday before, said, "He was in good spirits." She also questioned why no one noticed his bed sheet was missing. Suspecting foul play, she was quoted as saying, "No, I don't believe he hung himself." Even people on the street say, "That's crazy, that's not Bilal."

David A. Ruhnke, one of Bilal's lawyers said that he'd spent hours with him on Christmas Eve and he seemed upbeat and gave no sign that he might have been contemplating suicide. "It's just an awful thing. He wasn't an animal or a monster. He wasn't what the government portrayed him to be."

Meanwhile, Elizabeth's Mayor felt differently. Mayor, Thomas G. Dunn, told the press, "All I can say is justice has been served... at his own hands. I wish I could express some feeling of sadness, but when one knows all the damage, destruction and other human heartbreaks that (Bilal) caused, I find nothing within my heart to express sorrow."

The following is an up-close and personal interview with top members of the E'Port Posse, conducted by Susan Hampstead.

"The Aftermath" Interview

Susan: First things first, let's clarify the difference between the E'Port Posse and Faze II, were they actually separate crews?

Vincent Jackson: It's funny that you ask that question because a lot of people don't know the difference. EPP originally stood for Elizabeth Port Projects. Faze II signified "associates," which is the connotation of the word "Faze." EPP also represented E'Port Posse, which are those who are originally from E'Port. Mostly everybody from down in the port section are cut from the same cloth...one fabric...one texture. Basically, the whole downtown is E'Port. Faze II was what Bilal considered "taking it to the next level." E'Port is everyone from downtown Elizabeth.

Susan: Explain the difference between Bilal and Wakil to us

Vincent: Let me ponder on that for a minute because, honestly, that's a hard one to answer. Why? Because they both possessed leadership qualities. Two unique individuals, but if I had to determine the difference between the two, then I would have to say that Wakil was like the fox and Bilal was more like the lion. Like a fox, Wakil was very witty and more of a strategist than anything, self-taught book text. Bilal, on the other hand, like a lion, acts on animal instinct. He comes through to conquer and destroy anything that poses a threat or gets in his way. That's the best way that I can differentiate the two, because they're both of an authentic breed.

Susan: It's apparent that you and Bilal spent the most time together during the E'Port Posse's reign. Tell us how your life has been impacted the most.

Shawn Hartwell: That's hard because it means so much when someone gives you their all, from the heart, but overall, if I have to say, it would be his admiration for family structure. Bilal was about Unity, One Life, One Bond, One Love. Personally, I've never met anyone who loved me more than "The Late Great Bilal." Bilal was to Elizabeth what Biggie was to

25

Brooklyn and Wakil was what 2Pac was to L.A. In their own way they are both legends in our town.

Susan: Bilal was considered notorious. What do you think affected him the most before his death?

Shawn: A multitude of things. From Wakil's death to the incarceration of his grandmother, down to [his little brother] Samad being convicted for murder, but the thing that affected "E" the most was to see everything he worked so hard to build vanish right before his very eyes when he had a different goal he had set out to achieve.

Susan: It appears to be a lot of unanswered questions in regards to Bilal's death, the controversial case pertaining to his death penalty indictment, the involvement of his grandmother in the case, and current dispositions of the E'Port Posse. Can you elaborate?

Vincent: I'm put in an awkward position, because as much as I would like to elaborate on your sequence of questions, I can't. Only the books that are scheduled to come can answer them for you. I mean, you have a multitude of situations that are complex, such as mine for example, where I was tried and convicted under the RICO law and also as a Kingpin before I even reached the age of 17.

Susan: Yeah, I read that, but what books are you referring to?

Vincent: Basically, as of now, two out of several are in the process of being published as we speak. To my understanding, the first book will be "New Jersey's Finest: E'Port Posse–Minors who made it Major in a League of Their Own," and the second book I believe to follow is supposed to be titled *The Diary of an Underboss: Shawn Hartwell–Inside the Life and Times of a Don: Bilal Pretlow*.

Susan: Sounds interesting. I look forward to reading them.

Susan: Corey, I noticed that you were one of the two members of the E'Port Posse that received a life sentence for your involvement in the case. Why do you think you were given such a severe and extreme sentence?

Corey: On some real shit, I became what "White America" considers to be a ruthless menace… "America's Nightmare." First, understand that I was erroneously placed inside a judicial system that embodies racism and fabricates truths. Basically, I was made a statistic by not qualifying to meet society's standards at a young age. From a legal perspective, I was illegally transferred by the federal government to be tried and prosecuted as an adult. That's how a life sentence came about. There was prosecution misconduct and abuse of discretion by the district court judge…with those bullshit statutes and policies that stem only from politics…the red tape. The courts thought that a life sentence was more than lenient, unlike Bilal though, the equivalent "Machiavelli of Jersey," whom the government wanted to make a prime example of. It's crazy, because Bilal was only 18 at the time when he was eventually removed from the streets. It becomes intricate when you try to decipher why of all the infamous bosses that were ever brought to justice, only "EZ" was targeted to become the sacrificial lamb. I mean…come on now…the death penalty…locking his grandmother up for having natural birthrights…giving me life before my life even begun. This shit is absurd because the only facts that you will conclude is the obvious personal vendetta against us. Bottom line, the real gangsters just wanted to make examples out of us to show us who really dominated and monopolized the game.

Susan: Was that your reason for making an obscene outburst in the courtroom to the judge?

Corey: That's self-explanatory, but society is misinformed about the judicial system and court proceedings. As usual, the media only covered and reported what they wanted to sell to the public. It's odd how everybody was informed as to what I had said to the judge but was never informed about what the judge said to me. You see, the news coverage never reported how the judge made a sarcastic remark initially to me…calling me a "monster"…stating that I was a monster ever since the day I was born. I mean, where is the professionalism in that? Furthermore, what does a statement like that imply about my mother? So to answer your question, yes, because honorability was at stake.

Susan: How were you placed in an adult facility when you were only a minor?

Corey: We were all young, I just so happened to be the youngest of all of us that were charged in the indictment. At the time, when they just started the investigation, I was only 13. By the time they knocked me off, I was 16. At first, I was in the Union County Juvenile Detention Center, but because of the publicity of the case and all of the media exposure, I became a security risk and by the time the district attorney took a personal interest in the case, I guess he felt that the detention center didn't have strong enough security to house me, so they had me transferred to a federal holding spot, which at the time was Union County Jail, when I was 17.

27

Susan: At what point did you recognize the end?

Shawn: At our lowest point, which was at Wakil's death?

Susan: Why do you say that?

Shawn: You wouldn't understand, but Wakil was like the governor. His presence was astronomical. When he got killed, that was like the eclipse of the E'Port Posse. It derailed the course of what was supposed to come next. The plan was to get Keith out, but Wakil's death was the cause of Shamar, Wendell, Malik, Irvin, Bilal and me getting locked up. Out of everybody, I was the only one to get out. Instead of one getting out, everybody went in, with Wakil's blood on all of our hands. His death took a piece of our future with him to his grave. That was the beginning of the end of our "Dynasty," but let me clarify something [despite] what you read in the newspaper [there weren't] any type of masterminds behind [our] investigation. There's no validity or truth to Detective Swan taking us down. Overall, the only thing that he did was interrogate some people and stumble across a few major pieces of a puzzle, and just so happened to see what any other detective would have saw, given the same opportunity and the same pieces. Any adult could easily manipulate a bunch of kids. That's how all the cooperation from anyone that was involved in this case came into play. We were all under 18, even Bilal, at the time. Detective Swan did nothing spectacular.

Susan: Don't take this the wrong way, but I'm sure the readers would like to know, who now carries the torch of the E'Port Posse after Bilal?

Vincent: Before I elaborate on your question, let me put this out there right quick. After Bilal, or Wakil for that matter, there is no other that reigns supreme in my eyes, but it depends on what type of answer you're looking for, either the one who is entitled to it or the one who inherited it.

Susan: See, now you got me open. How about if you give me both?

Vincent: I somewhat figured you would ask that, plus I'm sure inquiring minds want to know. Technically, the one who is entitled to it is Shawn, but when you speak about inheritance, hands down it will always be within the family.

Susan: And what makes up the family?

Vincent: My family, the Jacksons, which is where the Grahams and Pretlows extend from namely my grandmother, my great-aunt Marcella, my great-uncle Sonny and my great-uncle Artis (who is an army of one).

28

On a similar note, my respect goes out to John Dozier, Johnny Poe and John Riggi.

Susan: Who are John Dozier, Johnny Poe and John Riggi?

Vincent: More of "New Jersey's Finest."

Susan: Is there anything else you would like to say?

Corey: Yeah. It wasn't easy growing up where I'm from, but harsh trials and tribulations are nothing new to a young black man in America. I wasn't actually given an opportunity in life, and it was an injustice of the highest order to imprison millions of young African Americans. I want my brothers and sisters to know that the greatest weapon in the world is knowledge of self and one's surroundings. Just having a conscious awareness of what's going on within the system is important. This shit here is designed to tear families apart and causes you to lose touch with reality. Since I've been in, I've already lost someone dear to me, my grandmother, and right now as we speak, I'm dealing with my moms fighting cancer. I should be there for her. Even my grandfather's health becomes weaker as every day passes. In my absence, I have a son who is forced to be raised without a dad. Not a day goes by without me thinking of them because I love them. My grandmother, Mrs. Shirley "Mother" Grant (RIP), my grandfather, Mr. Milton "Dad" Grant, my moms, Mrs. Valerie Grant, my aunt Cheryl and cousin Sherrell, my son, Jatise and my sisters Sharon and Missy.

Susan: Shawn... the same question to you?

Shawn: Despite what I'm sure many are anticipating hearing, unfortunately, I can't express my profound experiences at this time. All I can say is get it out of the book. (Shawn states, with a devilish smirk coming across his face.)

DD: What's behind that smirk?

Shawn: Nah, as I'm talking, things that my man E. once said are playing in my mind.

DD: Like what?

Shawn: Well, I'm reminiscing on some of the conversations we once had. I remember 15 years ago when they put me and E. together at our first arraignment. Prior to that I hadn't seen E. since Wakil's death, so you can only imagine how I felt, in spite of what we were all going through. For as long as I can remember he seemed to make situations and matters appear less than what they really were. Like at our arraignment, I said to him, "Bilal, they trying to give me life," and he turned around and said, "Shit, they're trying to kill me." There was another time when he had told me, "Don't be depressed because depression only brings more depression, besides you're a legend and you're not even dead yet." Even when the government was trying to execute him, E's only response at the time was, "I'm about t'win an Oscar for this one." It's crazy because I was up in the bullpen on Murder One and here he was, all humble...when it should've been the other way around. I had said, "I'ma kill all these niggas when I get out for what they did to us," and he said to me, "Forget all that bullshit. You gotta think about getting back out there so you can be there for the kids." Since then, I haven't thought of anything else except my responsibility. You see, all of our kids bear our names and our blood...from little Shawn, little Bilal, Jatise and Quindella (Vincent's kids), Wakil's three kids and all of the rest of the E'Port Posse members' kids. So, never do we want an E'port Posse II or...Faze III because that rests where it lay...with the lost... (RIP Wakil and Bilal). While I'm on the subject of family, I want to show love to the rest of my family members, starting with my grandmother, Ms. Ida Mae, my moms, Ms. MaryAnn, my aunt Ms. Gloria, my sister Tammy, my cousin Jermain, Jamil and Latiesha, and all the rest of my cousins, nieces and nephews and those who are gone but not forgotten, my uncles Tip and Bruce. To anyone who wasn't mentioned that may be outside the realms of my immediate family...if you are somebody worth mentioning then you're mentioned in the book and on a more worthy note to all [to] who[m] it applies... Be good to the game and the game will be good to you!

Susan: Vincent, do you have anything further to add?

Vincent: To keep things in their proper perspective, now that I'm looking back on it, I've come a long way and now I realize that a major responsibility has been placed on my shoulders, so by force, I have no choice but to continuously build myself up physically, mentally as well as emotionally, to carry the heavy load of my ancestors, in order to ensure that both theirs and my own legacy live on. Before I go on, let me pay homage to some people, places and things. "A-low" to the whole Elizabeth, from downtown (E'Port), midtown and uptown; and if you don't know what "A-low" implies, then you can't be reppin' Elizabeth. Also, "ONE" to Union County as a whole, from Elizabeth to Plainfield and "ONE" to our extended family in Newark and the surrounding cities that make up Essex County (those inside and outside these walls).

On a much more personal level, RIP to my Heavenly Divine Earth, my mother, Ms. Brenda Jackson and the G.O.A.T.s of Elizabeth (Greatest of All Times), Wakil and Bilal. I want to also send infinite love to my son and daughter, Jatise Lamar Oates and Quindella Monique Pough, my sister Lisa, my brother Jabo, my uncles Larry, Curtis and Gin, my aunts Cat, Carmen, Marla and Lenore, and my cousins Shamar, Hasana, Samad, Ray G, LaKiesh and all the rest of the Pretlows, Grahams and Jacksons who fall under that regime.

I also want to acknowledge a special someone, who gave birth to the generation that brought forth our generation, "The Diva of all Divas," my grandmother Mrs. Eleanor "Sister" Graham. I know I speak for all of us, including those who have fallen......WE LOVE YOU!

After serving 20 years Shawn Hartwell was released on September 9, 2009. Vincent Jackson was able to give back 8 years of his original sentence, and after serving 22 years he was released in April of 2011. Welcome Home Comrades.

"While interviewing a member of the E'Port Posse, in the heart of Elizabeth, several gunshots rang out approximately 50 feet away, causing people to scream and scatter for cover. This is just a taste of how real it sometimes got for Don Diva." –Susan Hampstead.

Bilal Pretlow's attorney David Ruhnke speaks with author Cavario H. about his client Bilal "E" Pretlow and his last days of life:

I came in because Bilal was facing the federal death penalty, he had already been convicted in state court a year or two earlier and he was serving 20 years for the state. This was back in the early 90s, late 80s; there wasn't a federal death penalty until about 1988–there hadn't been one for twenty years, and it was only for people involved with murders connected with large scale drug trafficking. There were at least two murders involved in the case-there was a guy, I remember, named Mutah Sessoms who was cooperating against what they called "the E'port Posse." Mutah Sessoms was found with his body dismembered in a suitcase somewhere, as I recall, if I'm recalling correctly, they never found his head.

Then there was a beautiful young girl (Melanie Baker) who was believed to have been "cheating" on the organization, and she was shot in a car, and those were the two murders that the government sought the death penalty on. Some of the evidence in the case was almost comical because there was some hardware store operator who said that this group of young males

31

came in wanting a chainsaw, acid, gloves, garbage bags and big suit case. It leaves you wondering what kind of home improvement project this guy thought this was all for. What the government said about the E'port Posse was "it was almost like a business," they had basically found a way to buy cocaine in New York in great quantity, bag it up and sell it for half of what it was selling for on the street.

They completely took over the cocaine market in the area of Elizabeth. They also stuck out like a sore thumb, there was lots of money– there was one raid on a motel where they (law enforcement) picked up like $118,000-$120,000 in cash; they were 18 to 20 years old, some of them were still juveniles. A lot of money was spent on cars, so law enforcement would see these 18-year-old kids with gold [jewelry] "dripping" off of them, driving a red Mercedes Benz with a $7,000 stereo system around downtown Elizabeth. It didn't take long for the police to figure out where they were getting the money, and it didn't take long for every law enforcement agency in the vicinity to want to take them down.

They were just sticking out and showing it off, it was just like sticking their thumb in their [police's] eye, like, "I'm doin' it right under your nose." I had a client once, an alleged drug dealer in Newark, who used to drive around in a Rolls Royce convertible, and I used to always tell him, "Well Wayne ('Akbar' Pray) what do you think [they're gonna think]?" So they moved in on the guys, they had wiretaps, they did a lot of searches and "flipped" some people and they (government) really did put together a very, very strong case where these guys were dealing drugs "big-time" and they got caught.

There were some things about the group that was kind'a interesting; a lot of them had no fathers, or no parents at all. They sort of formed their own family; they found something with each other. They had photographs together holding signs saying "The E'port Posse." Bilal would do things like get some boy who was like 14 years old who would be selling on the street, he'd take him out and spend $10,000 or $5,000, he'd buy him like 20 pairs of sneakers or something that the kid really wanted and that would buy undying loyalty that way. But Bilal was a very smart kid, he was very young when I met him, he was like 21 years old, and he had a brother who had been killed, and he was very close to him and he was very affected by his brother's death. I think he was really depressed by his brother's death.

I remember when he killed himself, it was the first part of the (federal) case, we had picked a jury, we had started the first part ('guilt' phase) of the trial and we had taken a Christmas recess. I told him, "I'll be back before Christmas comes, see ya'." He said, "Ahh, no you're not. You're just telling me that you're gonna come down to the jail but it's gonna be like Christmas Eve and you're not gonna show up–you're not gonna make it, you're gonna be with your family." I said, "Nah, I'll be here, I'll be here." I showed up. I had bought him a Christmas present and they wouldn't let me give it to him. That really pissed me off. Prosecutors and cops would like to confine everybody to an image, 'you're two-dimensional'; you're either a brutal, murderous drug dealer or you're somebody who doesn't hesitate to kill or you're ruthless.

They don't really meet people up close–very few people are actually like that. I've met some people who are like that but very few. Bilal was very young and that bothered me, here was a kid who probably at best, given the strength of the evidence that they had against him, could've hoped for a "life" sentence–meaning he'd spend every day of the rest of his life in jail. I believe it was New Year's Eve or a day or two before; I got a call from somebody who was working on the case with me, a social worker, who said she had just gotten a call that Bilal had killed himself. She was [also] getting hysterical calls from family members. So I called the Union County Jail and the Union County prosecutor at the time was Drew Rutolo, (he's dead now, he died of cancer at a very young age). But the jail wouldn't tell me anything, "I said look, here's who I am, I want you to reach out to the prosecutor and have somebody call me back." They said, "Well they're here." I said, "Well, that tells me a lot." Then I talked to the prosecutor, Drew Rutolo, and he told me that he (Bilal) had hanged himself in the cell [and] that he had seen the body hanging there.

For some reason the judge wanted to have the jury come back, and tell them what had happened instead of just calling them up and saying that the case was over, the defendant was dead. The first trial date of the new year, I went back to federal court and the judge told the jury he (Bilal) was dead–they had all heard anyway, because it was all over the street. That was the end of the case. People were asking why would he kill himself? Did he kill himself? Was there something else [going on]? I saw the autopsy reports, I don't remember for sure but I think I saw pictures of the body and it didn't seem to me that it was anything but a suicide but... you know. There were always rumors that I heard that he was supposed to be cooperating with law enforcement and testifying against some corrupt cops.

I'll tell you that I never heard that from him and I never heard it from any law enforcement agencies and it's impossible that could've happened without me being brought into the 'mix'. I just think that the simplest answer is the correct answer, and that is that he killed himself. He had no future and he was really affected by his brother's death. I had seen pictures of the body and it didn't seem to me that there was any foul play. It was sad, because I had grown to like him and I had never had a client kill himself. It wasn't like he had nationwide reach or anything, it was Elizabeth, it was Union County, but he sure was powerful within his community. It was a short run, it had to be three or four years from start to when they took him down. They weren't very sophisticated, they didn't know how to keep a low profile... they had a good time while it lasted. But it didn't last very long.

David Ruhnke was also my respected comrade Kenneth "Supreme" McGriff's lawyer in his highly publicized 2005 federal trial for murder for hire and drug dealing. He received natural Life without the possibility of ever seeing the streets again and he took it on his feet. Two extraordinary men brought together under unfortunate circumstances. Peace to you both.
–Cavario H.

This next story took me to Chicago for the first time; the subject was reputed to be one of the most influential underworld figures the Windy City had seen since the reign of Alphonse Gabriel Capone. I was met by my contact at O'Hare International and taken directly to the Harold Ickes Homes, called simply "the Ickes" by locals (pronounced: ick-ēēs). When we arrived it was after dark, the large neglected parking lot was basically baron but for a few cars. There were nine massive concrete structures separated by raggedy fields of cracked concrete and patches of grass. The building we went into sat directly in front of the lot, and there were two others to the left of that. There were four buildings set symmetrically behind those, as two others sat beyond the opposite ends of the parking lot–all creating a backward F formation.

It was one of those artic-like Chicago nights I had heard so much about, but I came prepared in a jet black, long haired fox jacket. It was put together by my furrier Stixx, he used eight full skins (enough to make a full length coat), each section, including the sleeves, was a single piece so once the jacket was zipped closed there were absolutely no signs of a seam–not even where the zipper was. Not at all the kind of thing you'd want to be wearing wandering around in the wild for fear of being mounted by a wild animal in some frenzied mating attempt. The Ickes were a GD (Gangster Disciples) stronghold and virtually everyone that resided there was GD or GD affiliated. We walked into the barely lit stairwell and trekked up a flight or two before emerging into a hall that was even darker than the staircase. We approached an apartment that had a folding security gate in front of the door, which was charred from top to bottom. I studied the diamond pattern of the gate as I surveyed the damage to the surrounding walls and ceiling.

"What the hell happened here?" I inquired.

"Oh, they tried to burn us out," my contact responded casually as he struggled to collapse close the metal barrier (which to me seemed hardly more than a threat to the safety of the occupants).

A little disturbed I asked, "What if somebody comes back and puts a lock on that gate and sets this muthafucka on fire again, what's the plan then?"

My contact merely shrugged and said, "They ain't gon' be comin' back." Then he pushed open the door.

There were several young men lounging inside the scanty pad, which was peppered with mixed-matched furnishings. None of the young men looked to be older than twenty-one. After the ritual hand slapping introductions we all went into a room where they had a makeshift recording studio set up. They played several songs for me while I studied the random patches of spiny, foam-like material stuck to the walls (their attempt at soundproofing the place) and then we got down to business. The youngsters explained in great detail what life in Chicago is really like when one is poor, black and growing up smack dab in the heart of the largest gang in the country. The following is the resulting article as it originally appeared.

LARRY HOOVER "KING OF KINGS"

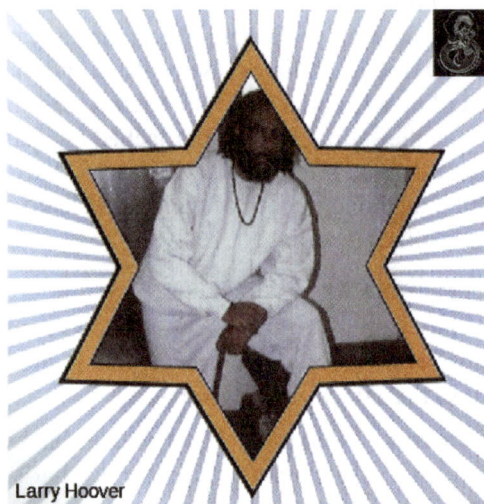

Larry Hoover

They call him Larry "King" Hoover; he is undeniably the uncontested, absolute leader of the Gangster Disciple Nation, which for a time was the largest and most powerful gang in the country with a membership that exceeded 30,000 cohesive members across 35 states.

As of the printing of this tome, Larry Hoover has been in prison for over 40 years and is now serving 6 life sentences in the worst prison on earth–the ADX Supermax Penitentiary in Florence, Colorado where he is locked in a small concrete cell 23 hours a day with no communication with any other inmates or guards. Because Larry Hoover is one of the most powerful and respected men on the streets throughout America, I hit the cold streets of Chicago to bring Don Diva's readers this incredible story.

It was evident early on that Larry Hoover was destined for leadership but it would come at a great price. By the time Mr. Hoover reached his 16th birthday he had been shot six times in various gangbanging incidents while elevating to the leadership of his own street organization. In 1967 a much larger gang, the King Cobras, tried to take Larry's gang territory but because he stood his ground, he got hundreds of Cobras to join him, merging into one gang which came to be known as the Black Gangster Nation. Two years later another merger occurred when Larry's following throughout the South and West sides of Chicago, which numbered more than 5,000 at the time, connected with David Barksdale's 10,000 Disciples... thus naming them the Black Gangster Disciple Nation.

Mr. Hoover was a recognized force on the streets but his power seemed to accelerate shortly after he began a 150- 200-year prison sentence for ordering the murder of William "Pookie" Young. It's supposed that Pookie robbed one of Larry's drug spots, and shortly after, Pookie was found shot in the head six times. It was this prison stint that lead Larry to his 1995 indictment in which, the government contends, Larry used his 30,000-strong GD Nation, to funnel some portion of $100,000,000 in yearly drug money to various political candidates as well as his own political activist group: 21st Century VOTE–which Larry created in 1990.

It is alleged that Larry Hoover lived better in prison than most people live in open society. Supposedly while in Vienna State Prison, Larry had keys to every door but the front door and women came in and out of the facility at all hours. It's also been rumored that a wall between two cells was removed to accommodate Mr. Hoover. Most fantastic of all, is the tale of weekend rendezvous in downtown Chicago hotels via helicopter from the rooftop of the prison to the rooftops of the posh pavilions.

In 1992, the US attorney's office, led by assistant attorney Ron Safer set its sights on Chicago gangs, more specifically the Gangster Disciples- reputably the largest, most organized and most notoriously violent gang in the country. The goal was to break the power structure behind the GDs, which in plain English means they set out to break Larry Hoover and his reign as "King" of the streets and prisons.

Initially the GDs proved too savvy for the government and although the government was attacking GD operations voraciously they were unable to do any real damage to GD businesses. The government was spinning its wheels and time was running out. Hoover had a movement on the streets and his popularity with various officials and politicians was growing. It looked as if Hoover might actually have had a chance at freedom after what was at that point more than 20 years in state prisons.

One evening Ron Safer, apparently frustrated and desperate, came up with a last chance idea. He knew Hoover received many visitors so he took a chance that could possibly pay off. The government placed miniature transmitters into paper-thin visitor's passes worn by individuals that came to visit Mr. Hoover in Vienna minimum-security state prison. They called it "Operation Headache." The visitors did not volunteer for this nor were they aware that the bugs were in the passes.

According to the media and government sources, the government caught Larry on tape bragging about the freedom he enjoyed at a minimum-security state prison. Hoover said on tape that one of his top lieutenants "could corrupt anybody at Statesville Correctional Center and he also claimed that the gang paid bribes to have keys made for "every door in the penitentiary except the doors to leave."

"For $100 at a time, one prison staffer let the gang use a key making machine, and we would be making keys in two minutes," Hoover is supposed to have said. This boasting purportedly occurred on December 11, 1993, as he met privately with alleged GD member John Baugh in the visitor's area of Vienna Correctional Center. Neither man was aware of the miniature transmitters in Baugh's visitor's pass.

It was stated that Larry continued, saying, "You know we used to cop down in Statesville, we got our reefer 30 pounds at once..." At another point in the tape where the reception was fuzzy, Hoover is supposedly heard saying, "I...to go up to the hospital unit on the third floor...be up there, me and...smoking for two hours laying there with my broad..." Most of these tape recordings are minor offenses on Hoover's part and only go to show the corruption and illegal activity that was present in the Illinois Department of Corrections. After all, what inmate wouldn't pimp a corrupt prison system?

Larry's federal drug Kingpin indictment wasn't served until Larry was allegedly caught discussing "Nation's Day" on tape with his visitors. The government's claim is that this is when Larry Hoover conspired to implement a street tax called "Nation's Day," in which gang members were to handover one day's drug profits once a week–bringing in an estimated $200,000-$300,000 a week. This "conspiracy" is what the government based its 1995 indictments on. If they could prove that Nations Day did exist they would be able to put Hoover into a federal maximum-security prison. Once there, Hoover would be locked down for 23 hours a day and no longer be able to control the Gangster Disciples or the streets of Chicago.

Here's where Larry's story gets even more complicated. There was a big dispute as to whether Larry Hoover himself actually implemented the Nation's Day tax. For more than 20 years, any laws handed down to the streets were given secondhand. The majority of the GD's growth was done while Larry was in prison, 90% of its members had never seen Larry Hoover in their lives, yet they followed what they believed to be his law, his word, as a way of life. There were entire housing projects in Chicago that represented GDs, and none of the members had ever laid eyes on or actually heard words come out Larry Hoover's mouth.

The government alleged that they had Larry Hoover on tape discussing the implementation of a Nation's Day tax. One media source printed the following excerpt from the government tapes recorded in November 1993.

November 7, 1993
Larry Hoover: "I want everybody doing, everything (unintelligible) reefer, cocaine...Tell them...everybody out there got to give me a day. Every week you get a different day...Tuesday I want to rake in two or three hundred thousand dollars...Tuesday."

Another tape excerpt reportedly caught Hoover allegedly changing his mind about doing Nation's Day. On those same tapes Mr. Hoover is quoted as saying, "We don't need that...any businessman would understand that." It's presumed that Larry was referring to not doing "Nation's Day" at all, although the jury was never allowed to hear this part of the tape. In total, the government had 55 hours of taped conversations between Hoover and his visitors–the prosecution only transcribed 4 hours and those were the only portions of the tape heard in court and by the public.

I went to the Harold Ickes projects in Chicago (which are no longer standing) and spoke with GDs directly to find out what was really happening on the streets. This was no easy task. No one talks about Larry Hoover or the workings of the GD organization. I was told that I was "crazy" for going into the projects and asking questions about the infamous Hoover. But real always recognizes real and I received nothing but bulletproof love from my comrades in the hoods throughout the Chi'– even to this day.

Cavario: How long have you been a Gangster?
GD: Since I was eight years old. My whole projects is GDs, that's the reason why you become a GD, 'cause it's the hood you raised in–you know what I'm sayin'. Nigga's mommas and nigga's fathers was GDs even though my father was a Vice Lord. When I moved to the Ickes GDs was around and I was raised over here, know what I'm sayin'.

Cavario: Tell me about "Nations Day".

GD: Nations Day ran all through Chicago, it wasn't just GDs, it could be any "nation," it could even be Stones. Nations Day meant you had to shut down for a certain amount of hours for the "Nation," for the crew, for the GDs that was runnin' the block. They put they own workers in for them hours to sell they shit, all the money go to them. That was in eleven states, St. Louis, Missouri, Alabama wherever you wanna name wherever 'Folks'* was at, them hours was goin' on, and all the money was goin' to Larry Hoover.

*Folks- members of a massive alliance "street gang" made up of various street gangs spread throughout the United States. The following is a list of past and present "Folk" gangs: Black Disciples, Insane Gangster Disciples, Northside Popes, Spanish Cobras, Gangster Disciples, Maniac Latin Disciples, Satan Disciples, La Raza Nation, Latin Eagles, Simon City Royals, Spanish Gangster Disciples, and Crips.

Cavario: Were there other types of 'Nation' taxes?

GD: Yeah, [on] parties... if there was a Folks party goin' on somewhere in the city, every other party had to shut down. If they found out afterwards that somebody had a party, the GDs would come for taxes the next day, if not the same night. When they [Folks] was throwin' somethin' you had to shut down, simple as that. They took attendance so they knew who showed up and who didn't.

Cavario: How did they take attendance?

GD: They used the people they had 'in play', "big hat" niggas, like some of the Coordinators. Hoover had count of everybody that was 'Folks' and the Coordinator would have all the members sign in after they paid. When the party was over, the coordinator and the treasurer would match the membership lists with the attendance list. If yo ass was on the membership list and you came to the party but didn't sign in or you just didn't come at all, they would come to your block or maybe even your house and give you a "mouth shot." If you couldn't take that mouth shot you was payin' that fine. It didn't matter how bad you was 'cause they comin' deep wit' a hundred niggas... project niggas too.

Cavario: Coordinators and Treasurers? What other ranks were there?

GD: From the bottom up, it worked like this; first you had your Soldiers, those the niggas on the street, then you had your Treasurer and Chief of Security and a Coordinator for each block. Coordinators ran the block, and then above them you had the Regents who ran the whole neighborhood, so each of them had a few coordinators responsible to them. The Regents had to report to the Governors though. The Governors ran entire sections of

40

the city like South Side, West Side, shit like that. The Governors had to answer to the Board members and only the board members spoke directly to Hoover... "The Chairman of the Board."

Cavario: How many board members were there and who were they?

GD: "Shorty G" (Gregory Shell) was a board member, and the dude "DD" (Andrew Howard) and "Pops" (Darryl Johnson), that muthafucka was mean as shit, you didn't wanna see Pops on your ass. They brought Nas and Wu-Tang and all them niggas down here way back. Ever since Mayor Daly and his people broke them niggas up the city of Chicago been fucked up, there ain't been no big concerts here. They broke 'em up 'cause they was comin' at them (mayor Daly's administration), gettin' political and shit. When we started 21st Century VOTE, we did a march on City Hall. It was called a "Politicalship for the Folk." It was mandatory that all GD had to be there, they had a list.

Cavario: Did all the GDs show up?

GD: They sent two or three buses to every project that had GDs in 'em. You didn't go to that, you got fucked up. You might think I'm bullshittin' but the GDs had that shit together, the Chicago crime rate was down when they was all out on the street. Hoover got all the other gangs in the city to do a peace treaty, even in the county jails. Larry Hoover was able to do this because he had the biggest gang in the city, they be sayin' its only thirty-somethin' thousand of 'em, but it's way more than that. It's like twice that. Anyway, it was really his members that was warring wit' all these small side gangs. Plus he was big in the joint, and Chicago is ran from the jails.

All these muthafuckin' members on the street, most of them ain't never seen Hoover, don't even know who he is, shit, I don't know who he is... but me and my whole projects is GDs. 'They' [local gov't] got scared of what Hoover was doing and they broke all the gangs up, not just the GDs. They broke the Stones up, the Vice Lords, niggas on the West Side, the "Fo's" (4 Corner Hustlers), them niggas was tryin' to buy a rocket launcher to blow up the police station. But the guy who was buyin' it didn't know he was dealin' wit' a undercover cop. When he found out, he went on the run. They had a manhunt for him but they never caught him. Eventually they found him in the trunk of a car with his throat cut and his tongue pulled through the hole in his neck (Columbian necktie).

41

"Gatorman" Bradley visiting Larry Hoover in Vienne State Prison

I got a firm denial that Nation's Day existed from King Hoover's long-time comrade, Wallace "Gator" Bradley, who was also once thought of as the "last man standing." But about a year and a half after the original article appeared in issue #9 it was rumored that he fell out of favor with Folk-kind and an attempt was even made on his life. In better days, Gator was the official GD political candidate and on behalf of the 21st Century Vote, he got into the race for Alderman (an individual elected to represent the interest of the common people and to be the voice of his community in political arenas) in the city of Chicago, with the support of thousands of GDs, their families and friends. Gator nearly won the election and caused a runoff. Gator met with me and dropped science about Chicago politics and how nothing has changed since the days of Al Capone.

Cavario: The government says that Larry Hoover and the GDs made $100,000,000 a year from drug sales. What is the government basing its claim on?

Gator: They're basing that on the one day a week program that Larry Hoover was talkin' about puttin' together. The program was to be that they go to the guys on the street that was selling dope and they was gon' shake drug dealers down. It was from a taped conversation that they got from Vienna, but they edited the tape [and] they excluded the part where Mr. Hoover said, "Nah, [we] better leave that program alone." They never came up with any money during the whole trial.

42

Gator's explanation of Nation's Day would make the GDs extortionist, not drug dealers.

Cavario: Well tell me how the fuck did Larry get 150-200 years for a murder?

Gator: Andrew Howard testified that he was the one who murdered William "Pookie" Young in 1973 and he was released on parole in 1993. People started askin', "If this guy admitted to the shooting then why is Hoover still locked up?" We all realized it was because Larry was takin' GD to another level, from a negative to a positive. From "Gangster Disciples" to "Growth & Development." The bug was put in the visitor's passes in '93; they didn't come and arrest Mr. Hoover 'til August of '95, right after the automatic election that I was involved in.

Cavario: I've heard the GD creed, it's one of the most powerful collections of words that I've ever heard. Do the young GDs today live by those words?

Gator: Well, you got those out there now that I say are pimpin' the GDs. They realize that Mr. Hoover is the leader of GDs and he's sayin' we no longer do what was done in the past. Now you must go to school, now we march to make sure we get jobs on construction sites. It's a whole new avenue now. We've become political; it's gone from the bullet to the ballot. They ain't doin' it like that so I gotta say, no.

I was told how GDs were required to go to school. GD coordinators kept attendance and the penalty for an unexcused absence was a "shot to the mouth."

After changing the name from Gangster Disciples to Growth and Development, and forming the 21st Century Vote Organization, Larry assumed responsibility for organizational activities. Among these were registering minority voters, instigating thousands of minorities to rally in a march on Chicago's City Hall and starting education rallies for the poor. He organized various charity events including "Save the Children Promotions" which sponsored free concerts for kids. He's also responsible for getting his spokesman Wallace "Gator" Bradley to meet with such political leaders as Rev. Jesse Jackson (who's half brother, millionaire businessman Noah Robinson is also incarcerated, serving several life terms for his alleged involvement with another Chicago gang–El Rukin) and President Clinton at the White House. Hoover required that if a GD wanted to be involved in the administration of '21st Century Vote' business, they were required to stop ALL illegal activity. It is also alleged that at this time Hoover ordered a ceasefire in the streets.

Through his political endeavors and outreach programs, Hoover gained favor with the Chicago community. During this time there were countless articles in the Chicago media defending Hoover and saying that he should be paroled. The community believed that Larry had the power to influence the youth of Chicago–namely the gang-bangers–a demographic that parents, teachers and conventional role models could not reach. Larry's legend, which gave him great influence and the ability to move people in a positive direction, was more than evident in the affect that he had when he conformed the Gangster Disciples to Growth & Development and began to focus on community development and outreach.

The government claimed that this sudden turn around from Hoover and the GDs was just a smoke screen for his criminal activity. They did not believe that the Gangster Disciples had turned over a new leaf and were now a political organization called Growth and Development. Hoover activists believe that it was Hoover's accomplishments in the political arena that scared the government most. If Hoover could influence thousands of people politically he would turn African Americans into a political force that would have to be heard and represented in the government.

In August of 1995 Larry Hoover, along with Adrian Bradd, Gregory Shell, Andrew Howard, Jerry Strawhorn, Darrel Branch, Tirenzy Williams and William Edwards were indicted for heading a multimillion-dollar organized crime syndicate that stretched across 35 states and into 40 major cities.

Within the four weeks immediately after Mr. Hoover was presented with his 1995 indictment for heading a Continuing Criminal Enterprise, police reported an eruption of shootings and 10 slayings of Gangster Disciples members. Apparent power plays...being done by members who were anticipating a change in ranking with the removal of communication from Mr. Hoover. Police braced themselves for GD infighting by starting up a special task force in an attempt to curb gang warfare.

While awaiting trial, more Gangster Disciple leaders were charged with the murder of two GD members that were working with the government-one an informer, the other a government witness.

The GDs showed up deep in the courtroom during the trial. You could hear hundreds of Hoover supporters all the way on the 19th floor, yelling

"FREE HOOVER!" Hoover had long ago won in the court of public opinion. The defense for Hoover called over 70 witnesses to testify to the existence and legitimacy of Growth and Development, 21st Century Vote and various other community programs Hoover started, but that wouldn't matter against the testimony of informants and the taped evidence the prosecution had against Hoover and the GDs.

Federal Judge Duff told assistant US Attorney Safer not to allow the recorded tapes of Larry and his associates to be heard by the public before the trial was concluded. Safer and the US Attorney's Office sealed one tape but not the two copies that were made. As a result, Judge Duff was on his way to court and heard excerpts of the tapes as then President of the United States Bill Clinton spoke about Larry Hoover and the Gangster Disciples "problem" on the radio.

Larry and the GDs were unable to get a truly fair trial by jury because everyone had heard some part of the tapes and of course, none of the positive parts. Attorney Safer was brought back into court and reprimanded, as Judge Duff told him that he "knew what they were trying to do" and he "wasn't going to allow it." Mysteriously, a short time later Federal Judge Duff removed himself from the case.

On May 9, 1997 after only 12 hours of deliberation the jury found Hoover guilty. US Attorney Safer appeared before the news media and said, "WE are the biggest gang in Chicago."

Larry is in the Florence ADX–Supermax Prison in Florence, Colorado serving six LIFE sentences, seven 2-year sentences and three 4-year sentences, all sentences running concurrently. At the time of the original run of this story in issue #9, Larry was awaiting word on an appeal from the United States Supreme Court. That appeal was denied.

After all was said and done, it was revealed by members of the prosecuting team that "Nation's Day," which was basically the foundation of the government's case, "Never happened." That means that on October 14, 1998, assistant US Attorney Safer and Styler, sworn officers of the court, had a duty to be truthful and reveal this imperative "exculpatory evidence" but decided to do the opposite and violate due process.
Inmates and prison sources said the Gangster Disciples' organizational structure remains largely intact behind bars in state prison and incarcerated GDs still celebrate Hoover's birthday.

Written and researched by Cavario H.
Interview conducted by Cavario H.

"That with which I cannot coexist must cease existence. This is what I understood..." —*from the autobiographical book Raised by Wolves*

Pete "THE PISTOL" Rollack

In just about all of its forms of entertainment the African American community tends to lionize outlaws, but glorifying the bad-guy is not just a "black thang," America's fascination with gangsters, drug dealers, hustlers, thugs and murderers dates back long before the inception of rap, the introduction of films or even the invention of television. Men who have made their mark in society by less than conventional means have been a part of the American landscape since this country began. Even our own heroic President George Washington violently rose to power and actively participated in one of the most nefarious Continuing Criminal Enterprises in history–the international slave trade. Yes, G.W. was an original bad boy.

On November 8, 2000, Peter Rollack a.k.a. Pistol Pete, was sentenced to Life in prison without the possibility of parole for his role in the murderous drug gang known as Sex, Money & Murder. Like those who came before him, Pete's crimes have earned him the description of "ruthless killer" with the government, but Pete's exploits have also inspired rap songs and made him a legend on the streets. SMMC was founded and incorporated by Peter Rollack and operated in the Bronx, New York; Pittsburgh, PA; and North Carolina. The government contends that the members and associates of Sex, Money & Murder agreed to commit killings in exchange for money or to acquire narcotics from other drug dealers.

Pete has been described by the office of Mary Jo White (the US Attorney in Manhattan) as a ruthless killer who hung pictures of Mafia members in his bedroom and called his murders "wet t-shirt contests" because his victim's bodies would be soaked with blood. They also said that his gang terrorized the Soundview and Castle Hill neighborhoods to maintain its grip on a lucrative crack business. The most heinous of his crimes was ordering the murders of David "Twin" Mullins and Efrain Solar in what has come to be known in the Soundview/Castle Hill area of the Bronx as the "Thanksgiving Day Murders." On November 27, 1997, David Mullins and Efrain Solar were killed in a burst of gunfire in front of about 30 people during a neighborhood football game between residents of the Soundview and the Castle Hill projects in the Bronx. In early August 2001 before he was sentenced, Pete reached out to me after he got his copy of the magazine–while he was in the hole. Just before Christmas, and after being sentenced, Pete made arrangements for me to meet with his mother to get his side of this explosive story. Because of the terms of his plea bargain, Pete was still in solitary with no outside contact and couldn't receive visitors, and he knew if he wrote us again, his mail would be confiscated.

The government is calling Pete's plea agreement an "unusual deal." He pled guilty to federal racketeering and the murders of eight individuals with the understanding that he would get life with no parole instead of the death penalty. Prosecutors agreed not to seek the death penalty against Peter Rollack as long as he agreed to the restrictive prison conditions that would limit visits to his lawyers and immediate family. Those conditions stipulated that Pete would be imprisoned in a maximum-security prison where he would be locked down 23 hours a day and segregated from all other inmates. His incoming and outgoing mail would continue to be heavily scrutinized, as would his phone calls. The media claimed that such harsh prison restrictions aren't widely used and sited that they were implemented only once before, in 1997 in the case of Luis Felipe, the founder of the New York Chapter of the Latin Kings, who was also accused of ordering murders from prison.

The government contended that these severe restrictions were necessary because Pete was so powerful and influential that he had the ability to continue his gang activities from prison. Many of the murders Pete pled guilty to took place while he was incarcerated and it was the government's contention that Pete ordered those hits through written correspondence with his gang members.

According to government documents, Sex, Money & Murder was founded by Pistol Pete around 1993. Its members and associates at various times included George Wallace, Andre "Dula" Martin, Robinson "Mac 11" Lazala, Shawn "Suge" Stokes, Rufino "Roro" Turner, Jasmine "Total Package" Mansell, Michael "MO" Gray, David Andino, Reginald "Big Boo" Harris, David "Twin" Mullins and Rafael "Scruffy" Moore. There were several other members involved in the court proceedings that were not indicted because they turned government witness, including Pete's right-hand man, Yaro Pack. At the time of the original release of this story in issue #5, Don Diva got it from a source that Michael Gray, who received 15 years, was soon to flip and turn government witness after sitting in prison for some time.

Although the media coverage on the Sex, Money & Murder gang had mainly focused on the violent murders that occurred, the indictment that came down on Pete and his associates included not only murder, but regular acts of violence, as well as robbery and narcotics trafficking. While it hasn't been focused on, according to the "streets," SMMC members were running massive amounts of narcotics up and down the East Coast. According to court documents, the members received their cocaine from Pete's uncle, George Wallace and John Castro, a former correctional officer who by the time this story was initially released was doing time for an unrelated murder, which occurred at Jimmy's Bronx Cafe. While it had not been confirmed at the time, it was believed by some of Pete's close associates that both Wallace and Castro had turned on Pete and snitched but verification of this was slow coming.

Pistol Pete in the Bronx with his new sports car

The members of Sex, Money & Murder legally incorporated under the name of *SMMC, Inc.* mainly to lease a fleet of luxury cars from a leasing company located in Pittsburgh, PA. It is rumored on the street that SMMC kept this leasing company in business with their own leasing contracts. The leasing company served two purposes for SMMC; it helped them gain easier access to all sorts of high-end vehicles and it helped them hide huge cash car purchases. To make up for the "corporation's" lack of credit, the leasing company got SMMC, Inc. deals financed by doing pre-paid leases. In an attempt to hide the massive amounts of currency being spent on some of the vehicles, the leasing company would make the paperwork appear as though the vehicles were leased but in fact the members would pay for these cars upfront in cash–often paying as much as $24,000 for a two-year lease before they drove the cars off the lot. Most of the vehicles leased through this company were equipped with secret compartments known as "stash boxes" used to conceal drugs, money and guns. Some of the vehicles obtained through the Pittsburgh leasing company were a fleet of Mini Vans used for trafficking drugs on the highway, a Hummer, an Acura NSX, Mazda RX7, Toyota Supra, two Cadillac STS models, as well as several BMWs and Mercedes Benzes. This crew had every hot street car imaginable in the early to mid 90s and they all had stash boxes–some as many as three.

Pete's prison nightmare began in late 1995 when he was arrested at Grant's Tomb in Harlem, NY for the murder of Carlton Heinz. He was incarcerated at the Riker's Island Correctional Facility in New York and it is here that the government claims Pete became a member of the Bloods. According to a "street" source, Pete and Carlton had beef over territory that Carlton controlled and Pete's associates wanted. Pete caught Carlton outside a car stereo installation shop off of Boston Road in the Bronx; he shot and killed Heinz and wounded another individual by the name of Carlos Mestre on April 8, 1994. A couple of months later, it's said that Peter caught Carlos Mestre coming out of a Hip-Hop clothing store known as "Jew Man," in the Bronx, and killed him because he was a witness to the murder of Carlton Heinz.

At the time Pete was arrested at Grant's Tomb for the murder of Carlton Heinz, he was carrying a gun and was required to do an eight-month mandatory sentence for the possession of an illegal firearm. Once this sentence was up, Pete's mother bailed him out. Pete walked free for two weeks. When he went back to court for the murder case he was remanded into custody because of a federal narcotics indictment out [of the Western

District] of North Carolina. Rollack was subsequently transferred to the Charlotte-Mecklenberg County Jail in Charlotte, North Carolina to await trial.

Pete in Federal Prison

While in prison in Charlotte, it is alleged that Pete continued to communicate with members of his gang and run his organization. Federal Agents intercepted Pete's incoming and outgoing mail while he was in prison in North Carolina. They claimed to have found evidence that Pete was in fact using the mail to direct the illegal activities of gang members. The government claims that through the mail, in the fall of 1997, Rollack ordered the "Thanksgiving Day Murder" of David Mullins a.k.a. Twin, a member of the SMMC organization, in order to prevent Mullins from testifying against Peter in his Federal Narcotics trial in Charlotte. The government also says that at the same time Peter put out an order to hit Damon Mullins, David Mullins' twin brother.

Most people believe that the government's investigations, and in some cases harassment, ends when they are sentenced to prison, but in fact for many, it is only the beginning. Men and women like Peter Rollack, who have developed reputations of being powerful and influential don't just do prison time; they do hard, confined prison time. Many people feel that this is rightly so. Pete's victims can't talk to their family and friends anymore, so why should he be able to? It was not Don Diva's role to take sides–only seek to enlighten our readers by disseminating the truth: it is–what it is.

Prison time is an ordeal in itself but when you add to it maximum security and restricted outside contact, you add a whole new level of punishment. Once in prison, outside contact with family and friends via letters, phone calls and visits is often the only thing that keeps inmates sane. When an inmate is being closely monitored and harassed it makes it very difficult for the inmate and his family and friends to stay in touch. This is no accident. Separating the inmate from the outside world is exactly the outcome the government has in mind.

For all prisoners it is a safe assumption that your phone calls, incoming/outgoing mail and visits are monitored but if you are an inmate that has been designated "a threat to the institution's security," you can bet that all of your communications are being monitored and recorded. Please believe that every rule that exists within the inmates' facility will apply to the designated inmate even if they are overlooked when it comes to other inmates. There is no "fair play"; designated inmates are public enemy #1 and they are usually cut no slack.

Oftentimes, monitoring an inmate's outside contact, and excessive restriction of their movement in prison is not an order of the court (as in Pete's case), however because of the inmate's reputation, the prison officials take it upon themselves to impose these conditions. You may believe that if you had a reputation of being a killer or a baller, it would earn you some respect in prison and guards and inmates alike would not trouble you. There is some truth to this–however, as with all things, there is a flip side to this. People fear what they don't understand and they often resent what they admire. In other words if a person wants to be you, he is more than likely going to "hate-on" you; this goes for prison officials as well as other inmates. You can bet that as soon as something goes down, like contraband being brought in or drugs being sold, you will get blamed, because you are the resident "bad ass."

Whether it is fear for the prison's security or just good ole' fashion playa hatin', prison officials will harass, confine, over-punish and scrutinize an inmate who seems to be influential or who has achieved a certain level of notoriety. Once you become "known" it is impossible to be anonymous, and in prison being "invisible" is the best way to stay out of trouble and bullshit.

The bottom line is that the "killer" reputation you develop on the streets, which will more than likely will play a major role in you getting locked-up, will also affect you while you are in prison. For most this means being affected for the rest of their lives. So while you're out there trying to make the newspapers, remember once you're "known," the attention you will receive, both good and bad, won't end even when you want it to.

Research and Interview by Cavario H. & Tiffany Chiles
Written by Cavario H.

SMMC, Inc.: The Inner Circle

Those of us closest to the situation might say that the demise of Sex, Money & Murder began long before Pete's arrest for the murder of Carlton Heinz. I'm going to take you back to early 1992, maybe late '91, back to a town in North Carolina where a good deal of cocaine was being bought and sold by many of the town's residents. Their supplier in the instance I write about here was a hungry young pusher named Yaro. Yaro was from the Soundview area of the Bronx and under the tutelage and sponsorship of a New York Correction Officer named John Castro, Yaro became a cash millionaire, just barely in his twenties. He moved across the country bouncing from state to state and city to city making a killing and doing a few as well. From Pittsburgh to Boston and all ports in between, Yaro made moves. A demure young fellow with a fair complexion and a large nose that scarcely overshadowed the festive smile beneath it, Yaro hardly fit the profile of a hardened drug lord or killer, but he was in fact silent and quite deadly. And at the point when he was no longer silent, he became even deadlier but mostly to his friends and comrades.

While in Charlotte, N.C. on one of his many money missions, Yaro, having apparently gotten too close to one of his local customers, carelessly exposed a concealed compartment built into his Nissan Quest mini-van and at some point during that ill-fated trip his vehicle was reconnoitered by the local authorities. In their "investigation," which was really nothing more than an illegal break-in based on their informant's tip, the police discovered several pounds of cocaine and a large sum of banded cash.

There was no one in the vehicle at the time, but Yaro and his associates were soon located and summarily arrested. But now here's where the story gets "unique"...Yaro and his associates were released, the story that he told Castro was (and I quote), "They confiscated the coke and then they said that they were keepin' the money as taxes on the money that we would've made off the coke." I strongly advised John against the likelihood of such a turn of events, "JB, I've been around this shit all of my life and I'm tellin' you there's absolutely no way that that happened that way." But his love for Yaro grossly impaired his judgment and he accepted the loss, which had to add up to about a quarter of a million dollars total. Neither the coke nor the money was ever spoken of again, and everything went on as usual, the whole potentially career-ending experience was chalked up to a very fortunate fluke.

Fast-forward a couple of years and many millions later...Yaro is on the move in Pittsburgh, the word is he was making a lot of moves this particular day preparing his crew for his routinely scheduled departure. Supposedly he had met with several individuals, given out several kilos of cocaine and collected close to, if not exceeding, a half million in cash. But before he could complete his day's tasks, federal agents snatched him out of his vehicle. The first thing that we had to be determine was if it was in fact the feds that had grabbed him, and if it was, then how long had they been on him? What did they see, what did they get? And most of all, who told what?

The following is an excerpt from my autobiography Raised by Wolves: *As we pulled side by side into our parking spaces, the Mustang pulled in behind us and sort of blocked us from the back. Two white men dressed in light colored jackets and worn-out jeans popped out of the Mustang. "Excuse us, we're from the Sheriff's department, can we speak to you for a moment?" I showed no expression I just opened my door and stepped out. "Do you have any weapons on you sir?" "Nah, I don't carry no weapons," I said. They informed us that they were instructed by the federal prosecutor in Charlotte to wait for us to return, "We been out here for two days...where y'all been?" O and I looked at each other and kind'a smirked. They asked us if we were going to the apartment, we said no, we were there to meet with a friend, to help him move. They didn't seem to know what to do with us, they didn't seem to really care to be there either– I guess the babysitting detail didn't appeal to them. The lead Sheriff told me that the feds didn't even tell him what the whole thing was about, "'Just wait here, check their vehicles when they pull in,' is about all they said. They told us that we should look for portable car battery chargers too but they didn't say why. Personally I could care less." With that statement O and I locked eyes again. We were starting to form a clearer picture as to why they were there.*

Inner Circle continues: In less than five hours after the news of his capture there was a story that reeked of weird, coursing through the crew in several cities across the east coast. It came down the wire that Yaro had been making moves in a "hooptie" (inconspicuous vehicle) and the feds were supposed to have had it bugged and therefore must have heard as well as seen everything he did on that day. Here again, another wild story surrounding Yaro. No one took time to analyze the sequence of events as they were described because the first focus is always to liberate the comrade whenever possible–"Let's get him out and then we'll figure this shit out."

To compound the situation, by this time John Castro was already in jail for shooting two brothers in front of Jimmy's Bronx Café on Fordham Road. The incident was the result of an altercation over a bottle of beer that one of the siblings had snatched from behind a bar. Jimmy and John were enjoying drinks and talking business when Jimmy noticed one of the young men reaching over the bar before drawing back with a bottle of Heineken. He turned to John and said, "Hey John, you gonna let them rob us like that?"

John glared as he focused on the young Latin gentlemen. He too was Hispanic but his medium brown complexion and Afro-affected features made that fact impossible to discern. He approached the young man and told him that he'd have to pay for the beer or leave. John told me that the guy was belligerent and bit the top off of the bottle before spitting it at him, hitting him in the chest. "I just looked down at where the top hit me and then I looked back at him, he was laughin' and looking at the other kid. That's when I punched him in the mouth."

The other brother jumped up but he was subdued before the squabble could escalate. They were both taken forcibly from the club. John went outside almost immediately after them, and was approached by the men. Some words were spat back and forth and then one brother instructed the other to go and get the gun. He spoke in Spanish and the brother was ready to comply but John stopped him, holding up one hand while his other hand pressed against his waistline where his pistol was. "Don't move pa'pa. I already got it right here."

When the brother heard John speaking his language with stark fluidity he paused. He understood Castro's body language even more clearly, indicated by the way his eye followed his hand to his mid-section. "I'm ready to die!" the brother responded in Spanish while nudging his brother to continue on his charge. I could see John's face contort with anger when he repeated the guy's words, and I could've finished the story on my own from there.

"When he said that I was like, 'Oh yeah? Okay!' Then I just blasted the both of them right there."

One of the brothers died from his wounds. The irony in this little sidebar is that it was said that the mother of the two victims worked with the New

York State liquor commission–she was probably the one that gave Jimmy's their liquor license–life's a bitch huh?

Back to Yaro, days passed and although everyone is doing business as usual, it is now clear that Yaro isn't going to slip out of this one–or is he? Maybe months past before the whole thing began to unravel; other people in the crew were getting visits from federal agents in places that no one (save the closest members of the team) was supposed to know about. Full-scale raids were waged at homes, and girlfriends' apartments and even stash cribs–something was very wrong but Castro could not see it. He was still blinded by the love that he had for the scrambling soldier that he had transformed into a millionaire general.

In fact it wasn't until after Castro was finally apprehended in Florida after purchasing 20 kilos of cocaine during one of the harshest droughts of 1995 from a connect that not only managed to have material when no one else seemed to but who had a price that was far below what it should've been considering the state of the market at the time.

Against everyone's advice and implorations, John, who was still a fugitive from the Jimmy's shooting, decided he would go himself and meet with this Florida connection. After copping the coke John decided that he needed to get to Charleston, S.C. to lay low and instead of using his alternate identification and taking a plane, he decided that he would ride back with the material in another Quest van. They weren't well on the road before they were pulled over and searched; of course the cocaine was found and John immediately took the blame for the work (drugs). After they were taken to the precinct, the young woman and her mother, who had come along to assist with driving during the intended multiple-stop jaunt, were released. John, under an alias, was held and charged with the cocaine.

The call came as soon as the ladies were released, "They got him, but they don't know who he is."

The next few weeks were a constant back and forth with the lawyer and the court, "Can we get a bail?"

"No… maybe… it's still undecided." And it went on like that.

"Do they know who he is? Hasn't his fingerprints comeback yet? Do they fingerprint Correction Officers and if they do, would the Florida authorities think to check New York Corrections' fingerprint files?"

There were many questions but only one real answer and after a couple of months of false releases, it finally revealed itself–"Hey, John... you know we knew who you were all the time, right?"

The cocaine 'fairy' that had come to our rescue, not only with the elusive product but with the primo price too, had himself been turned and allowed an agent to sit in on the buy; Castro was busted before he even entered the room.

Now both Yaro and Castro are in a pickle and it still isn't clear whose standing where or saying what but one thing was for sure–the shit was being slowly fed into the proverbial fan.

After a while the feds and Yaro dropped their ruse and from then it was all the way on. They went on a full-scale hunt for all the violent primaries in the Sex, Money and Murder organization.... first up, "The Pistol."

ACTUAL COURT EVIDENCE IN THE US V. ROLLACK TRIAL

MMC organization chart as displayed in
the court room during Pete's federal narcotics trial.

US v. Rollock

John Castro (Cocaine Source)	Peter Rollock "Pistol Pete"	George Wallace (Cocaine Source) (Pete's Uncle)

Yaro Pack "Savon Codd"

Xavier Williams

Tawana Lumberton, NC Bronx, NY			Efram
"Hat" Pittsburg, PA			Derious Covington Rockingham, NC
Mike Hanna Pittsburg, PA	Brian Boyd	David Mullings "Twin" Wil./ Lumberton,NC Bronx, NY	Andre Martin
David Evans Charlotte, NC Bronx, NY			"Chubby" Lumberton, NC Bronx, NY
Hershel McNeil Charlotte, NC Bronx, NY	"Bemo"	Emilio Romero "LeadPipe"	"Little Nat"	David Gonzales Charlotte, NC Bronx, NY
Sebastin Mathis Charlotte, NC Bronx, NY	"Big Ant"		"Scotty Bo"	"Calvin" Columbia, SC

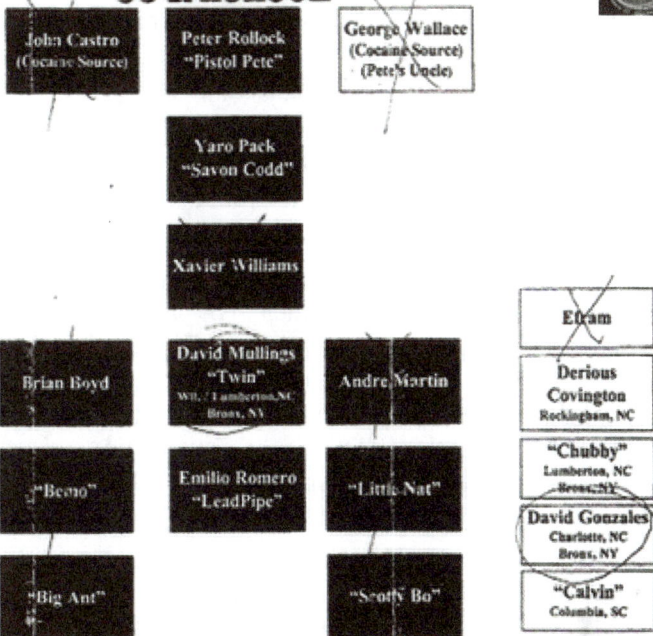

Peter Rollack

Hershel Mc Neil

David Evan

Savon Codd Yaro

Sebastin Mathis

David Gonzalez

57

Yaro had revealed to the authorities that we used vehicles equipped with stash boxes that were generally situated anywhere between the back seat and the trunk, and that they could only be opened when the red and black clamps of a portable car battery charger were placed in exactly the right position. Placed properly the positive and negative charges actuated the hidden lid on the box, which opened to reveal its contents. This was the reason that the Sheriffs were instructed by the feds to search Obie's truck and my own for the portables.

Before long even John had to face the irrefutable facts, Yaro had gone from, "Death Before Dishonor" to "Ball till I fall and then...tell everything that I know."

John was apparently prepared to fight his own battle for his own indiscretions and lapses in judgment. His philosophy was, "I got money, my lawyers will fight it, whatever it is." Granted not an entirely new concept for the field but it got him through his days. When the cards began to stack against him, his tune, of course, changed–"This nigga Yaro is sayin' that I did all this killin' that he actually did...am I supposed to just sit here and let him dump his shit in my lap?" John had the answer long before the situation had gotten that far... "That's what lawyers are for."

John received 11-years for the murder and 8 for the cocaine (apparently, 44 pounds of hydrochloride salt isn't that uncommon in the state of Florida) a relatively light sentence in view of his transgressions against many state and federal legislations. John's a free man now.... funny phrase "free-man." The reality is, in the life of a drug dealer, it costs to be a MAN–the only question is, "How much are you willing to pay?

Erick Bozeman "THE GENERAL"

"The first thing I want to address is Don Diva Magazine and the importance of a magazine like this. One of the things I feel this magazine does is give the prisoner, the 'grassroots', the individuals that don't have a voice, an opportunity to speak."
—Erick Bozeman

While everyone was watching OJ's trial on television there were three other trials simultaneously in progress. These trials took place in Los Angeles', New York's and Atlanta's federal courts. All three were connected to one man: Erick Bozeman. Had his trials been televised it could have brought in more ratings than the former football star and Heisman trophy winner.

"It is one of the largest cases we have ever prosecuted and one of the most sophisticated," U.S. attorney Kent B. Alexander boasted before the trials began.

Out of the 1,100 wire tap recordings, FBI agents were said to have acquired, they reported hearing Bozeman order as much as 300 pounds of cocaine at a time in conversations with drug sources in Columbia on his cellular phone.

However, while invading his privacy, what seemed to raise their eyebrows even more were other things they claimed to hear. Bozeman winning $50,000 gambling in Las Vegas, spending $150,000 a month on travel, restaurants, and business expenses and details of his stay at a very posh resort in Hawaii.

"It was so expensive, we freaked out when we heard. It was unbelievably expensive. It would be a lifetime before we could spend that much money," one of the officials said.

Erick Bozeman, born and raised in South Central California, was being accused of masterminding an operation that shipped cocaine inside of hollowed out computers throughout the United States, as well as laundering money through shell corporations [Shell Corporation: a dummy company that only exists on paper.] to off-shore accounts. Law enforcement authorities claimed this earned him more than 30 million dollars within a two-year time frame.

His indictment stated that he covered over 10 major black cities including, Memphis, Tennessee; Jackson, Mississippi; Baltimore, Maryland; District of Columbia; Detroit, Michigan; Chicago, Illinois; and Cleveland, Ohio; crossing geographical lines coast to coast–not at individual times, but simultaneously.

Records showed that Bozeman maintained multiple residences from the Eastside of Manhattan to Lakeshore Drive in Chicago, Buckhead in Atlanta and Miami's South Beach, just to name a few. He changed addresses and identities with ease. When asked where he lived, an official once stated, "He lived wherever he felt like living."

While more than half of Bozeman's fifty (50) codefendants made plea agreements with prosecutors, Erick did what no one ever expected or recommended he do–become his own lawyer and represented himself in federal court!

The feds charged Erick with multiple counts of conspiracy and money laundering and the main count, an 848 Kingpin charge, at the Atlanta Federal Courthouse along with two of his Chicago and D.C. codefendants. Eric enthralled everyone in the courtroom, including his co-counsel, with what was said to be one of the most unusual and unheard of courtroom cases ever to be tried.

Here are some excerpts from Erick's opening argument:

"…I'm sorry to inform you that you are all participants in a game by the government. I intend to expose that… I will not pretend to be Johnny Cochran or F. Lee Bailey in these proceedings: however, I come with the voice of reason and sound logic…

"…the War on Drugs. Ha, Ha, Ha. This war has taken on many forms in America, many forms and many faces. It has existed in one way or another since African prisoners arrived in 1619 as slaves. It was showing different faces of that war that said slavery was legal. It showed different faces of that war that codified Jim Crow into law… institutionalized Apartheid. It was showing different faces of that war that condoned lynching and made it socially acceptable."

Ms. Gordon (Prosecution) began speaking, "Your Honor, I am going to object. Race has nothing to do with this case. He's supposed to talk about the evidence."

Erick countered, "…I want you to be aware of the fact the law's engaging in what's called undercover entrapment, breaking the law in order to catch law breakers…."

"…The evidence in this case will show that right and wrong are of no major importance to the government. The evidence will show that, no matter what crime you commit, if you plea-bargain and work for the government, your crimes will be forgiven…."

"…The evidence will show that government witnesses are hostages of the government…"

"…Because I refused to accept a plea, I refused to work for the government, when I was first arrested in Los Angeles… (I am now a hostage.) The evidence will show that they offered me a job, they said, 'Mr. Bozeman, you are a young man. Your whole life is ahead of you. Will you accept a plea, work for us, inform, lock up everybody that you know?' In other words, they call that being a snitch. I call it selling your soul. So, in other words, I was told if I sell my soul that I would be turned loose…."

"…You know it would be a slap in the face and an insult to all of your intelligence for me to stand here and tell you that I had nothing to do with these activities, but I'm not going to say that, [or] that I received no profit…."

"…The evidence will show that I was born in the urban war zone of South Central Los Angeles where the real law is money and survival…."

Erick in St. Maritz

"...I was a broker just like Michael Milken [on whom the movie "Wall Street" was based] and Ivan Boesky [the original inside-trader that stole hundreds of millions on Wall Street.] Except I don't have six million dollars to pay a fine to the government and go home in three years, or just go totally unpunished like the people who ran the S and L's in America, for which every taxpayer is paying... [S&L: Savings & Loans "scam," in which more than a billion dollars were loaned out but never paid back to the banks. The debt was then passed on to the government and in turn to the taxpaying citizens of this country. Zeb Bush, son of then U.S. President George Bush, and the brother of former president George W. was "heavily involved" in the scam.]

"...I am not a drug dealer. I am not a Kingpin...."

"...In closing I say, do you remember, when Ali was a champ, his matches had names: 'The Thriller in Manila,' 'The Rumble in the Jungle.' But I entitle this trial: 'We The People, Don't Believe The Hype.' Thank You."

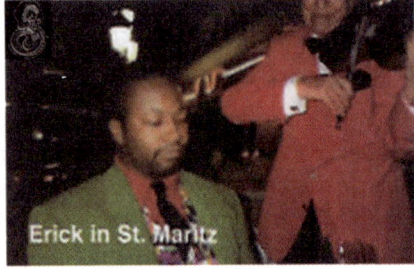
Eric in Paris

Susan Hamspstead: What made you decide to represent yourself?

Erick Bozeman: A couple of days after I got arrested a friend of mine sent me a book and that book was called, "The Autobiography of Assata Shakur." As I read that book her strength, defiance and revolutionary spirit throughout her unjust trial and the inhumane conditions of her confinement inspired me. Assata used her trial as a political stage and I decided to do the same because I always felt the "War on Drugs" was a war on blacks in America! Representing myself was the only way to present my views because no lawyer that wanted to continue his practice could have said the things I said in trial!

Eric's palatial Virginia Estate

Susan: Were the things you said during trial recommended and agreed upon by your co-counsel?

Erick: Prior to trial I had a lot of experience hiring lawyers and my opinion of them was very low in general. Brothers need to understand that federal court has a 95% conviction rate and that lawyers are not saviors, so stop putting all of your faith in them. During pre-trial I argued a motion very poorly so the prosecution laughed and thought that the trial was going to be a joke. I had never discussed strategy with co-counsel, being that this was my life they had to just follow my lead. I set the tone, I set the pace, and I set the direction and strategy. In my opening statement they had no idea what I was going to say, so it wasn't up to them to agree or disagree, not only was my co-counsel shocked at my delivery and presentation, the prosecution stopped laughing and did not think that 'Erick Bozeman' was funny anymore!

Susan: Who was the "tipster" that made them start an investigation?

Erick: The case started way out in Los Angeles as a money laundering investigation conducted by the IRS. It spread nationwide resulting in a multiple count indictment and a national sweep of arrests. However, I could not be located and only a few people were able to contact me. One of my closest friends called me, I went to the hotel lobby to call him and the call was being traced. His name is Marvin Epps. He betrayed me,

"Treason!" That's something that's characteristic of individuals in the streets these days.

Susan: How close were y'all?

Erick: Like brothers.

Susan: How long did you know him?

Erick: All my life.

Some excerpts from Erick's closing argument:

"Good afternoon, ladies and gentlemen. I would like to take this opportunity to thank all of you for the attention given to my case for the past two weeks. Even though at times it has moved at a snail's pace, it is important to you, but it is my life and my liberty at stake."

"To all the ladies in the jury I would like to apologize to you for being subjected to listening to conversations with me and my associates that are not befitting of a lady. However, in the environment in which I was, in that is the language, which is used. And, to the men, you have heard it all in the locker room before."

"I remember once, when I was younger and I had my first piece of money, I went home to my grandmother's house. She looked me in the eye and said, 'Son, whatever it is you are doing, you need to stop'."

"And there's a lady sitting on this jury that reminds me very much of my grandmother. In fact, she said that she had seen just about all the things there was to see in life, and I contend that, if I got before you and told a lie, she would know."

"I told you in the beginning of this case, I made certain promises to you. I stated that I would not insult your intelligence, that I would expose the whole picture. That I would simplify this mass confusion that this trial was not about right and wrong and that I would show you that, and that I was a capitalist, and that I was a broker."

"I also told you that I sold no drugs in Atlanta or in Georgia [and] that this case was about me snitching for the government, or the government wanting me to be a snitch for them, as you have heard it from the agents when they testified. And I said that I was the only one that could win this case."

"Ladies and gentlemen of the jury, I would like to say that this is a trial by jury to make a decision on the truth of each defendant and that this is based on the evidence presented in this case and also the absence of evidence presented in this case."

"Also something that you will have to take into consideration is reasonable doubt. Those are the things that you question when you say 'I think,' 'I guess,' 'It could be'. –That's doubt."

"I told you that I would expose the whole truth, and you notice every attempt that I made to expose the truth the prosecution here objected. If they didn't have anything to hide, why would they have objected to you hearing the whole story—-."

————Prosecution: "Objection, Your Honor…"

"…Well let's talk about a few facts. Let's talk about the C.C.E. [Continuing Criminal Enterprise] first, which is a very, very serious charge. I want you to be very confident in your decision. That carries Life without parole."

————Prosecution: "Objection, Your Honor. The penalty is not to be revealed to the jury."

"…She [prosecution] stated that I had substantial income, [and] that I went on vacation. She talked about millions of dollars that belonged to me. The evidence does not show that. Nobody has testified that Mr. Bozeman has a bank account with so much money in the bank account…"

"The absence of evidence, that's what I want to talk about. I don't want to talk about what she [prosecution] showed you. I want to talk about what they *didn't* present."

"Let's talk about the wiretaps for a while, which it was presented that everybody had a fundamental difference with. There were 1100 tapes… They brought to you 400 tapes [out of] 1100 tapes. If all of the conversations were criminal, why didn't they play the 1100 tapes? Because the conversations were not criminal. Because they taped me talking to girls, my mother, my family, everybody. Why didn't they present all the tapes to you?"

"…Why did the judge have to strike one of the tapes because she interpreted it as being criminal, because I was talking about Snoop Dogg, about my friend who was in the music business, talking over that contract. That's what we have here, the government's interpretation…."

"Well, let's get to the real, real meat of the case now. You saw one witness, Nina Stewart [and another] Bronwyn Burroughs...these were witnesses that were available to the government."

"...Why do we need interpretation of the truth when we have witnesses? These people signed plea agreements with the government. Part of their plea agreement was to come in here and testify. Didn't Bronwyn tell you that she had to testify, that it was part of her plea?"

"Why didn't they present Nina Stewart to you? Why is she interpreting what Nina meant? Bring Nina Stewart, put her on the witness stand, and let her tell you the whole truth."

"...She interpreted once again for Nina."

"...She wants you to find me guilty of something that was flown on a plane, and the person who was on the plane now works for the government, as a government informant, [and] has signed a plea."

Prosecution: "Objection, Your Honor..."

The jury deliberated for four days and came back with a hung jury on the Kingpin charge causing an upset for the government. Now news reporters and television crews wanted answers, including Dan Rather who was refused a visit by officials to speak with Erick the day before sentencing. CBS News ran the story regardless. Headlines of Erick's verdict flooded the papers: "Californian Acquitted of 5 Big Drug Charges..."

A black man representing himself, playing the race card he was dealt, was relieved of some of his charges by his peers! Now everyone waited with bated breath for the sentencing. Judge Clarence Cooper, an African American, had the spotlight on him.

Excerpts from the sentencing:

Judge Cooper:

...Let the record reflect that the statutory penalty for counts two and ten is ten years to life and/or a four-million-dollar fine as to each count. The statutory penalty for count twenty-eight is 20 years and/or $500,000 fine... the custody guideline range is life.

Erick Bozeman:

...First of all I would like to ask that I be placed at USP Plantation Atlanta...

...I would like to ask that I be allowed my last words before being sentenced to death by incarceration...

Eighteen months ago I stood before this court and stated that I would represent myself. Everyone in the court fell out laughing. You (Judge Cooper) smiled. The clerks looked in disbelief.

And the prosecution fell out of their chairs laughing, anticipating an easy victory. Afterwards I sought the help of an African American firm. At that time I began to mentally formulate my strategy, which was centered on the following elements: One was to be judged by a group of my peers.

The next was to expose, like never before, the hypocritical and unethical, in my eyes, power of the prosecution's office which started from the day of my arrest when, as the agents testified in trial, the F.B.I. asked me to work with them.

The second thing was exposing the great lengths that the government participates in breaking the law in order to achieve its goals.

The third thing was showing the jury that right and wrong are irrelevant and that somebody that's facing a large amount of time is subject to the power and discretion of the D.A. They have the power to pardon that individual in exchange for favorable information or testimony.

...The reality of the situation is based on economics and that the drug laws are draconian and racist in nature.

And, lastly and most importantly of all, that, when taking these things into consideration, that, not only does the jury system in America have the right to decide guilt or innocence, but something much greater is that the government is supposed to work for the people, and that the people have the power to pardon an individual, [and] to change the law.

However, that is one of the biggest problems facing America today. The people have lost that control of power to lobbyists, [and] to lawmakers with their own agendas, to economists that have the desires of Corporate America ahead of the desires of the average American.

However, with this case they had the opportunity to tell America, especially when it came to the unethical, biased courts: 'Enough is enough. We have pardoned Mr. Bozeman from a life sentence... We do feel that he should be punished, but we do not feel that he should deserve a life sentence'.

Since that time your honor, you have become quite a popular fellow, and America has sent its agents of propaganda to hear your decision. The jury reached a decision that rocked the federal building, and, because the D.A. presented a very poor case based on speculation and assumption, with no first-hand witness testimony to come forward, how do you present the biggest drug case to ever be presented in Atlanta and not bring forth one person to testify confirming the speculation and direct involvement of the alleged activities? And now the ministers of propaganda have the audacity to imply that I played the racist card, that blacks, Negroes, African Americans don't have the ability to make a rational decision in the jury box based on their own reality, based on their lives and the lives that exist in their community.

...One last statement, I most definitely want to take this opportunity to salute all of my brothers that refused to cooperate with the government in exchange to be free. Death always, before dishonor.

Judge Cooper:

Mr. Bozeman, you are obviously bright and very intelligent, and I don't understand why you chose to pursue the career you chose, that is, a career trafficking in drugs. It's really regrettable that a person with your ability would use his talents in such an unlawful way...

...I see a man standing before the court who acts as if he is being sent to jail for doing nothing wrong, and that just upsets me...

...someone having done all of this, has the gall to put everybody else on trial...

Let the record reflect that, pursuant to the Sentencing Reform Act of 1984, it is the judgment of the court that the defendant, Erick Bozeman, is hereby committed to the custody of the Bureau of Prisons to be imprisoned for a term of life on each of counts two and ten and a term of 20 years on count twenty-eight, all to be served concurrently.

Susan: Explain to me the verdict and what that verdict meant and the sentencing and what the sentencing meant.

Erick Bozeman: The verdict was a victory and an alarming message to the government at the same time. Most jurors and especially black jurors have no idea as to the amount of time given to defendants in a federal trial, nor would they agree to participate in what equals a Legal Lynching! This was part of the foundation of my trial strategy, which proved correct. My indictment consisted of 29 counts, I was found guilty of only three counts.

Although it's against court rules to inform the jury about the amount of time a charge carries, I did it anyway and after the verdict the jury stated that they refused to find me guilty of any charge that carries a mandatory life sentence.

Although the jury clearly made its wishes known, during the sentencing phase the government and the courts have what they called "Preponderance of the Evidence" which means that a judge can hold you responsible of relevant actions (previous arrests for similar crimes) although you have been found not guilty of them by a jury. This process strips away from the jury the right to be the final "tryer" of the facts and removes from them their unified voice that says, "He's not responsible," "He's not guilty of what you charged him with!" This was the method used to raise my guidelines and increase my sentence to Life!

Regina Austin and Paul Butler, two black legal scholars, have written in Law Journals that as a defense mechanism, not only should certain laws be ignored, but that black jurors should stop finding the defendants guilty of certain crimes, i.e. drug sales. This strategy is called Jury Nullification!

Erick is currently teaching black studies in Edgefield Federal Correctional Facility to fellow inmates that before their incarceration were never taught their history and worth.

"To all of my family, comrades, conscious and unconscious POW's: Death Before Dishonor! Victory is the only option."
–The General E.

Original interview by Susan Hampstead

Edited by Cavario H.

"Fear not the racist, for he has no power. Beware the class'ist that lives in the tower."

–Cavario H.

GET OUT OF THE MATRIX

What is the Matrix? Imagine a room with only three walls, each fifteen feet high; your challenge is to escape this room. There's no question as to which way you would go, obviously your direction would be the path that presented the least resistance. But who designed this room? I pose the question because whoever put the walls up in the first place is the same whoever that determined the direction you would be taking and this was determined before you ever entered the room. This is the illusion of choice–this is the Matrix.

It's a fact that twenty-and-some-odd-number of years ago, a kilo of Heroin averaged at a cost of about $225,000 (give or take $25,000) –and after traveling thousands of miles from, let's say for the sake of conversation, Asia's Golden Triangle to a New York City drug mill, it could be cut as much as 100 times, to be bagged for street sales. By the mid 90s the price was as low as $70,000–and the 'dope' could barely hold a '10' (10-grams of additives, commonly referred to as "cut," to every 1-gram of Heroin). In the late 70s until about the first half of 1982, just as free-base (later to be named "crack" by the mainstream media) became more regularly accessible, a kilo of Cocaine was going for something in the neighborhood of $60,000, and you could hit it three or four times and still have "nitro," which is what we referred to "good" cocaine as back then. But by 1986-87 the common price was as low as $13,000 (per kilo), and if you tried to put anything on it (in the line of cut), it had better be more cocaine–because that's all it could withstand.

In the "old days" there were just a few cats that could get either Cocaine or Heroin, in large quantities, and they were basically supplying the suppliers who were supplying everyone else.

But in the last twenty-five years or so it seems everybody and their mother has or is a connect.

There's no doubt in my mind that the availability of drugs is being manipulated, and I can see why. The more prices drop, the more "opportunity" becomes available, and more people are able to spend more money, to buy more groceries, more cars and more clothes, etc. Before you know it, an economy is stimulated.

But when the availability on the street is abruptly decreased, it brings about increased desperation and mindless behavior: "panic," especially in those who have become accustomed to the more, more, more. They're being shook from the Matrix (temporarily).

When drugs become increasingly more difficult to get, most dealers and wholesalers assume that the "panic" (shortage) is due to a major bust. A "major bust," or even the rumor of one, can affect the streets in the same way that a forecast of severe cold in Florida does the price of Orange juice– prices soar when people anticipate scarcity. Whether the bust does or will affect supplies that are already in the country or even shipments slated to arrive (but feared by connects to likely be on hold because of the potential of a compromised transport route) it is assumed by most that the price will go up and availability will decrease because simply, "There ain't no coke on the streets!" But in the mid 1980s, in lieu of a major raid on the largest cocaine processing plant in Columbia, "Tranquilandia," and the subsequent limited embargo of the chemicals necessary for the processing of coca leaves (ether/acetone), the cartels were forced to come up with a way of circumventing the policies being put into practice by the various interdiction forces, severely limiting their ability to manufacture the literally tons of cocaine base that their organizations were producing a month.

The cartels realized that although the chemicals were being closely monitored when leaving the states, there was little scrutiny on the coca leaves coming into the country. So, they "brought the mountain to Muhammad.

The first coca leaf processing plant discovered in the U.S. was in an upstate New York farmhouse in a sleepy, little, burg called Minden, a town in Albany. The year was 1985; this signified the beginning of a new era on the streets of America. The domestic dispensation of the popular powder opened a floodgate of new jack entrepreneurs. Without decree, coca had left her mountainous, green, southern American homeland and migrated to the hamlets of the United States. She was now the newest neighbor to North American cities, and although incomparable to the serenity and beauty of her tropical homeland, the America's concrete jungles had much to offer- natives ever restless for her.

These processing plants were set up in small towns largely in the southeast and often just a few miles away from the highway. There were instances where as I drove down I-95, dubbed the "cocaine pipeline," I was positive that I smelled massive amounts of acetone. At the time I was unaware of the plants having been transplanted to the states but I always thought that the way the prices had dropped so drastically from what they were in 1979 to what they were in 1990, somewhere in the processing something had changed. I was sure that the work was being done in the states by this time

71

but I, like the rest of America, was oblivious to the transplanting that had occurred.

Cocaine has been illegal for over 90 years, deemed so after falling from grace as the "wonder drug" used to treat Asthma, digestive disorders and morphine addiction. And most Americans have heard that cocaine was used in Coca-Cola prior to the enactment of the Harrison Act in 1914 after coca was deemed a "narcotic."

Meanwhile, back on the street, when the material (cocaine and heroin) got cheaper, it also began to get weaker, we had to hustle harder, only to make as much money as we used to; then the material got even weaker and we had to hustle harder still, only to make less. I don't believe that at any point nature decided to produce a less potent strain of the plants from which heroin and cocaine come. I suspect that the processing labs, where those plants are converted to their narcotic forms, are where those changes are occurring. Some people might assume that the drug lords of Europe, South America, the Middle East and Asia just got greedier, and decided that they would make more money off of less material, and those who assume this may be partially correct but let me point out two things: the first is that the drug lords are not hurting for material or money. I mean, let's face it, in some countries the stuff grows wildly out of the ground.

Second, I think they would have continued to flood this country with the highest-grade product they could possibly produce, until the sun itself burned out– what do they care about the people in America going to prison at an unbelievable rate or dying slow, agonizing deaths from using drugs? I'd venture to entertain that there was a new arrangement thrust upon the foreign drug lords by their greedier North American counterparts, the ones whose jobs are made easier and whose political careers are furthered through better "public image." Better public images are made possible when "less drugs" (at a higher profit margin) are let onto to the streets. The desired result is that it looks as though "They" give a fuck about the masses. You may have heard about this arrangement, it's often referred to as, "The War on Drugs."

The prices of drugs on the street are often manipulated through "panic" tactics. That means that material is being held back in order to drive the price up, to maintain a market 'plus-point' that makes dealing with narcotics a seemingly worthwhile venture to the desperate and disenfranchised.

At their heights, these man-made panics have driven cocaine's street price up to as much as $40,000 per ki'. I say "man-made" as opposed to a natural occurrence causing the mass destruction of coca crops over in South America and affecting the availability in this country to such a degree that it drives the prices through the sky. It ain't nothin' but game. But that level of game means decreased availability for people on the street– in an environment of increased risk. At the same time, that game has resulted in greater profits for the many multi-national conglomerates that are building new prison facilities in small towns all over the country, creating jobs and thriving mini economies in little upstate towns that most of us have never heard of. And brothers wallowing in desperation resulting from a lack of quality education and opportunities in their communities, frustrated by the day-to-day strain of hood life, are all but lining up for a spot in those fine, new facilities; all for chasing the dream of curvy women, quick cars and lots of cash.

During my nearly two decades in the street, I had come across dudes that presumably had a lot of cash, they may hav   e even been "millionaires," they most certainly qualified for the more popular term: "nigga-rich." Back in the 80s it wasn't uncommon to find several sneaker boxes full of cash, 10 and 20,000-dollar stacks, in a tenement or housing projects apartment in any ghetto, in most American cities. This seemed cool– I mean if you came up hard and hungry and at some point found yourself able to actually put your hands on a couple of hundred-thousand dollars; having all that money at your immediate disposal, you might feel a sense of control over your own destiny.

Who wouldn't feel a sense of security, having cash like that around? You'd most definitely believe that with it you could handle any problem– it may even feel like power. But there are many flaws in that type of power. One of the major flaws is that paper doesn't belong to you, it belongs to the Federal Reserve. And since it is the property of that privately owned corporation, as is stated on each and every "document," it does not matter how much of it you have under your mattress or in your closet. If the Fed's enforcement agency, alternately referred to as the "federal government," does not acknowledge your stash as legitimate, then it may as well be old newspaper. If "your" money isn't flowing in this country's mainstream economic system or at least recognized by an established banking organization, then it really doesn't provide you leverage, and it really isn't power at all. It's sitting there in shoe boxes and you can look at it and count it over and over again, but you know you had better be careful where and how you spend it. At some point you may realize that all that paper is somewhat of a burden, "What am I gonna do with it, where can I hide it? How many chains and whips can I cop?"

Although these dilemmas may be less burdensome than hunger or despair, they are still burdens (if you haven't been there, I really don't expect you to appreciate that point). But as with any burden you'll probably seek to relieve yourself of its stress. So for the lack of better ideas you may go to car dealerships, jewelry stores and malls, which is fucked up because most colleges and trade schools will take that paper just as quickly, and they won't ask any questions either. But you're gonna look kind of silly walking around with a degree on your neck or trying to put 20 inch rims on a certificate of achievement–so fuck that, right?

Question: When is a profit not a profit?

Answer: When the *definite* risks far outweigh the *potential* rewards. When this is the case, it is just not a worthwhile chance to take. Believe me, I know about "Right-Now-syndrome" and "I Don't Give a Fuck-itis," but many of the judges in this country's court system care even less about you than you do. Many of them (not all) especially "don't give a fuck" about giving you 30, 40 or 50 years in a prison cell. In fact they have a more difficult time deciding what to order for lunch than they do serving you a Life bid.

The sentencing for drug-related crimes has become more severe over the years, almost in direct correlation to the decreased profitability of selling them (makes ya' say, "Hmmm" don't it?) and the people that are most affected by that increased severity are probably the least aware of it. Mandatory minimums are so rigid that even first time, nonviolent offenders are more often being imprisoned– is it because of the "War on Drugs?" No. It's because a prison without inmates is like a hotel without guests. Where's the profit in that? The people on the street, including cops, are no more than lubrication for the life-grinding wheels of "the system."

A system that's making the rich richer and is condemning the poor to an existence that rivals generational indentured servitude until death. This is the case in the world as well as in prison. "America" is a business, run by businessmen under the auspices of "government." From the viewpoint of people from the street, it has become painfully obvious that the main commodities in this "business" are drugs and human lives. Not a bad stock and trade when you think about it, plants and people are two resources that are not likely to run out anytime soon.

In his governmental expose, *Behold A Pale Horse*, ex-Naval Intelligence Briefing team member and author William Cooper (RIP) exposed many common practices of this "system." In chapter 1 of the book, "Excerpts from Silent Weapons for Quiet Wars," under the excerpt heading "Energy" (second to last paragraph) it states; "In order to achieve a totally predictable economy, the low-class elements of society must be brought under control, i.e., must be housebroken, trained, and assigned a yoke[1] and long-term social duties from a very early age, before they have an opportunity to question the propriety[2] of the matter. In order to achieve such conformity, the lower-class family unit must be disintegrated by a process of increasing preoccupation of the parents and the establishment of government-operated day-care centers for the occupationally orphaned children."

[1] Yoke: subjection, servitude.

[2] Propriety: rightness or justness.

I was taught, "The game is to be sold, not told," and I believe that the price is substantially greater than the cost of a newspaper. Most criminals believe that they are operating outside of the system– but the truth is they are doing just as the circumstances being systematically perpetuated, through a campaign of information manipulation and greed, religious anesthetizing and blindfolding, dictate they do. Information is and always will be power; for one to believe that the privileged few who possess the greatest degree of that power are going to just give it away for the cost of a daily rag is, in my opinion, unrealistic.

Consider that, and this as well: people want to be entertained more than they want to be informed. The privileged few, overstanding this fact, provide as much entertainment as they can and keep the majority of information for themselves– in their own, "more responsible, more capable and more deserving" hands.

And for what we do not know, those of us on the street have paid, and will continue to pay, with all that is dearest to us: our families, our freedom and our sanity. I've shared this theory with different people over the years, and whether they are civvies or soldiers, "black-hats" or "white-collars," the common response is, "If they can control the drugs flowing into this country, why don't they just stop it?" To which I can only respond with a shrug of my shoulders and a simple one-word answer, "Control." You probably thought I was going to say, "Money." If that's so, then you really haven't been paying attention, I'll make it plain…Information is power, money in the hands of the uninformed is just paper. They may as well wipe their asses with it.

"I'm the first and only man, Black or White, to enter the system as an alleged Organized Crime Boss (Drug Kingpin), taught myself the law to the extent where I rivaled the skills of the best attorneys, made new law for lawyers to argue and courts to follow, obtained the release for other prisoner as well as myself, witness the suicide of the man who put me in prison and made history in the process. I rewrote the book on what it means to be an O.G."

Isaac Wright

Issac Wright in Las Vegas November 2000 wearing a custom made Milan Edition Lambskin designed by Robert Cavalli worth $45,000.

Isaac Wright, after being convicted as a drug Kingpin, was sent to prison where he was to remain for the rest of his life. While incarcerated, he taught himself law and the art of litigation to a degree unimaginable and unprecedented in the penal system and then, single handedly, embarked on a journey that resulted in the judge who presided over his trial being sent to prison; the prosecutor, who tried him and obtained his conviction, committing suicide; and his release from prison with convictions being vacated and all charges dismissed.

On July 25, 1989, Isaac Wright Jr. was arrested in Passaic County, New Jersey by a joint task force of law enforcement officials from Passaic, Middlesex and Somerset Counties. The arresting officers beat him. One officer led the beating while Wright's wife was forced to watch the beating.

"...The next step is to take a bullwhip and beat the remaining nigger male to the point of death in front of the female and the infant. Don't kill him, but put the fear of God in him..." excerpt from "The Making of a Slave" written in-line with Willie Lynch's manifesto, delivered in 1712.

Upon arrival at the Franklin Township Police Department, Isaac was charged with narcotic offenses, including being the "Head of a Narcotic Trafficking Network" (New Jersey's Drug Kingpin Statute)– a crime that carries a mandatory Life sentence. Authorities accused Wright of being the leader of a $20 million dollar a year drug trafficking network throughout four of the largest counties in New Jersey. According to the authorities, it was a profound and complex criminal case involving a large and sophisticated drug organization with 12 major codefendants. In Stark contrast, Wright possessed only $96 in cash at the time of his arrest, and ultimately, the prosecutor could only locate about $600 to forfeit.

According to Isaac Wright, it was a treasure hunt by the lead and head prosecutor, Nicholas L. Bissell Jr. The plan was to set Wright up, confiscate his wealth and possessions, skim their share off the top, and then force Wright to set his friends up. Wright refused and, in retaliation, Bissell set out to convict him. Everything was going as planned for Bissell and those other law enforcement officials working with him. They had arrested Wright, used illegally obtained evidence and perjured testimony to indict him as a drug Kingpin, falsified police reports, altered wiretap tapes, coerced his codefendants to lie in testimony against him at trial in exchange for secret non-custodial sentences, and somehow got the cooperation of the presiding judge in order to make it all work smoothly. Accordingly, Wright was convicted and sent to prison for the rest of his life. Specifically, he received a sentence of Life imprisonment on the Kingpin conviction and in excess of seventy years on nine other convictions.

Isaac decided to try his criminal case himself (proceed pro se). He knew he had been setup and understood the obsession associated with convicting him. He realized that there was no one that could help him. He was going to be convicted regardless of whether he was rich, poor, guilty or innocent.

In fact, Bissell was prosecuting him personally. Therefore, proceeding pro se was even more important because it would make it personal (him against Bissell). Isaac knew that making it personal would invoke mistakes on the part of the prosecutor.

In 1991, Wright would begin a civil suit against all the law enforcement officers and entities involved in his case. On the surface, this civil suit was based on all the wrong that was done to him by these officials. Deeper, however, was the fact that the suit allowed him to gather evidence against the prosecutor that he would never have been able to obtain under any other circumstances.

Wright constantly and consistently submitted various motions to the court after he was convicted and awaiting appeal. He knew these motions were going to be denied regardless of merit. However, they served two main purposes; they kept attention and focus on his case by the media and they bought him time to gather evidence and to expose certain portions of that evidence that could not be exposed in relation to his case. For example, through the years Wright acquired evidence that the presiding judge was corrupt and that the prosecutor was a thief and had engaged in tax fraud. This had nothing directly to do with his case and could not be used as a means to request relief (lesser punishment or exoneration).

However, it was a matter of public importance. Exposing it to the public would mean weakening the powerful and corrupt hold Bissell had over the county and county officials, including the judge. Thus, at one of the motion hearings, in 1994, after the judge had denied his request for relief, he saw and took the opportunity to expose both the judge and prosecutor in open court by yelling out their transgressions as prison officials were escorting him back to prison. Just as he had anticipated, the media jumped on the statements, quoting Wright word for word. Thereafter, citizens with personal knowledge of these acts as well as those that had been victimized by Bissell came forward and the government began to investigate them both. The judge was eventually removed from the bench and sent to prison and Bissell was indicted on 33 counts of tax improprieties such as fraud and evasion, as well as other crimes, including threatening to plant cocaine on a business partner. He was removed from office by then Governor Christie Todd Whitman.

Wright knew his case was very political and that his appeal would probably be denied because of the politics. Therefore, he used the case of another prisoner serving life for being a drug Kingpin. He began by creating a brand new legal theory regarding the jury instructions that explained the Kingpin crime. He reasoned that the instructions that were being used forced the jury into rendering an unjust verdict. He then argued that theory in the other prisoner's appeal and won. This victory created a new precedent in New Jersey courts. Wright then took this new interpretation of the law and had his own Kingpin conviction reversed on appeal in 1995.

In 1996, Wright motioned the court to dismiss the entire case against him and release him from prison. This motion was based on newly discovered evidence and prosecutorial misconduct. The court allowed Wright to have a hearing and call witnesses. During this hearing, and under examination by Wright, a police detective, James Dugan, confessed to falsifying his police reports, giving false testimony to a judge in support of arrest and search warrants and illegally confiscating evidence. The Chief of Detectives and Bissell's close friend admitted thereafter that there was a meeting between officials where a decision was made to cover it up and to use the illegal evidence to indict and convict Wright. Other instances of corruption came out when a defense attorney admitted he made secret and illegal deals with the prosecutor, on behalf of one of Wright's codefendants who testified falsely against him, to aid in the conviction of Wright.

The moment these confessions became public, Bissell, fearing more time in prison, took flight with his former co-law-enforcers in hot pursuit. U.S. Marshals eventually cornered the fugitive in a sleazy casino hotel in Laughlin, Nevada. When they attempted to lure him out of the room to arrest him, Bissell screamed, "I can't do 10 years!" then placed a gun in his mouth and pulled the trigger, killing himself instantly.

In December of 1996, the court granted Wright's motion and released him from prison. In 1997 all charges against him were dismissed.

A fundamental difference in the outcome of Wright's plight was his uncanny and extensive knowledge of the law. It was this knowledge that not only gained him unconditional respect in the legal community, as well as his freedom, but Wright's legal quest has affected the lives of over twenty prisoners, many with life sentences. Wright's work gave them new hope for relief, got their sentences reduced or gained their release from prison completely.

Isaac Wright (& date), Cavario H. at Wendy William's 1st Dons&Divas party

I hooked up with Isaac Wright to get his side of the story. Recognizing that only Don Diva would represent Isaac as the Legal Don he is, Isaac gave me the following exclusive.

Cavario: Who is Isaac Wright, Jr.?

Isaac Wright: Isaac is the third son of a black man. I was born in Orlando, Florida in a military family. My father spent 30 years in the Army before retiring. He also worked for the South Carolina State Police before retiring from there too. I lived all over the world, spending over seven years in Augsburg and Bremehaven, Germany. I have four brothers and one sister. I grew up in a household of gladiators, with a father that trained and prepared us, and a mother that nurtured us. Character and discipline are necessary virtues to me. Winning is everything. How you play the game is not important unless you're losing. Accept death before dishonor or defeat. Sharing with the people around you is [also] an important rule of life and living.

81

Cavario: Are your parents together?

Isaac Wright: Yes. They've been married for over forty years.

Cavario: What do your brothers and sister do?

Isaac Wright: My oldest brother was a Golden Gloves boxer. My second brother lives in New York. He used to be the City Planner of Brooklyn, which means that no construction could take place in the streets of Brooklyn without his approval. Now he's in charge of all of the bridges and tunnels in the entire city of New York. My third brother, who was also in the military (Army) has his own private security firm. He provides security for individuals, corporations and many celebrities in the entertainment and sports fields. My baby brother is twin to my sister. He's a contractor and has his own construction company. My baby sister was the General Manager for one of the largest apparel store chains in the country.

Cavario: How did you wind up in New York?

Isaac Wright: When I came to New York, I found myself, in many ways, in the street. I didn't come to New York a rich person or a momma's boy or a person with handout intents. I came to New York as a kid believing with everything in his soul that he was a man. I had $60 dollars in my pocket when I got off the Greyhound bus. I didn't consider where I was going to live. Didn't consider it until it was too late. For a good part of when I first came into New York, I was in the street. Until then, I had never experienced the streets before. I was totally green and completely oblivious to the harsh reality of what was in store for me. I can remember sitting in Penn Station contemplating my survival. I can remember rejecting all of the options that I had like calling my two older brothers, who were both down south at the time, and asking them to help me [or] calling my mom or dad for assistance or guidance [or] going to my grandparents in Boston. Or just going back home to a warm house with large bedrooms and a huge yard until I was financially ready to make that move. I had no family here at that time.

I didn't consider the fact that it might be very difficult for me to make my way in New York, a young kid all alone with no money. I had an unstoppable character, and in a lot of ways I still do. I felt that whatever came my way; no matter how hard, no matter how rough, I'll get around it. In an attempt to survive, I actually studied the migration of bums and homeless people as they moved throughout the city at night. In essence it was the derelicts and nomads that indirectly contributed to my survival

82

until I was able to hustle up the money needed for me to find my way out of the streets.

Cavario: What were you doing before you were arrested?

Isaac Wright: Well, I married very young. She was my high school girlfriend and we had a daughter. We were very poor at the time but that changed as our entertainment careers began to blow up. I was a producer and owned a label called X-Press Records. My roster on the label included the Ultimate III, ESP & 2 Much, the female rapper (La Shawn) who did the original song "Doin' It" (it was actually called "Wild Thang" before LL Cool J sampled it and called it "Doin' It"). My wife (Sunshine Wright) was a platinum recording artist with the group The Cover Girls (best known for the songs, "Show Me" and "Wishing On a Star".) She was also one of the top Black models in the City at that time.

Cavario: Are you and your wife still together?

Isaac Wright: No. In fact, my imprisonment completely destroyed my family. It scattered us like a tornado. I was in prison in New Jersey. My wife [was] in upstate New York with her family and our daughter was with my parents in South Carolina.

Cavario: Tell us about your arrest and charges?

Isaac Wright: To begin, it was the first and only time I ever went to prison. I was arrested in Passaic, New Jersey and charged with being a Drug Kingpin and the leader of a $20-million dollar a year drug empire operating throughout Passaic, Essex, Middlesex and Somerset Counties in New Jersey. At the time of my arrest, I was placed in handcuffs. The police then removed the shoes from my feet, escorted me to a mid-street location and forced me to my knees. Upon forcing me to my knees, the guys who arrested me along with other police began beating and kicking me. One of the officers told the others how they should beat me. He kept telling them not to hit me in the face. Simultaneously, he pushed my head down, forcing my chin to touch my chest in order to prevent the other police officers from punching me in the face. I was going to have to take mug shots so they did not want any evidence that I had been beaten to show up on the pictures. A female officer grabbed my wife and pulled her by her hair to the scene where I was being beaten.

They then forced her to watch the beating at gunpoint as they screamed at her. They were saying things like, "look at the bastard now," "look at the nigger," "he ain't so big now is he?" I didn't even realize she was there until I felt her tears falling on the back of my arm. I forced my head up and saw her being silent in her agony, not wanting me to know what she was seeing. After they had finished, they grabbed me by my groin and pulled me up until I was completely off the ground. They carried me like that with my face towards the ground, keeping me balanced by pulling on my elbow. They then threw me in the back of a utility vehicle and transported me to the police station. Although I had 12 codefendants, I was ultimately tried alone. Everyone else had taken deals. Earnest Ervin, who now lives in Atlanta Georgia, Fred Dickerson, who was and is probably still living in Connecticut, and John Sumkins who lives in New Brunswick, New Jersey, testified against me. Dickerson was actually an informant. Sumkins testified for no reason at all but later changed his story and Ervin who the police claimed was my right hand man, turned stoolpigeon also.

Cavario: Really, why?

Isaac Wright: Well, you know there's a thing called "Selling Out," exchanging your misery for the misery of someone else.

Cavario: Right. "Your ass for mine."

Isaac Wright: Right. So when the police present a mindset that they have a certain level of greed (desire to arrest) for a particular individual, it doesn't take a man that is in trouble, very long to understand he has a way out. The police wanted to get me and they used the vulnerabilities they inflicted on people to their advantage.

Cavario: Once you were arrested and you said, "I didn't do that." What happened?

Isaac Wright: They wanted a million dollars in cash for bail. I stayed.

Cavario: Oh right, the ol', "We definitely have something on him if he makes bail."

Isaac Wright: Right. I knew that the moment a million dollars in cash was brought to post bail, it was going to be confiscated as drug money and my bail would then be immediately raised to a higher amount.

Cavario: What made the police focus on you?

Isaac Wright: I believe the focus was a result of my lifestyle in the beginning. Or maybe it was the chrome plate reading "Get Jealous" across the side of one of the cars. (Laughing.)

Cavario: What was your lifestyle? How were you 'carrying' it?

84

Isaac Wright: I was carrying it like I had it. I really don't like to get into exposing myself in that manner but some things were a matter of public record like the cars, jewelry, money and things of that nature.

Cavario: This is Don Diva Magazine; you got to tell us what kind of cars?

Isaac Wright: (Laughs) A few Benzes, including an AMG Hammer, limousines and a few others. (Isaac crosses his legs, leans back in his seat with his finger under his chin). Listen, my first apartment in New York was a hole in the wall on Edgecombe Avenue and 145th Street in Harlem. I watched Dreads (men with dread-lochs) drag bodies in the basement of abandoned buildings damn near every night. I went from there to Far Rockaway projects where I ducked bullets every time I wanted to go in and out my house. I moved to a better neighborhood in Crown Heights Brooklyn but still had to barricade my door at night. There are those who say I went from that to making over $350,000.00 a week. I was accused of running a $20-million dollar a year drug enterprise in some of the worst ghettoes in New Jersey. Throughout my life I have learned the ways of cultures all over the world. I've eaten with Aristocrats during the day and broke bread with Thugs at night. I've been to Paris, London and Japan, to name just a few. I've lived in Italy, Switzerland and Germany.

I'm an international, multi-cultural muthafucka. Yes, I was arrested and sentenced to Life in prison but I ran through the system like Ali ran through Foreman. I walked away with my freedom during a time when people convicted of drug crimes got no relief. No court in this country has released drug Kingpins and leaders of organized crime from their Life sentences. No one has ever done what I have done. Yo, it's hard as hell being Isaac…it ain't easy being me. I know now that going to prison was my destiny. It was God's plan to throw me into that hell so that I could make a difference. Can't nobody walk in my shoes. I am the first and only man, black or white, to enter the system as an alleged organized crime boss (drug Kingpin), taught myself the law to the extent where I rivaled the skills of the best attorneys, made new law for lawyers to argue and courts to follow, obtained the release for other prisoners as well as myself, witnessed the suicide of the man who put me in prison and made history in the process. I re-wrote the book on what it means to be an O.G. I didn't really care about money as much as I cared about enjoying life. I lived by little or no rules when it came to enjoying life. Money was always there for me to get and I spent it like that.

Cavario: When did your mind tell you it was time to start fighting?

Isaac Wright: The moment I got arrested. I come from an environment and was raised in a household where battles were healthy and necessary if it was for a good cause. My father was a warrior. He fought in wars for this country and he taught us in those ways. I was conditioned, way before my arrest, to fight. And to fight in the hardest battles to the death– even in the most hopeless situations. I was convicted of being a Drug Kingpin along with ten other counts. I was sentenced to Life in prison plus 30 years. I was supposed to die in prison. And, through all of that, I never considered a day without a fight or a time to take a break. I know this though, if for any reason, I did not win my freedom and I died of old age, I would have died in the law library or in a courtroom in the middle of an argument.

Cavario: What did you do?

Isaac Wright: I'll kind of give you a summary. When I was arrested, the head prosecutor (DA) got out of his bed and came to the jail where I was being detained. He walked up to the cell where I was, reached through the bars, introduced himself and shook my hand. He then let me know that he was going to be handling and trying my case personally. By doing that, he allowed me to understand his mindset and his disposition. The man that shook my hand was arrogant, cocky, completely self-absorbed and sure of himself to a fault. Immediately, I made a decision to try my own case because I knew that trying my own case would make it personal to him. Because of his disposition, making it personal would cause him to make mistakes. He made those mistakes and as a result of those mistakes, I was released from a life sentence of imprisonment. Now please don't get me wrong. I don't want anyone to think that this was as simple as understanding a man's mind. I fought and studied my ass off for years. And, that was my greatest asset. Yes, I ultimately won my freedom but that episode and those years were years of unimaginable pain and suffering. To this day, I am experiencing fallout from what happened to me. I suppose the fallout will diminish with time but I don't think it will ever disappear. If I died and at judgment I was given a choice between an eternal existence in the pit of hell or to live again but with a life sentence in a maximum security prison doing hard time, I would not be able to make a choice because I'd think it was a trick question. There is no difference between the two.

November 18, 1996– jumping his 300,000 bail two days before his scheduled sentencing, former prosecutor Nicholas Louis Bissell Jr. stood to forfeit his home as well as his elderly mother's condo. He was scheduled for sentencing on 33 counts of corruption, tax fraud, perjury and official misconduct. According to information that surfaced during his trial, Bissell was engaged in criminal activity from the very day in 1982 when he was sworn in as Somerset County's top law enforcement official.

Cavario: How do you feel about the D.A. killing himself?

Isaac Wright: I really have no feelings about it, only to say that the gun he had on me, he turned on himself.

Cavario: Do you believe the D.A. killed himself because of what you did to him?

Isaac Wright: I don't know. It's hard to determine the motives of a man in distress. I do know that he went on the run when my case unraveled. The Feds tracked him down at a trashy hotel in the desert. When they forced their way into his room he was sitting on the floor, in his underwear, with a gun to his head. They tried to talk him out of it but he yelled, "I can't go to prison" and then killed himself before they could get to him. (Isaac mumbles sarcastically under his breath, "but I can do life"). They found later that he had been gambling, looking for an apartment using a fake I.D. and having sex with prostitutes in Vegas before they caught up to him.

Cavario: Exactly what did the D.A. do in your case that forced them to release you and make him run?

Isaac Wright: He condoned or ordered the police to falsify their police reports and give false statements to the judge in support of arrest and search warrants. He also conspired with my codefendants' attorneys to have them lie on the witness stand during my trial, to the extent that he actually told them what they had to say. He made secret promises to those codefendants that they would not go to jail even though they accepted plea bargains requiring them to do prison terms. This was done so that I could not destroy their credibility on the stand by showing that they were really getting better sentences than what was required in exchange for their testimony. All of these things began to come to light when a police officer broke the code of silence and confessed on the witness stand under my cross-examination.

I remember distinctly. He began crying, stating that he had been holding that secret in for over seven years and it was eating away at him. He said he was fighting to tell the truth and although he was getting ready to destroy his career and contribute to my release, he had to tell what happened. After his testimony, everyone started telling what was done to me. That's when the prosecutor ran.

I mean, these are the things that came out. There were so many things that no one knows and has yet to come out. For instance, one of my codefendants, a female only 19 years old at the time was placed in a room. Three police officers came in. One forced her mouth open. Another placed the barrel of his gun in her mouth. The third asked her questions about me. Every time she gave an answer they didn't like, the officer with the gun in his hand dry fired the weapon. I remember hearing her screams from my cell all the way from the other side of the jail. It was so horrific, it sounded like death. I remember hearing her screaming my name, calling for me, begging to be allowed to talk to me. I remember these things as if it were yesterday.

****

Rhoda White was arrested along with Isaac in this alleged narcotic conspiracy and she was subsequently forced, through threats, to make false statements against Isaac Wright. According to an article printed in the Star Ledger on May 30, 1997, during the initial trial, Ms. White's attorney told her that she would, "definitely go to prison" unless she accepted a plea bargain from Somerset County prosecutor, Nicholas L. Bissell Jr. "They told me exactly what to say, my lawyer and Bissell." A Mr. Hurley, vice president of the Somerset County Bar Association testified that the full scope of the deal between the District Attorney's office and White was never put on record. Instead, jurors at Isaac's trial were told White, despite her cooperation with the prosecution, still faced up to five years in jail; purportedly this farce was perpetrated to give her more credibility.

Hurley later revised his testimony, denying there was a secret deal. Hurley too was charged with violating a legal standard of ethics for not disclosing the plea arrangement to the trial judge, Michael R. Imbriani. Under cross-examination by Hurley's attorney, Michael Rogers, White said repeatedly that she had been assured that Imbriani was aware of the deal...she said Hurley told her, 'The judge is right up there in on it too.' White readily admitted that she had lied to avoid going to jail and being separated from her young son.

Cavario: What about the judge?

Isaac Wright: The judge disliked me to hatred.

Cavario: Did the judge believe that you were who the district attorney said you were?

Isaac Wright: I'm certain that he probably did. At times, I felt he wanted me dead, both of them. In order for the prosecutor to have obtained a conviction on me the way he did, the judge had to be in on it. One of the defense attorneys admitted to my codefendant that he was in on everything.

Cavario: Where's the judge now?

Isaac Wright: He went to jail and was disbarred. He did his time and he's home now. He was prohibited from ever practicing law again.

Cavario: Did you help other prisoners while you were incarcerated?

Isaac Wright: Yes. I was a paralegal with the Inmate Legal Association in Trenton State Prison. As a result of the legal work I did while I was there, over 20 people got relief. Fifteen of those twenty had Life sentences and were either released or got significant time cut to the extent where they all were going to go home.

Cavario: Tell me about the letters that were written by judges and lawyers regarding your legal skills?

Isaac Wright: Well, let me read an excerpt of one of the letters. It will give you an idea of what they all say. I quote, "I found Mr. Wright to be highly intelligent and articulate and thoroughly prepared at all times. I also found Mr. Wright's legal writing to be lucid, pertinent, well organized and analytical. Indeed, I consider Mr. Wright to be a better brief writer than most attorneys I have encountered. I was most impressed with Mr. Wright's ability as a legal strategist." This letter was from the prosecutor assigned to fight against my appeal. He was out of the same office and county where my case was tried.

Cavario: What would you say are the worst things about incarceration?

Isaac Wright: Well, outside of the devastation that is associated with the loss of your freedom and the removal from your family, one of the most tragic events I have encountered was: the reality of incarceration. There are thousands of prisoners aggressively and obsessively researching the law, moving through the law library, trying to put together arguments and situations where they can get some sort of relief in court. Even down to just throwing anything together. Just the fact that they have a court date is hope for them. Most of these people, even the ones who profess to know the law, have no idea of what they are doing. What's more tragic is that they don't even know that they don't know what they are doing. I have sat in the law library on numerous occasions and have watched this thing perpetuate itself and have been stirred with emotion because I knew that they were going to be there for a very long time and I couldn't tell them. I knew that they would never go home and they don't even understand that–they don't know what they are doing. I mean how do you tell somebody that they are going to die in prison without ever seeing the streets again. Who am I to destroy their hope, the only thing they have left to live for? Exposing that reality to them could get you killed or force you to kill someone.

Cavario: What are your thoughts about the system?

Isaac Wright: I personally believe we have the best system in the world. However, I equally believe that those who are in charge of facilitating, monitoring and administrating the system are, for the most part, incompetent and humanly lacking in the kind of standards, character and honor necessary for running a system like ours. They bring havoc and chaos to the system. *They* make the system flawed and unjust.

Cavario: Are you back into the music?

Isaac Wright: Yes, I have a female R&B group. These chicks are the hottest shit out there. Ain't nothing touchin' them and I would put my reputation on that. I also have some rappers and producers signed to my production company. And I got some bangin' shit. Please excuse me but I need to get ghetto when I talk about this subject 'cause the shit is fucked up. The level of hate in the game nowadays has reached critical levels. If niggas ain't hatin' on a muhfucka', and tryin' to keep them out of shit so they can't eat, [then] they're just full of shit. I spend 85% of my time duckin' suckas in this music shit. Most of these cats don't know who I am and I don't tell them. Plus, I was already in this music & Hip-Hop shit gettin' crazy cake. Prison caused me to lose contact. Russell Simmons, Jermaine Dupree, Chris Lighty, LL Kool J, Teddy Riley, I dealt with all these niggas and more. When Flex was carrying Chuck Chill-Out's records, I was there. When Chris Lighty was being taught the game by Red Alert, I was there riding them around in my limo with much love and respect. When Jermaine Dupree was breakdancing and being tutored on the back of a tour bus, Ike was there. When LL Cool J was brought by Run DMC to witness the first Hip-Hop concert ever (New York City Fresh Fest), Ike [Isaac Wright] was there. When Teddy Riley was a member of his first group ("Kids At Work"), I was there riding him on the back of my motorcycle in a small South Carolina town called Monks Corner, listening to him tell me how much he liked my sister. When Russell Simmons and Ricky Walker had to make the crucial decision of dropping Curtis Blow as a headline act and replacing him with Run DMC, I was backstage, right there, a part of that history. I was just a kid doin' my thing at that time. All of these niggas I just mentioned would look out for me today if I could contact them. It's been so long that a couple of them probably wouldn't remember me until they saw me. But it's these new cats that's runnin' shit that ain't tryin' to look out. Lucky for me I get money and I ain't starving. That's cool though because I will not be denied. Believe me, there ain't nobody out there that's gonna stop me. And, I ain't forgettin' shit.

Interview by Cavario H.
Research by Cavario H. & Susan Hampstead

The End of New Jersey's Forfeiture King

On May 10, 1990, homebuilder James Giuffre (jif-fray) was arrested on charges of selling $700 worth of cocaine. After arresting Giuffre, Prosecutor Nick Bissell had him taken to the Somerset Trust Bank building where the county rented a second floor space. Giuffre stated he was handcuffed to a chair for nearly two days during which he was not allowed to contact an attorney despite his repeated requests. He was also physically threatened. The officers even threatened to shoot his dog. Bissell offered to drop Giuffre's charges if he willingly forfeited two plots of land to the prosecutor's office. Believing he'd be taken out back and shot, Giuffre relented and signed over the two lots valued at $174,000. The lots were sold at auction for $10,000 apiece to the girlfriend of an individual in Bissell's office. Giuffre's charges were dropped and in 1992 he sued Bissell for extortion and won. This got the attention of the Internal Revenue Service and the FBI. Bissell was arrested, but released under the condition that he wear an electronic bracelet. He cut the device off and fled to Nevada, leaving his wife, Barbara Bissell, to face fraud and tax evasion charges. Bissell's mother was also left dangling as she was to be evicted from her condominium, which he'd offered up as part of his bond security. Nine days later the disgraced lawman was tracked down, through his cell phone, to a small gambling town, where, after a 10-minute standoff, he fatally shot himself.

Today Isaac Wright is a respected lawyer and continues to help people who fight against legal injustice.

History of the Game

This next article was originally printed in the 1ˢᵗ year anniversary issue (#4) of Don Diva magazine. I feel it really clarifies the principal causes behind the behavior that plagues our communities today. If we don't know where we've been then there's no way to know where we can go.

"Our" game is only an outgrowth of the game that was played and is still being played on us. Now meet the Original "BIG" Willie.

The following speech is purported to have been delivered by a white slave owner named William "Willie" Lynch, back in 1712.

"Gentlemen, I greet you on the banks of the James River in the year of our Lord, one thousand seven-hundred and twelve. First I shall thank you, the gentlemen of the Colony of Virginia, for bringing me here. I am here to help you solve your problems with slaves. Your invitation reached me on my modest plantation [he had hundreds of acres, and hundreds of slaves] in the West Indies where I have experimented with some of the newest and still the oldest methods for the control of slaves. Ancient Rome would envy us if my program is implemented. As our boat sailed south on the James River, named for our illustrious king, whose version of the Bible we cherish, I saw enough to know that your problem is not unique. While Rome used crosses for standing human bodies along its old highways in great numbers, you are here using the tree and the rope.

"I caught the whiff of a dead slave hanging from a tree a couple of miles back. You are not only losing valuable stock by hangings, you are having uprisings, [and] slaves are running away.

"In my bag, here, I have a foolproof method for controlling your black slaves. I guarantee every one of you that if installed correctly it will control the slaves for at least 300 hundred years. (Author's note: By the print of this book, 2014, we will be in year 302, and it seems that Willie has already exceeded his minimum prediction.) Willie continues, "My method is simple. Any member of your family or your overseer can use it.

"I have outlined a number of differences among the slaves and I take these differences and make them bigger: use fear, distrust and envy for control purposes. These methods have worked on my modest plantation in the West Indies and it will work throughout the South. Take this simple little list of differences, and think about them. On top of my list is 'Age' but it is there only because it starts with an 'A', the second is 'Color' or shade… [and then] there is, intelligence, size, sex, size of plantations, status on plantation, attitude of owners, whether the slaves live in the valley, on a hill, (this is this author's favorite part) East, West, North, South... (where you from nigga?!) have fine-hair (AKA "good hair"), coarse-hair, or is tall or short.

"Now that you have the list of differences, I shall give you an outline of action– but before that, I shall assure you that distrust is stronger than trust, and is stronger than adulation, respect or admiration.

"The Black slave after receiving this indoctrination shall carry on and will become self re-fueling and self-generating for hundreds of years, maybe thousands." (maybe thousands!)

"Don't forget you must pitch the old Black male against the young. You must use the dark skinned slaves against the light skinned slaves and female against male and the male against the female. You must also have your white servants and overseers distrust all Blacks, but it is necessary that your slaves trust and depend on US, they must love respect and trust only US.

"Gentlemen, these kits are your keys to control. Use them. Have your wives and children use them, never miss an opportunity. If used intensely for one year, the slaves themselves will remain perpetually (forever) distrustful (of each other). Thank you, gentlemen."

The following section is part of a manifesto based on BIG Willie's doctrine, it also appeared in issue #4 along with the speech you just read; it's titled:

The Origin and Development of the Negro:

Part 1: Let us make a slave.

What do we need? First of all we need a Black nigger man, a pregnant nigger woman and her baby nigger boy. Second, we will use the same basic principle that we use in breaking a horse, combined with some more sustaining factors. What we do with horses is that we break them from one form of life to another. That is, we reduce them from their natural state in nature; whereas nature provides them with the natural capacity to take care of their needs and the needs of their offspring, we break that natural sting of independence from them and thereby create a dependency state so that we may be able to get from them useful production for our business and pleasure.

Pay little attention to the generation of the original breaking but concentrate on future generations. Therefore, if you break the female mother, she will break the offspring in its early years of development and when the offspring is old enough to work, she will deliver it up to you because her normal female protective tendencies will have been lost in the original breaking process. For example, take the case of the wild stud horse, a female horse and an early infant horse offspring. Take the stud horse and break him to prevent sudden attack. Completely break the female horse until she becomes very gentle whereas you or anybody can ride her in comfort. Breed the mare (female horse) and the stud (male horse) until you have the desired offspring. Then you can free the stud until you need him again. (Thus, the question: Where's my daddy?) Train the female horse, and she will, in turn train the infant horse to eat out of your hand also. When it comes to breaking the uncivilized nigger, use the same process.

Part 2: The Breaking Process of the African Woman.
We have reversed the relationships. In her natural uncivilized state she would have a strong dependence on the uncivilized nigger male, and she would have a limited protective tendency toward her independent male offspring and would raise the female offspring to be dependent like her. Nature had provided for this type of balance.
For fear of the young male's life being taken from him, she will psychologically train him to be mentally weak (Thus, "You 'ain't shit', just like your father!") and dependent, but physically strong. Because she has become psychologically independent, she will train her female offspring to be psychologically independent (Thus, "A black man 'ain't shit'! You don't need that nigga!") What have you got? You've got the nigger woman out front and the nigger man behind and scared. This is a perfect situation for sound sleep and economics for the slave master. THE END.

So there it is. The choices we are making today, and the conditions under which we make them, basically come from Willie Lynch's business plan. So to all my "don't give a fuck," gangster-thug, muthafuckas– you think you got game? Well "nigger" you are game.

You think you're "representin'" when all you're really doing is replicating. I feel that these documents that I have reprinted, thanks to the Black Arcade Liberation Library, reveal the greater "game" in play. The game is perfect and it is old; it is perfect because it has us, the game "pieces," playing ourselves; it is so old that many of the children of the game

94

"masters" don't know that they're keeping it on the board and in perpetual play; they are just following the teachings of their forefathers. Remember, "...Have your wives and children use them...never miss an opportunity..." –It is now their nature.

Original article: Cavario H.

What about Black Gangsters?

A book titled "The New Ethnic Mobs" (Kleinknecht FREEPRESS 1996) states "…even if black organized–crime groups are "badder" than everyone else, they have never lived up to predictions that they would one day replace the Mafia as a dominant national crime syndicate. If anything, black crime groups have become less organized since those predictions were first made 25 years ago. They remain imprisoned in the pathology of the American ghetto, their ranks filled with reckless young drug gangsters who live wildly and extravagantly for a few years and then self-destruct, ending up with long stints in prison or a plot in the graveyard. With a few notable exceptions, black crime groups have rarely been around long enough to build a criminal legacy like those of the Italians, the Chinese, the Cubans and others." –That paragraph basically translates, "Blacks can't do 'wrong' right."

The line "…imprisoned in the pathology of the American ghetto" loosely interpreted reads like "Blacks are stuck in the mindset of the lowest social group in American society and will not collectively aspire to improve their conditions no matter how much drug money they make."

The New Ethnic Mobs by William Kleinknecht, is an informative book, which provides a great deal of fascinating detail in its description of the migrations, inceptions and evolutions of humble immigrant communities, through to gangs, and up to organized crime syndicates. It's pretty well known that most all of the ethnic groups that make up the "melting pot" that is America today, braved great peril crossing daunting seas, leaving their families behind, in many cases to never see them again. These facts contributed to their communal adherence to the ways and practices of their original countries and cultures– regardless of any personal differences between the individuals representing those countries or cultures. What was not mentioned is the one major difference between the descendants of African "immigrants" (bear with me) and all the other migrants–everyone else came with their own cultures, religions, beliefs and societal practices intact…everyone else came of their own volition. It's not an excuse (because there is none needed, it is what it is) but it is nonetheless a fact that has played a major role in how Black people and Black males in particular are perceived and interacted with in American society.

The same book goes on to say

"…[B]ut Dominicans are not inherently immoral, lazy or criminal. They just come from a country that is frighteningly impoverished and whose emigrants, through accidents of timing and geography, have found themselves being tempted more than other ethnic groups by the siren call of the drug trade."

Statements like, "…through accidents of timing…" and "…found themselves being tempted more than other ethnic groups…" actually makes me wonder about the ethnic background of the author. To imply that any group of people are more prone to commit an action as deliberate as selling drugs just because of their geographical origins, makes me wonder if it's fair to say that a black man isn't more prone to abandon his woman and his children because he's "irresponsible," "self-centered" or "callous"–it's just that for the first few hundred years that his ancestors were on American soil they were used largely as studding machines, moved from one plantation to another, and made to impregnate as many kidnapped African females as possible. But to say that would be ridiculous– right?

It's unfortunate that blacks were taken from a resource rich continent like "Africa" before we could initiate our own (voluntary) mass departure across the water to the shores of this great land of opportunity. If not for that fact of misfortune I could write about an "accident of geography" and our irresistible propensity for controlling the diamond trade or the gold market or even the heroin importation business. I'm not saying that slavery robbed black Americans of the chance of being better criminals with greater goal orientation than a few years of living fast and dying young– but we were certainly robbed of the option of knowing where we were from, where we had been and subsequently where we could go… legally or illegally. With that said, I say now, "GAME OVER! STOP PLAYIN' OR GET SERIOUS!"

The Practical Application for Pragmatic Learning

I know, it's an odd title so before I go any further I'll break it down: 'Practical,' according to Webster's Dictionary means "applicable theory", more precisely "it actually works the way you think it works." 'Application,' Webster says, "putting into effect," (Hood translation) "Gangstas do what they want."

Now here's my favorite, "Pragmatic"– crazy ass word right? But dig, it's heavy in its simplicity, I'll elaborate further of course; beginning with Webby's definition which says "dealing with events in the light of practical lessons or applications." (Yeah a'ight, try this) "The last time you thought it wasn't serious, you took a fuckin' loss so now yo' ass know better what to do."

Last but not least is 'Learning' and we've all, no doubt, heard this one many times since we were children. But I dare to wager– nothing major (but wager still) that many of us still don't get it. That goes for you four-sided cats too. Webster says to acquire knowledge or skill 'in' by study, instrumentation, practice or experience. (Streets say) "Listen a lot, live a little, survive it all and then lay it down."

Now that we've gotten that out of the way, I hope the title has more meaning to you, but don't feel bad if it doesn't yet, it will soon enough– one way or the other.

Dudes in the street are seldom "practical," for some reason it just doesn't fit the creed; live fast and (if you're lucky) die young. If you don't believe in luck then you have an alternative, you can die slowly– rotting away in a prison cell for the rest of your natural life. The old saying, "if you're in for a penny then you're in for a pound" (pound is what the British call their "Dollar") still stands. It doesn't matter that you weren't making as much as the next guy, if you are named in a conspiracy then you stand to do at least as much time as the guy at the top of the pyramid. There can be no whining, bitching or moaning about, "I hardly made any money…" or "Dem niggàs was the onlyest ones gettin' paid!" because no one cares that you didn't know you were part of an ongoing criminal enterprise and therefore subject to Mandatory Minimum sentences. There is NO justification for informing, cooperating, telling, ratting, "doin' you," or passing the buck (even if you never really saw any). The name of the game is "If you catch it, it's yours".

The reason that ANY game works, whether it be the Wall Street game, the Real Estate game, the Politics/Government game or the Drug game, is because its participants adhere to some sort of guideline or rules of conduct enabling the game to sustain itself. When individuals who do not recognize, respect or even know these rules exist, are allowed into the game (any game) what we have is anarchy. Where there is no order, there exists a weakness for the enemy to exploit. When the 'hood-fathers' got strung out on Heroin or began freebasing, or received a super-long stretch in a super-max or just simply went broke trying to out Cadillac each other while simultaneously increasing the enemy's war chest by buying up everything he was trying to sell us and not manufacturing a damn thing for ourselves— they ('hood-fathers') left us naked and alone in the brick and asphalt wilderness to fend for ourselves and undoubtedly repeat their mistakes– for the lack of the benefit of their experiences. Where's daddy?

Why do you sell drugs? Why are you willing to risk life and limb to achieve infamy and acquisition? Why when things come to a bad end do you believe that you can and should blame someone else for this end? Even if someone you trusted with everything were to betray your trust, you still are to blame for the ultimate outcome. If you ended up on a hill in a mansion you wouldn't be too quick to credit someone else for it, no matter how important to your operation they were. So why is it the next man's fault when he 'twists' your brains out and runs with the stash or turns gov' witness on you? You were the one that determined that this would be the individual that you would bestow such a degree of access and information upon that he (or she) could exalt you or destroy you. It is always your decision.

If this sounds like "rubbish" to you then you probably aren't built for the game. What it comes down to is, you are always responsible for you. If you relinquish your existence to unseen forces or the actions of others then you are subject to all things. You will be blown with the wind. This wind is cold, cruel and life damning. It will blow away your house, cars and jewelry and will creep back around the corner and smash your woman and children too (especially sons). I say sons in particular because they will be left to fend against and then adjust to the reality of their actual state in the vacuum that is left by your absence, as they struggle to take the unmanned reigns and regain the glory of ghetto-illustriousness. The environment I grew up in fed me its misery, its fears, and its hunger; these were the elements that I was nursed on. I didn't have to adjust to the streets; I was in the game from my first moment of consciousness.

Even when I was a baby, when shit was fucked up on the street for my family, I could feel the pressure...I could sense the desperation. Although

99

I was too "new" to be conscious of the effects of these feelings, the conditions they caused still thickened the air in my home...the air I had to breathe. I was then like so many children are now, a sponge...and I absorbed everything around me. When you're growing up, everything seems practical. By that I mean you feel as though you can do whatever you see the people you admire, love and trust, doing. Although you interpret what you see through the eyes and understanding of a child, you believe that you can be as good or bad (as the case may be) as your elders. The implementation of pragmatism at such junctures would save many-a-life. But the infinite ignorance/ arrogance of youth (especially left unguided) is the stuff that both dreams and nightmares are made of.

Don Diva first came into contact with the Don known to many as "Akbar," in the course of doing our 2nd issue. We were determined to come back with a piece on a significant individual that had never been reached by the media before. By significant I mean a knowledgeable man whose experiences could lend life saving power to our text. Akbar epitomizes the character and charisma necessary to command men and run an organization and therefore affect the choices of those that come into his circle. We wanted to show the hoods and the world at large that we were indeed the streets...its voice, its heart and its spirit. By meeting the standards of integrity and intelligence that Mr. Pray holds dear, (regardless of any crimes the court alleges he's committed) we achieved our goal– this next piece is the result.

I met with Attorney David Ruhnke who represented Wayne Akbar Pray in his federal appeal case. This is what Mr. Ruhnke had to say, "He (Akbar) was the first one to face that Mandatory Minimum thing...He was the first one who was indicted as what 'they' call the "principal administrator" of a CCE (Continuing Criminal Enterprise), which is like over a hundred kilos of cocaine....once you got to that level it was a mandatory Life sentence. And that's what he wound up with."

Wayne "Akbar" Pray: BRICK CITY DON

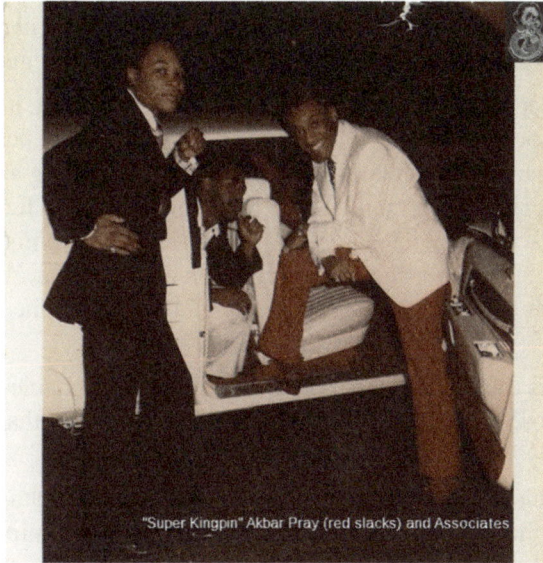

"Super Kingpin" Akbar Pray (red slacks) and Associates

If I told you that you could be indicted just because of the full-length Black Llama mink you had tailor-made or the S500 Benz with the 20-inch Lorinsers you drive up and down the avenue in, would you believe me? If I told you that the same $60,000 platinum and 'ice' Rolex that you so lovingly sport would be "article #12211 of evidence" that gets you convicted of being a Drug Kingpin, would you believe me? If I told you that sitting in floor seats at the All-star Game, flying first-class to the Caribbean with your "mommi" of the week and staying in a five-star suite would get you life in jail, would you believe me?

****

On June 21, 1988, Wayne "Akbar" Pray was arrested in Boca Raton, Florida. Unknown to him he had been indicted April 15, 1988 by a federal grand jury in Newark "Brick City," New Jersey. This indictment came in part due to Martha Gomez. Martha Gomez was arrested in Florida on October 1, 1987 for drug trafficking in an attempt to import 126 pounds of marijuana into the United States. She in turn agreed to cooperate with the federal government for leniency in her sentencing. At the time, Martha

101

Gomez was romantically involved with Akbar. During DEA debriefing, it is alleged that Martha Gomez linked Akbar to the importation of 200 kilos of cocaine into the United States from Columbia.

It was called "The Family," a Newark based cocaine, heroin and marijuana trafficking organization that operated in several areas of the country, and commanded millions of dollars in annual revenue.

Although Akbar's indictment covered only a 2-year period, it was the government's position that Wayne "Akbar" Pray allegedly headed "The Family" for nearly 20 years until he was convicted of being a drug Kingpin and sentenced to mandatory life without parole in federal prison in 1988. Akbar was convicted of being the "principal administrator" of a substantial cocaine importing and distribution organization. At its height, the government believed that Pray's group had about 300 members and associates.

For many years the government considered Pray untouchable because he never came close to the narcotics. The government claims that Pray built up "The Family" through "fear, intimidation and violence."

The DEA Special Agent in Charge, Ashton, detailed the status of the Family in testimony, "The Muslim name Akbar means omnipotent, all-powerful, or The Great One. In fact, Akbar referred to himself as 'Akbar the greatest of the great.' He lived up to his name by assuming control over a vast and durable criminal network...At its height Pray's network had at least 12 mid-level supervisors classified by the DEA as Class 1 Violators."

A Class 1 cocaine trafficker is defined by the DEA as one who has the capability of distributing at least fifty kilos of cocaine on a monthly basis and manages at least five subordinate drug traffickers.

During Pray's 1989 federal trial for leading a continuing cocaine and marijuana trafficking enterprise, DEA witnesses testified that he was responsible for possessing and distributing approximately 188 kilos of cocaine and 544 pounds of marijuana in a five month period between February and June of 1987. It was estimated that Pray's organization was receiving millions of dollars of gross income annually. During the trial Akbar testified that he had wide ranging business interests including a car dealerships and a promotions company that promoted boxing matches, but the government argued that Pray was unable to produce any business records to justify his large income. The courtroom was usually packed throughout the trial with Pray's family and supporters. The few who

102

waited through the days of jury deliberations sat quietly as the verdict was being read. The jury reached its verdict after seven months of trial and 3 days of deliberation: GUILTY.

Sentence: Mandatory Life with No Parole.

In January of 2000, through one of our Don Diva sources, we contacted Akbar for his side of the story. Akbar had, by that point, been in federal prison for over 12 years and despite his conviction, maintained he was innocent. The only link ever made between Pray and actual narcotics was the testimony of cooperating witnesses. Akbar's most incriminating snitch was Martha Gomez.

Susan Hampstead: What were you thinking while your girl was on the stand testifying against you?

Akbar: "Oh Poppy"... and all the other Spanish words of love she used to whisper in my ear when we were together...I felt betrayed because of the emotional level we got to, but I didn't feel betrayed because she did lie... I had five people testify against me and she was the most incriminating... she testified for 18 days.

Susan: Why do you think she turned on you?

Akbar: She was a very rich woman...a multi-millionaire. She never did a day in jail in her life. She was indicted on the importation charge which I didn't get arrested on...she cooperated on that case and would have had to do 6 years but she didn't even want to do that, so she got me Life.

****

Aside from snitch testimony, the major focus of the prosecution's case against Akbar was called "Substantial Wealth." Basically this means that the brother had too much paper, lived too well, flossed too much and looked too good, and the government felt like he couldn't show any legitimate sources of income to support his lavish lifestyle. When Akbar was arrested the government seized a white Rolls Royce worth $110,000 and one of his homes in New Jersey worth about $210,000, which is equal (more or less) to $518,700.00 today. During the 80s, Akbar was known in and out of the hood for his flamboyant dress-style. The brother donned full-length furs of all kinds, and his trademark was lemon yellow, pink and canary yellow tailor-made suits with matching gators.

Akbar: I grew up in Newark, and compared to most I probably lived a very flamboyant lifestyle to whoever may have observed it. I always liked fur coats and I started having them made at a young age like 19 or 20– I

103

guess it was too much. Our boys always had new cars...back then people weren't buying Mercedes they were buying Eldorados (Cadillacs)... I was a kid [but] I always had a new car.

Susan: Did you floss a lot...hang out at the spots while you were on the streets?

Akbar: No I spent most of my time in the company of women. I dined out a lot, went to the theater and to shows...I traveled...I didn't hang out with a crew. If you saw me I was out with my woman or my kids. I have 23 kids...I didn't do the after hours clubs...I went to Sweetwaters (A Manhattan bistro/discotheque and live performance lounge, which once stood on the Upper West Side at 68th Street on Amsterdam Avenue in Manhattan) and one or two other clubs.

Susan: Do you believe that you became "hot" because people were talking about you and gave you a name?

Akbar: You become hot because you have a high profile lifestyle. There are probably a few guys who slip through the cracks because they have a lower profile lifestyle... so they may have a longer "run", so to speak, in that particular 'theater'...but on a whole when you do have a high profile lifestyle, people see you and if they can't see a legitimate form of income they assume you are selling dope...a lot of times people don't do anything to discourage that (image) because they think it is a hell of a calling.

****

In an effort to prove their claim of substantial wealth, the prosecutors even tried to subpoena his lawyer's records and receipts to see how much Akbar had paid him. The information was being sought to try and establish that Pray had substantial assets and no legitimate way to account for them. Now while subpoenaing a lawyer's records is highly irregular and must be approved in Washington– it is legal. The government also brought in a circus of 126 witnesses to testify to Akbar's lifestyle and only 5 witnesses to testify in regards to drug activities. There were no wiretaps and no one that said Akbar sold them any drugs.

Akbar: They brought people in that I spent money with from all over the country. Every hotel that I went to, every time I checked into a suite...anytime that cash money was spent. They brought in 126 document witnesses...and these people were from clothing stores, car dealerships...even the guy who did my lawn, my plumber and the guys who installed my carpet were brought in...they brought in the people at the Louis Vuitton handbag store where my wife used to go buy our luggage…they brought in every possible person that I spent money with in an 18-month period…and that is what they used to convict me. I had a lot of jewelry…about $500,000 worth of jewels. They showed every individual piece of my jewelry to the jury.

Susan: So what you are saying is that if you live in a certain manner, they are coming after you.

Akbar: Absolutely…If you have a legitimate means of income that is visible, like record producers, sports figures…computers…then maybe you can justify it but you will pique their attention.

Susan: You had legitimate businesses that could "show" for your income. Are you telling me it didn't matter?

Akbar: No, it didn't matter…It is very hard to disprove an accusation. All you can say is I didn't do it…It's not only a matter of credibility, it is a matter of what the jury wants to believe…I had eight blacks on my jury and back then the average income was probably $32,000. So when you bring out a piece of jewelry that costs $32,000 that's their yearly salary…it doesn't look good to them. They don't have any comprehension of the lifestyle.

****

Akbar owned car dealerships, two abortion clinics, an ambulatory service, 2 supermarkets and a luncheonette. Akbar founded in 1978, Akbar Promotions, a company that managed and promoted boxing matches. Akbar was one of the largest closed circuit fight distributors in New Jersey. Although it would appear that Akbar's emergence in the sports and entertainment arenas would have quieted the whispers about the source of his income, it seemed to have had the opposite effect. Local authorities became more interested in the business dealings of Akbar and even more so when he became involved in Politics. In 1983 Akbar co-founded the Young Black Businessmen Association. Sixty members strong, the YBBA quickly became a political force to be reckoned within Essex County (Yes, the same Essex County that Isaac Wright had his problem in).

Susan: Has this experience made you wish you lived your life differently?

Akbar: Yeah, I probably would have not met Martha…(his snitch girl-friend). I would probably pay a lot closer attention to my business records and taxes…I enjoyed my life and I still try to find quality in my life not withstanding my circumstances…so I am not mad with the life that I lived…I am still fighting to try and rid myself of this nightmare.

****

Early on, Akbar was offered a plea bargain of 10 years with "cooperation" but he adamantly refused this deal. He is still working on getting back into the courtroom to clear his name. Akbar released two books: *Death of the Game* and *Last of A Dying Breed*.

Susan: Do you have any words to the brothers coming up into the GAME?

Akbar: If they are involved in what they call the "Game"…they should know it's a vocation (trade) not an 'advocation'…in other words if you are doing it as a job to catapult you from point "A" to point "B" then perhaps you may be successful long enough to get yourself out of the streets…and live a comfortable life. But if you want to be a "dope boy" then you're going to have what they call a short shelf life. A lot of people want to be portrayed as a "dope boy" and if that is your thing [then] they have a place for you and it's called a Federal Penitentiary. The whole playing field has changed. The streets are washed with undercover informants, UOs' (undercover operatives), confidential informants and snitches. So it has altered the playing field…trust has been reduced to a rumor and a "stand-up" guy is a real rare commodity. Knowing this, if you choose to continue…you should know that your next deal could be your last deal. Know that "bling-bling" has consequences and that there is no parole in the feds. A 10-year sentence is a miracle, a 20-year sentence is considered a blessing and 30-years is par for the course…Know that thirty years is with no parole, that's 26 years and 6 months counting good time. You come in at age 25 you leave out at age 51.

Susan: What is your take on the "Game" today?

Akbar: More often than not, during the course of a day, I am confronted by some young brother imploring me to give him what he perceives to be the "GAME." In truth survival or life in the streets was never, nor is it now, a game. Even the term is a misnomer (a name that does not fit the thing it is attached to) for nothing can be more serious for those who have elected, or are forced through limited options to survive, than life played out in the mean streets of big cities. Perhaps, it was a game for those who did not take themselves or life seriously…for the few that did– the streets and its unwritten code was and remains grimly serious. To the would-be thoroughbreds and gamers, it is no more than a game. This point made evident by their lack of loyalty to life-long friendships and their broken

106

alliances to one another. When the game is no longer "fun"… when there are consequences to bear and pipers to be paid, like children playing a game, they want to gather their toys up and run.

For many of them it was not difficult to hide behind the facade of stand-up guys, thoroughbreds and comrades, when the consequences were less dire. However, their mettle was to be severely tested with the enactment of the amended 848 Kingpin Statute in 1986 and the new Federal Sentencing Guidelines on November 1, 1987. These new statutes and guidelines and the punishment that they carry were destined to make cowards out of killers and informants out of enforcers. Collectively they would sound the death knell of the GAME– such as it was. Now snitching or "flipping" is called "getting down first," "getting on the team" or "helping yourself." When someone flips or snitches now, and is then confronted, they are often heard to quickly respond, "Don't charge me…charge it to the game." Such is the state of what is called the GAME. Hence, in answer to the often-asked question…is the GAME dead? Yes it is! And good riddance– may it rest in peace.

Interview & research by Susan Hempstead
Edited Cavario H.

****

Although all of these stories involve death and the destruction of lives, the next story is likely the most tragic. This particular narrative is the saddest because it begins with family betrayal and ends with the death of the purest innocence. Much of the harsh reality that results from street life is difficult to accept, but when a child's life rests in the hands of greedy, loathsome and evil adults, it makes hope and reality difficult to reconcile. I met little Donnell Porter one summer night in 1987 in Harlem outside of a parking garage in his neighborhood on 132nd Street, just off of 7th Avenue (Adam Clayton Powell Boulevard). I had just pulled up on my all black Kawasaki Ninja 1000 to park for the night when Donnell approached me and began asking question after question, "Why do you have two pagers?" "What's that man on your chain with the two dogs?" "…This your bike? This a Ninja, right?" Donnell was a beautiful, bright little boy; he was friendly and seemingly unsoiled by his surroundings.

The story you are about to read is mostly about those surroundings and how they came to bear in a little boy's life.

"If free will is God's gift then ego is the Devil's curse."–Cavario H.

The following is the real life incident that Jay-Z referenced on the song "December 4th" (*The Black Album*) when he said, "And niggas get tied up for product and little brothers ring fingers get cut up to show mothers they really got 'em."

HELL UP IN HARLEM

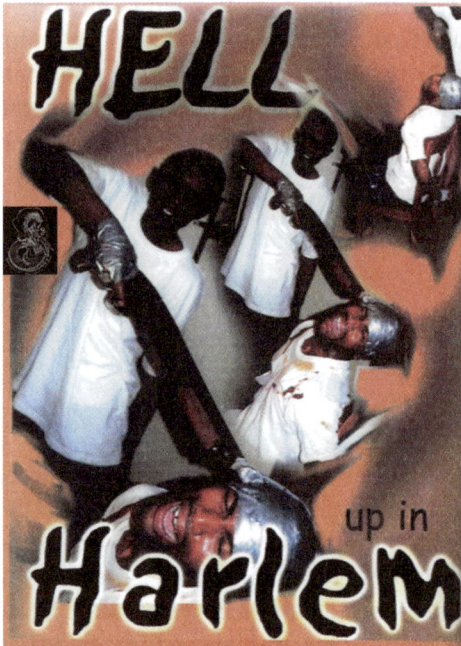

For almost a decade prior to the original publishing of this story in Don Diva magazine, rumors and speculation had been the primary source of information regarding Harlem's infamous underworld. Stories have been told and movies like "Paid in Full" have been made, but it would be Don Diva that put together the most detailed and accurate account of the fall of Harlem's Underworld, possibly Harlem's last notorious decade. This story was compiled from various law enforcement documents, confidential informers, court transcripts, FBI files and ultimately, through Don Diva's undeniable street credibility. Nowhere will you find a more factual account of what went down in Harlem during this era, which spanned throughout the early 80s to mid 90s. This story was so hot that shortly after it was published it was aired on cable as a law enforcement documentary.

December 5, 1989

Twelve-year-old Donnell Porter was walking to school alone on a Harlem street when a van "screeched" to a stop next to him. A man wearing a mask and gloves jumped out of the van and grabbed Donnell while the driver, who was also masked, opened the van door from inside. Donnell was thrown into the van and the first masked individual jumped in after him and the van sped off.

Donnel Porter age 12

Later that afternoon Donnell's older sister Patricia Porter received a phone call from a man stating Donnell had been kidnapped and was being held for $500,000.00 and that he would be killed if the police were notified or the ransom not paid.

December 6, 1989

A second call was made and the ransom was lowered to $350,000.00. The man on the phone spoke nervously as he demanded the money and instructed the family to go to the restroom of the McDonalds at 125th street on the southeast corner of Broadway in Harlem. The caller instructed Donnell's family to look under the sink, "There's something there that will show you just how serious me and my people are," he said. The family was warned again not to involve the police, the caller then states that he'll "be in touch" before abruptly hanging up the phone.

A Porter family friend entered the McDonalds restroom; he moved cautiously, checking the stalls to make sure that no one jumped out on him. He noticed a coffee can underneath one of the sinks and he moved slowly toward it. When the unidentified man picked the can up and looked inside of it, he was horrified as he stared into the can in disbelief. Inside the can was the severed pinkie finger of little Donnell Porter with a ring on it baring the initials, "D.P." accompanied by a cassette tape. Later that night Patricia Porter contacted the FBI. The FBI told Pat to contact her local precinct. Later that evening Pat Porter was interviewed by a detective in the 32nd Precinct– she pointed to the can on the table and handed the cassette tape to the detective.

The last call was received at approximately 9 o'clock on the evening of the 6th. Once the police were notified, the kidnappers did not contact the family again. The family told the police that they didn't know who would do this, the police had very little to go on.

At the station detectives working the case placed the tape in a player. On it they heard Donnell crying as he says, "They 'cutted' my finger off. They said if you don't do as they say they are going to cut my hand off. Please help. I love you mommy." The recording made investigators realize that the kidnappers were desperate and brutal; the cops knew their time was short.

It is believed that several phone calls were made to Richard Porter, Donnell's older brother– an alleged Harlem cocaine Kingpin. Apparently mutually agreeable terms on where Donnell would be exchanged for the ransom could not be arranged.

The investigators already had a file on the victim's brother Richard "Richie Rich" Porter, a well-known local drug dealer. The investigators concluded that Donnell's being kidnapped and a ransom of $500,000.00 being demanded from a relatively poor family from Harlem was tied to Richard's involvement in the drug trade. They stated it would be a tough case and that Donnell's chances of living diminished as each hour passed.

110

Rich Porter on vacation in Hawaii

December 7, 1989

Two detectives pulled up to the corner of 132nd street off of 7th Avenue where Richard Porter and Alberto "Alpo" Martinez were talking. They began questioning the two. After both their identities were verified, Alpo was allowed to leave. The detectives asked Richard to come in to the precinct to talk to them. He reluctantly agreed and got into the car with the detectives.

Rich's family building; W.132nd St. Harlem, NYC

The detectives interviewed Richard at the 32nd Precinct on 135th Street between 7th Avenue (Adam Clayton Powell Jr. Blvd.) and 8th Avenue (Frederick Douglas Boulevard).

The detectives told Richard that they knew that he was a "major drug lord." They told him that they would like for him to "cooperate" with them so that they could get Donnell back. Richard stated that he had no idea what was going on or who would do something like this. Finally Richard announced he was leaving and promptly did so. Richard denying that he knew anything frustrated the detectives– time was running out.

111

The family received a note that read, "We still want money, the child (Donnell) is in pain and needs medical assistance." No more calls were made and investigators tried for weeks to get a lead on the kidnapping, nothing came.

January 4, 1990

Nearly a month after Donnell's kidnapping, Richard Porter's body was found in Pelham Bay Park in the Bronx. He'd been shot in the head and chest. He still had his jewelry and a few thousand dollars in cash on him so robbery was immediately ruled out. This further frustrated the detectives– they knew now that Richard was dead that Donnell surely wouldn't be returned. The detectives hit the street harder now pulling in anybody associated with Richard Porter. There were several arrests made and all the people arrested were questioned about the murder of Richard and the kidnapping of Donnell.

An informant, threatened with being taken down for the distribution of narcotics, began to talk. He stated, "Maybe it was one of the big drug dealers Richard owed money to, I don't know; maybe it was Alpo or John-John or Lou from 142nd Street... maybe it was Preacher."

After bringing in several individuals, on mostly petty charges, the police were still no closer to figuring out the case than they were the first day.

The hours that passed were like days for Donnell's family and the days quickly turned to weeks of agony and desperation without a word from the kidnappers, but the Porters still hoped. Donnell had to be returned safely.

January 28, 1990

Less than a month after Richard's murder, another body was found in the same Bronx Park. It was the small, frozen body of a Black male wrapped in more than a dozen plastic bags. The child hadn't decomposed because of the brutally cold temperatures but his skin had turned grey and his eyes were devoid of color. The victim's head was noticeably misshapen and his petite mouth was agape as though he may have been crying out. Investigators noticed right away that the child was missing a finger.

January 29, 1990

The Porter family is notified that a body fitting Donnell's description had been found and they needed to come down to identify the remains. Donnell's family identified the small boy at the morgue. The medical examiner determined that he was killed by blunt force trauma to the head, the kidnappers had smashed Donnell's little skull. The M.E. (Medical

Examiner) had also determined that Donnell was alive when his finger was cut off. The M.E. could not determine whether the body was kept in a freezer or if it had frozen from the extremely cold weather.

At this point NYPD detectives as well as a special task force called C-11 squad– a FBI task force involving different law enforcement agencies– was "running the show." On an unspecified date, a meeting was called in connection to the drug trade in Harlem. The case agent took the floor and reviewed the major players in Harlem, referring to a chart set up like a hierarchy or "pyramid." Alberto "Alpo" Martinez, the 142nd Street Lynch Mob: Leon Brown, Louis Simms and several subordinate members. Clarence "Preacher" Heatley ran Preacher's Crew (sometimes known as the "Black Hand") along with his associate John "Big Cuz" Cuff– a former police officer; there were also several underlings in this crew– members were referred to as "the janitors." The pyramid showed crews and city blocks but the information on most of the main subjects was vague.

The objective of C-11 was to slowly work their way through the crew's ranks, to begin at the lower levels and place "flags" on all known crew associates, and it was established that if any crewmembers were picked up anywhere, C-11 would be notified.

June 1990

Nathaniel "Nut" Watkins (first cousin of Richard Porter) was arrested in Washington D.C. with little drugs and little cash and a pocket full of pawn tickets, he was charged as a "Kingpin".

C-11 was notified of Nut's arrest because Nut was a known associate of Richard Porter and Alberto Martinez. Agents from C-11 went to D.C. to interview Nut who at this point was facing a sentence of 20 years to Life in prison. Upon meeting with Nut the agents explained how they would "help" him if he were willing to cooperate with the government. Nut agreed, he told the agents that he received drugs from Alpo and distributed them in D.C. (Don Diva investigated these allegations and found contradictions to Nut's claims.)

Nonetheless, the information that Nut provided allowed the FBI to hit Alpo with a federal conspiracy charge. At that point FBI agents in Washington D.C. joined the investigation. A confidential informant told federal agents Alpo's whereabouts and connected several unsolved murders in D.C. to Alpo. Federal agents received information that Alpo lived in an apartment complex with his wife. After several days of

113

stakeouts off and on at Alpo's wife's house, the FBI spotted Alpo. When they arrested him in the car with his wife, they found drugs and money.

Alpo was first charged with drug conspiracy and money laundering. Later in a superseding indictment the FBI added five murders. He was a major prize– a "big name" in the Harlem drug trade. He knew the prosecution would be successful and decided to cooperate.

Investigators in New York debriefed Alpo. Among other murders he admitted to killing his former partner Richard Porter in a van then dumping his body. Alpo stated that a man named Terrell shot Richard Porter in the chest first, and then he (Alpo) shot him in the head. When investigators asked Alpo about the kidnapping and murder of Donnell Porter, he denied having any involvement.

Another case that the FBI was working on involved the 142nd Street Lynch Mob. Agents had come in contact with individuals looking to "help themselves," these individuals were giving information on the Preacher Crew, the FBI's "real target" –the top of the pyramid.

Investigators found their case moving very slowly because most people refused to talk about the "Black Hand." The agents and detectives of C-11 knew that they needed to somehow get inside of that crew in order to break them. C-11 found an opening when one of Preacher's main men got scared and went to the FBI for help.

April 4th 1990

Former Preacher crewmember Larry Jones aka "Larry Love" contacted the FBI. He said his life was in danger. He agreed to cooperate if federal agents would protect him from Preacher and his crew. Jones provided investigators with their first insider information. He told investigators where the crew held their meetings, how Preacher ran his organization and what he did to people when he felt that he had been crossed. Jones explained the voting "ceremony" that was held whenever a crewmember began to distrust another. In this ceremony if the majority voted "thumbs down" Preacher ordered them killed. March 1994, a crewmember named Maalik came up for a vote– he got thumbs down and Preacher ordered his murder.

Jones told investigators that Maalik went into hiding in Georgia because the investigation on him and the others was getting too hot. When Preacher decided he (Maalik) was too much of a threat to the crew he lured Maalik back to their headquarters by telling him they had a problem and he (Preacher) needed to speak with him. When the loyal Maalik arrived, he was made to feel comfortable. He had no idea what was about to happen to him. Maalik and the others were told to go down to the basement because there was business to take care of. John "Big Cuz" Cuff was waiting in the basement.

Preacher explained why Maalik was being killed despite his former friends' protests. Once Maalik was dead, Preacher ordered him dismembered. Jones tells the investigators he and another crewmember were given the job of disposing of the body parts. Jones gave explicit details of the process: acid was poured on Maalik's arms to remove tattoos that could possibly be used to identify him thereby linking him back to the crew.

"Maalik was done dirty! Make no mistake about this! Why? Just a call of the day by the Ol' Man. He was tied to a chair, gagged and tortured. He was sodomized, burned with cigars, and beaten beyond recognition. When I got to the basement I found him in this condition and was briefed on the session that had taken place. My job was to clean up the mess and break down his body and that is what I did. Maalik had burn marks all over him, his eyes were swollen shut, he was fucked in the ass by the ol' man and he was very dead when I arrived. So basically I didn't play a part in the killing itself on this particular incident, but I cleaned up after the dirt was done. Too many times this was the part I played. Other times I actually took part in the torturing and killings." –Larry Love

The severed limbs were left in a crumbling abandoned building. Jones told investigators that after seeing what happened to Maalik, he realized that the same thing could happen to him. That realization led him to the FBI and the protection of C-11.

Agents of C-11 stated in documents that one day they almost lost Larry Jones.

115

Larry was leaving a Manhattan courthouse on 100 Centre Street; he was there for another case. On his way out of the courthouse Jones spotted Preacher and some of his crew. Due to the fact that the area around the courthouse is heavily patrolled by all kinds of law enforcement, Jones was able to get to his car. Once inside his car, Jones drove off and was followed by Preacher's car. The two cars drove down a one-way street the wrong way, (it wasn't a high-speed chase) forcing other cars to the side. As Preacher continued to follow Jones the investigators were racing to his location. They arrived within moments with two cars, informed by Jones as to the route his vehicle and the pursuing vehicle were taking. It was at a stoplight that the agents made their move. They converged on Preacher's car from everywhere.

Jones escaped and Preacher and his men were arrested for reckless endangerment. In Preacher's car was a rope, a knife and Larry Jones' license plate number written on a piece of paper. Preacher was finally in custody, but the agents were further frustrated when Preacher and his men had to be released. It seems no one could prove that they were there to kill Jones.

C-11 continued its investigation of the drug trade in Harlem. They busted known buyers and sellers and pressured them to roll. During interrogation of one of the dealers in custody, investigators were told what had happened to Sheila Berry, the daughter of a correction official. The dealer provided the information hoping to receive leniency on his behalf.

Sheila Berry had been reported missing by her family in January of 1995. The dealer said Sheila had become addicted to crack and ran errands for Preacher's crew in exchange for a constant supply. The dealer also said that Sheila was sent to pick up drugs from a supplier and deliver them to Big Cuz Cuff. Cuff decided he didn't want to pay the supplier and told the man Sheila had run off with the drugs. To cover his lie Cuff and his men decided to get rid of Sheila Berry. Not one for wasting an opportunity, Cuff put out the word that she had stolen from Preacher's crew, thus killing her would serve two purposes: one, as a warning to others that might consider crossing them, and two, as a cover-up of Cuff's own greed and larceny.

The informant tried to direct the agents to where Sheila's body had been dumped but his information was vague. C-11 investigators continued to watch the crew, logging their activities and contacts around the clock; during that time investigators noted unrest within the crew. C-11

116

investigators stated the pressure was getting to Preacher as well. Thinking everyone was out to get him he began to appear paranoid.

While listening to a wiretap the investigators were able to hear Preacher order his main lieutenant John Cuff killed. As soon as the agents heard this they knew that Cuff had to be told. Agents sat across the street from Cuff's house in a parked car. When Cuff exited his house he was approached by the agents and told of the hit Preacher had ordered on his life. Cuff smiled, shrugged his shoulders and said there were lots of people that wanted to kill him.

August 1996

Agents of C-11 and the US attorney on the case met. They were reviewing the case, outlining the crew, their enterprise and their crimes. At the end of their meeting the US attorney agreed that they had enough and should make the arrests. Finally after more than five years of meticulous investigation, the US attorney's office of the Southern District of New York decided there was sufficient evidence for an indictment and arrests on a Federal RICO charge (Racketeer Influenced and Corrupt Organizations).

The first indictment listed Clarence "Preacher" Heatley and John "Big Cuz" Cuff. The plan was to bring Preacher in first, they figured if they started with anyone else Preacher would be warned and they might lose him forever.

Three arrest teams were set up in three separate locations. The investigators weren't sure where the Preacher was. Finally the team waiting outside of Preacher's Grand Concourse headquarters in the Bronx saw him emerge from the residence. The investigators' main target seemed to be alone, but with a man like Preacher caution had to be taken, the agents stated. The investigators waited until they could be sure Preacher wasn't being guarded and was alone. They approached the drug lord, identified themselves and took him into custody.

Agents said that Preacher, always calm, barely reacted. The team radioed in their catch. The other arrest team captured Big Cuz Cuff without incident as well. Now the two main players were in custody, but the case was far from over. C-11 and the US attorney met again. The US attorney stated the case still required hundreds more man-hours. The US attorney was still not satisfied that they had the crew solid. Neither C-11 nor the US attorney was clear on what had happened to Donnell Porter.

Apple Porter and Nephew Richard Porter

They needed to get John "Apple" Porter– a known associate of the Preacher Crew– in custody to complete the sweep.

They (C-11 and US attorney) persuaded "Apple" to meet with them. The US attorney explained to Apple Porter that as a major member of the crew, his not being in custody would likely have him labeled as a "snitch". Apple felt even with the Preacher and Big Cuz locked up this would still be a death sentence. Apple stated that he barely survived an earlier attempt on his life by some other members of Preacher's crew. Realizing he would eventually be killed if not placed under federal protection, Apple Porter decided to cooperate. Apple confessed to five murders and told investigators what happened to Donnell Porter, his nephew.

Apple revealed to investigators that he and Maalik put on masks and gloves and abducted Donnell on his way to school. Apple stated that Maalik jumped out of the van grabbed the child and threw him into the van. They brought Donnell to a building controlled by the crew. Investigators reported to the family that when Donnell was first grabbed his uncle thought he would have the key to Rich's mom's house with him.

118

It was further alleged that Apple had seen Richard counting substantial amounts of money at his mother's apartment on occasion and he figured they would be able to grab the money and run. Once the kidnappers had the boy they realized that he didn't have the key and the plan changed. They then began to make calls to the family. After unsuccessfully attempting to negotiate Donnell's release they decided that they needed to show Richard Porter how serious they were so they cut off the little boy's finger. Then they taped the message from Donnell and called Apple's niece Pat Porter.

Apple Porter and his nephew Donnell

Allegedly, Apple told investigators that he wanted to take what his nephew Richard Porter had built (referring to what he believed was a major drug empire) while he (Apple) was in prison. Apple said Richard wouldn't allow him to be a part of his operation. Apple promised Preacher half, and then Preacher and Apple agreed to grab Donnell.

It is alleged Apple also said that when he was made aware that Richard had been killed, he talked to Preacher and they both realized the ransom would most likely not be paid. Preacher told Apple that Donnell saw their faces; therefore, he would have to die, ransom or not. Apple told the investigators that it was Maalik who actually killed Donnell as well as being the one that cut his pinkie off. But Maalik was already dead by this time so there was no way to verify this. John "Apple" Porter was subsequently sent to prison for life.

119

The head had been successfully removed but the body still twitched. There were remaining crewmembers on the street that C-11 wanted to take down.

November 1996

Fifteen more members of Preacher's crew were indicted based on information offered by Preacher himself. The first names given to authorities by Preacher were that of his own son and daughter whom he alleged worked for his organization. Federal arrest teams fanned out all over the city but four of the men could not be found. Once everyone else was in custody they started talking. They gave the agents the address where bodies had been dumped, including Sheila Berry's and Maalik's. Several technicians wearing hazardous material suits sifted through a ton of crumbled building for days before they found something the medical examiner would later identify as the body of Sheila Berry. This evidence was necessary to support the testimonies of the confidential informants or CI's.

The arrested members of Preacher's crew explained to investigators how they were ordered to scrub the "killing room" down with boric acid after each murder. After securing a search warrant, crime scene technicians processed the basement of 2075 Grand Concourse in the Bronx. They found that Preacher's men did an excellent job with their clean up. They had completely cleaned everything...but they apparently didn't do windows. Although the room had been meticulously cleaned blood splatters were identified on the windows.

Fourteen gang members went to prison and more than 50 murder investigations were closed. John "Big Cuz" Cuff went to prison for life as did Clarence "Preacher" Heatley aka "The Black Hand of Death," and there is no parole in federal prison.

When a man takes another man's or woman's life, their thoughts rarely go beyond that instance or that individual. Rarely do they think about the mother, child, husband or childhood friend that may be waiting for that individual's return– the loved one never thinking that the last time that they spoke to, saw or hugged the individual would actually be the last time.

On the streets this is the reality everyday. Most often, thinking about the loved ones of your opponent or enemy is a luxury that you cannot afford. The things that make you blink, can leave you stink, so my question to you is…do you still wanna play this "celebrated" game?

Special thanks to Pat and Thelma Porter for their participation. –Written by Cavario H.

The following article was done with Jack (John) Cuff aka "Big Cuz." It originally appeared in our issue #10. It was another chapter in the "Hell Up in Harlem" saga that we felt needed to be brought forth for public scrutiny, too often rumors take hold and people's imaginations run wild in a vacuum of ignorance. Regardless of what anyone thinks, or believes, the word of the individuals directly involved in these situations have to be heard because if they can't speak on it...who can?

Jack "Frost" Brings the Heat

Jack Frost

I was contacted by John Cuff from Leavenworth Penitentiary. Cuff said that he had heard some disturbing "non-truths." He went on to explain that it was necessary that he set the record straight, both for the streets and the prisons. *"I don't give a fuck about this magazine shit, BoPp. Those that know me know [that]. But I don't wanna go somewhere else [another prison] and some muthafucka' gets it fucked up and I have to do something I really don't want to do."* I responded, *"I can dig it, comrade, and I agree, the people need to get it right. What do you suggest?"* He said, *"I'm sending you the necessary documentation to shut the rat, and those that support rats, down."*

Ninety-six hours later I received 5 government documents and a letter from Cuff. What you are about to read is the last word on the subject, the indisputable facts, documented by the government and the main player in one of the most notorious crews in Harlem's recent history.

My name is John (Jack) Cuff aka "Captain" aka "Jack Frost." I was part of the "Family." We had certain rules, [and we] lived by them wherever we were, with allegiances only to our Family & friends. We handled our business, much to the dislike of others, since the early 80s. Bad Boys move in silence, with no picks [favorites] or compromises!! Eye for an eye!

I want to thank Don Diva for giving me a chance to express myself and clarify a few things on a factual basis, with verification. Then put everyone on the right page in this struggle of survival we're all involved in. To keep those who are free, free and on point and to help those who aren't [free], to become free!

Other "publications" may think it's cool to entertain those individuals who think they're being shrewd, vindictive and selling your soul by becoming CWs [cooperating witnesses] & CIs [confidential informants] dealing in misinformation and deception with weak smoke screens being blown at the rest of us to justify their actions. Not wanting to be recognized for who and what they truly are. I'm not feeling "your" bullshit, nobody in their right mind is sympathetic to you. Certain individuals made a choice, live with that shit and stop fuckin' cryin'! Nobody forced you to make statements in the agent's jeep when they got you. Nobody made you go to the prosecutor's office with a smile on your face and with your pants around your ankles or on ya' knees with your mouth open!! When it's crunch-time and you're "The Champ" (supposedly) you [are] supposed to step up, not smash your own title at the feet of those who despised your existence since birth.

On August of 1996, I was surrounded by over 30 federal agents on 8th Avenue, at 144th/145th Streets. Unknown to me at that time, in the Bronx the other guys were surrendering to the government. All 4 of them immediately made statements! At 26 Federal Plaza, it wasn't me who made a post-arrest statement to the agents, then called the prosecutor at her home to inform her that [I] wanted to cooperate upon arraignment.

****

The following are excerpts from evidentiary hearings, pages 12, 13, 23 & 41:

Prosecutor being questioned in court:

Q. When was Mr. Heatley arrested, if you recall?

A. August 12, 1996.

Q. Did you become aware after Mr. Heatley was arrested that he had made a post-arrest statement?

A. Yes, I did.

Q. Can you tell the court the circumstances–how you became aware of Mr. Heatley having made a post-arrest statement?

A. I received a telephone call at my home on the morning of the 13th from detective Vincent Flynn one of the case agents, and he informed me that Mr. Heatley had waived his constitutional rights after he was arrested and had made a statement, and he described, summarized briefly some of the details of that statement and told me that Mr. Heatley had expressed an interest in cooperating with the government.

Q. Will you tell the court what conversation you had with Det. Flynn with regard to potential cooperation from Mr. Heatley and Mr. Heatley having made the statement?

A. Again, Det. Flynn indicated that Mr. Heatley had expressed an interest in cooperating, that he had given them a brief statement after his arrest, that he had expressed concern about Mr. Cuff to suspect that he (Heatley) was cooperating. He also told me that Mr. Heatley had assigned much of the responsibility for criminal acts to Mr. Cuff; that he, Mr. Heatley, had expressed to Det. Flynn that Mr. Cuff was the person that we needed to be most concerned about.

Q. How many hours, if you can estimate, did you spend in total debriefing Mr. Heatley during the five proffer sessions?

A. I would estimate between 20 and 25 hours.

****

John Cuff's letter continued:

...we had a 4 page, 4 count indictment, serious but not unbeatable. I was sent to the box [segregated cell within prison], the other guy [Preacher] was housed on the 7th floor in General Population where he really made his move with his lawyer and participated in 5 days of proffer [volunteer] sessions– August 21, 23, 27, 28, 30 of 1996. Then going on visits with his daughter and girlfriend, trying to convince his son to turn himself in but all along crossing each and every one of them!

While this was going on I was in the box, going on lawyer visits and family visits from the box, basically holding my nuts but keeping my mouth shut!!!

123

Then his godson D.H. came—yes, the same person from the Anthony Jones case in B'more, yeah, D.H. a, multi-platinum rat-coward showed up in court after he was banished out of NYC 2 years earlier. The godfather [was] coaching the godson on how to lie on people. I guess we're lucky NY, NJ, Penn., MD, and Georgia still have a population, NC too! But a seeping 47-count, 85-page indictment was handed down and on Nov 21, 1996— the T.V. and radio "amped" our case publicly. The [Preacher's] daughter, [Preacher's] girlfriend, [Preacher's] son, me and 18 of us were sitting in Manhattan Federal Court, sick with that indictment in our hands. Orange suits and blue shoes, wondering what happened. Sixty agents & NYPD [were] clapping [and] laughing at us. We all knew what happened, he [Preacher] went 'platinum' but his godson went 4X platinum. He was resented by the government so much he talked us onto the Death Penalty statute—real smart! To go a step further, in desperation he and his lawyers wrote a motion on March 25, 1997 to compel the courts to give an evidentiary hearing which was held December 2nd and 5th in 1997. Five hundred and fifty-eight pages of lawyers and prosecutors arguing the "great thing" he [Preacher] said about others since 1984 and why he should or shouldn't get a deal. Ruling in this by our judge—you get nada, shut-up and go to trial if you want to! (Cuff addresses Preacher, stating) You knew better than to try to out snake a bigger snake!

I did the first 22 months of this case in the box, but I kept my mouth shut through and through. I exercised my 5th amendment rights; I made NO STATEMENTS, PARTICIPATED IN NO PROFFER SESSIONS, NEVER IMPLICATED MYSELF OR OTHERS BY WAY OF PROVIDING ANY INFORMATION TO LAW ENFORCEMENT!!!

****

Excerpts from pages 7-9 of the Death Penalty motion:

This court is well aware, from extensive pretrial submissions and testimony, that codefendant Clarence Heatley engaged in lengthy and detailed proffer sessions with the government in an effort to tender his cooperation in exchange for leniency. There can be no doubt that during the course of these discussions Clarence Heatley provided the government with detailed information about the commission of crimes, including numerous murders, and the structure of an "organization" which provides the foundation for the government's theory of the case. It has even been alleged that Mr. Heatley provided information to law enforcement, which allowed them to protect a police officer whose life was allegedly in danger. This court can readily anticipate the following: if convicted of capitol murder, Mr. Heatley will claim, during his penalty trial, that he should be

124

spared the death penalty in part because he cooperated fully with the authorities after his arrest and provided truthful information about the activities of his cohorts, including codefendant John Cuff. He will argue to the jury that he came forward voluntarily, that he had no obligation to do so, and that he was offered nothing in return for providing substantial cooperation to the authorities. He will emphasize the lengthy nature of the proffer sessions, the fact that he implicated himself as well as others in criminal behavior, and may well have saved the life of a New York police officer. By contrast, the jury will hear no such evidence with regard to John Cuff. Mr. Cuff participated in no proffer sessions, made no statements to the police regarding the allegations for which he was eventually indicted, and has not implicated either himself or anyone else by way of providing direct information to law enforcement. In short, John Cuff has exercised his rights under the Fifth Amendment.

Cuff's letter closes:

February 1, 1999, 3 weeks before trial with 3 codefendants out of about 20. Seventy-one new crimes were brought against us and 37, which named me, crimes of very serious nature– unbelievable. Nevertheless I kept a straight face with a capital death case looming over my head. On March 20, 1999 I wore mine (took responsibility for his criminal charges) and some others' [charges] also, like a fresh baldy, a new butter-soft (leather jacket) [and] Gortex boots and jewels–that was my choice. I am who I am– a "Headbanger," a "Bad Boy," [a] "Villian"! I got no person arrested or indicted, none of that shit. I was sentenced to life plus 145 years on June 29, 1999 and I'm still wearing mine like a trooper.

All those who jumped ship to the prosecutor's office, you knew what this was about from day one, you didn't get drafted, you volunteered to be in the Family. Stop all that cryin' about being called a "Rat"!

A fish wouldn't get caught if he kept his mouth shut! Nas said it, "How could'a Kingpin tell?"

John Cuff #39012-954

Interview by Cavario H.

In response to the article that I did with former Black Hand associate and ex-police officer John "Big Cuz/Jack Frost" Cuff, I was contacted by the "Black Hand of Death," himself, Clarence Heatley, the following letter is in his own words, word for word without a single edit. Outside of the executive staff at Don Diva, no else has ever seen this letter.

Clarence "Preacher" Heatley: The 'Talking' Hand

Clarence "Preacher" Heatley AKA The Black Hand of Death

I'll start by introducing myself. My name Clarence Heatley a.k.a "Preacher." Don Diva has seen fit to publish an article laced with numerous unsubstantiated ugly, allegations concerning my family and me.

As a rule, I ignore media for that reason, but you have seen fit to publish such a blistering attack on my character, as well as question my integrity as a man and a parent. I am now compelled to respond with the facts of the situation. Now let me make this fact clear to your readership. I am not and never was a drug dealer/murderer/gangster. Nor do I have anything to do with any of those activities.

I, like so many others, am just another victim of this federal Frankenstein. The fact of the matter is at no time have I ever been before a grand jury and

126

or took the witness stand on anybody. This case was made by people who were never men in their lives and wouldn't stand up even in the shower.

I have no doubt these are the same kind of people that are supplying your magazine with this government propaganda. Most are just innocent dopes, but the others have a very sinister agenda. They take this kind of thing and run with it. It's called "case jumping." For the sake of your readers who may not know what that means, I'll give you the short version. A man enters a jail or a prison and will be approached by certain individuals, he will be asked to show his papers... to prove he is not a rat. After they read the paperwork, they go into who you know, what you know...where you know it from etc. The next thing you hear is your lawyer telling you, "You are going back to court because you have a new case!" Why?

Because those same people you spoke to made a beeline to the phone to tell the government you have confessed to a murder, drug deal etc. Welcome to the real world. You have made yourself a get out of jail free card for some rat!

It gets better or worse depending on your perspective. The government gases a man up who has Life already to do something to the person in question. The person is attacked. He is either killed or kills his attacker. The government doesn't care which way it goes. They just make sure they see it. Get the picture. These undercover agents now have a "get out of jail free card."

It is a ugly but serious game and if you can't think...like the game of tag...you're it. In the case at hand, what do you owe people that call the feds and turn their self in, then implicate you and your family. What do you owe cops that play both sides of the fence, until their master (the government) catches them out there. Then they implicate you in murder, kidnapping, drug dealing...etc. In my book, something I was told by a young man...something I shouldn't have forgotten... "Once a cop always a cop." What do you owe people that cross that line? As far as I am concerned ... I owe them nothing. All bets are off. When a fool takes a shot at you, you shoot back or you die.

I played the hand that I was dealt. I took my eyes off the deck, so they stacked it on me. It came down to lie on people that had no hand in this game, who did nothing to me, to put me where I was. So I had to fold. You can't win that game unless you go all the way. I took this headcrack so that my children would see daylight. The only place I ever brought my children was into this world. How in the hell could that ever translate into bringing them to jail? Both of my children are fine and all mines love me. Most parents will kill over their children, I took it to another level...I died for mine...I am doing LIFE plus 225 years.

The real problem is a lot of clowns never gave it a thought, I would sit down with these people and confess to a lot of lies and half truths. They are mad I got their 5K1 letter torn up. (Author's note: A 5K1 motion is filed by the Government when a defendant provides substantial assistance in the solving of other cases and the Government seeks a reduction in what otherwise would be his sentence.) They now have their federal agents and prosecutors working overtime to put enough pressure through this kind of slander so I will give in and make that call...their strategy is obvious.

This is nothing more than psychological warfare. They first divide a man's camp by turning his peers against him and that leaves him nowhere to turn but the government. So they keep their jailhouse agents stirring the pot, you know the more you stir the more it stinks. These tactics have worked for them over and over again.

The government doesn't care about me they have me right where they want me. They want what they think I know...which is nothing as far as I am concerned.

Now here is what you don't know...why they would even put their machine to work on me: I had a company based in Washington D.C. that did electronics and security. I had men working in the Pentagon of the U.S. We did work in the FBI academy. The CIA. We put the nurse call system in the navy hospital where they take the President of the United States. The list goes on and on. My company went up against the political machine of the Republican Party in Virginia and gave fundraisers for Doug Wilder to put him in office, as the first black governor of the state of Virginia. Get the picture! They would very much like to know who paved the way for a black man from Harlem to not only walk the halls of big business but the halls of government as well. What do you owe people that cost you at least fifty million dollars?

Don't let these jailhouse agents play you out of yours, so they can get out of jail on you.

The best agent the government has against us is not the guy with the 5K1 but rather those of us who are the minions of the agents and prosecutors running around reading papers and pushing papers.

Signed, Clarence "The Preacher" Heatley

This next related section is, for most of the public, a first glimpse into the obscured proceedings of the federal court system where the concepts of right or wrong are blurred by deal making and life bartering, purportedly in the name of a "greater good" oddly named, "justice."

UNITED STATES OF AMERICA,

Government,   *

                              *

                              *

                              *

v.   *

                              *

KENNETH SIMMONS,   *

RONALD ALFRED, JAMES ALFRED   *

FRANKLIN SEEGERS,   *

DEON OLIVER, KEITH McGILL,   *

                              *

Defendants.   *

* * * * * * * * * * * * * *   *

DAY 20, AFTERNOON SESSION
TRANSCRIPT OF TRIAL
BEFORE THE HONORABLE ROYCE C. LAMBERTH
                                   UNITED STATES DISTRICT JUDGE

November 3, 2003

PAGE 31... LINES 17 & 18.

Mr. Martinez, who has been cooperating since February 1992...

PAGE 36... LINES 10, 11, 12, 13, 23, 24 & 25.

LINE 10. THE COURT: Would the witness stand, face the

LINE 11. clerk and take the oath, please.

LINE 12. ALBERT GEDDIS MARTINEZ, GOVERNMENT'S
WITNESS, SWORN

LINE 13. DIRECT EXAMINATION

LINE 23. Q: Are you known – do you have any nicknames?

LINE 24. A: Yes.

LINE 25. Q: What nickname are you known by?

PAGE 37... LINE 1.

A: Alpo.

PAGE 38...LINES 11, 12, 13, 14, 24 & 25.

Q: Okay. Sir, are you here testifying today pursuant to plea agreements in both the Commonwealth of Virginia and in the District of Columbia?

A: Yes.

Q: And how long have you been in jail, sir?

A: Twelve years this month.

PAGE 39... LINES 3, 4, 5, 6, 8, 11, 17, 18, 19, 21, 22, 23, 24 & 25.

Q: What sentence did you receive in Virginia, sir?

A: First I received – I copped out to 35 years, and it was reduced to 16.

Q: What sentence are you serving?

A: Twenty-eight and a half years.

Q: Sir, can you tell us where you're located?

A: Yes, I'm housed in a secure area in the BOP (Bureau of Prisons) system.

Q: Can you tell us specifically what prison you're located at?

A: No.

Q: Why is that?

A: Because I'm under the security program.

Q: All right. The part of the prison that you're located in, does it have some kind of a name?

PAGE 40... LINES 1THRU 24.

A: The Witsec Program.

Q: Witsec is short for witness security?

A: Yes.

Q: All right. And is this –would you tell the ladies and gentlemen of the jury about its geographic proximity to the remainder of the prison?

A: Yeah. Well, the Witsec Program is a very – the housing areas are very small. A perfect example is, you take this room right here and you put all the guys that did what I did, and the rest of the building is for the general population.

Q: Meaning the rest of the courthouse?

A: The rest of the courthouse, yes. The rest of the whole building. We're housed in a very small area.

Q: Okay. Are you physically separated from it?

A: We're separate.

Q: All right. Sir, this Witsec Unit, is it some kind of country club?

A: No.

Q: Why do you say that?

A: Well, actually, in the Witsec Program you – the time is a lot harder because the facilities are very small and the movement is very limited.

PAGE 41... LINES 1, 2, 3, 4, 5, 6, 13, 18, 19, 20, 21, 22 & 23 .

Q: Limited, what do you mean?

A: Well, because the general population, they get to move around more because of their status and all. And our status is a little more high security and all that, and so when we move, stuff has to be locked down and things of that nature.

Q: Would you tell the ladies and gentlemen of the jury what your initial introduction to the drug world was?

A: ...[A]s a kid – as any kid growing up in, you know, in Harlem, I mean, especially in my neighborhood. I mean, when you came outside it was – it was right there. And I was introduced to the game by – by – by someone, and – and that's basically it, I mean.

PAGE 42... LINES 13, 14, 15, 16, 17, 18, 20, 22, 23 & 24

Q: You indicated that you had somebody who introduced you into this world.

A: Yes.

Q: Who was that?

A: At the time, he was – I guess I was around 16 years old; he was probably around 19, 20, older guy.

A friend of mine named Randolph Jamison.

He's now doing 40 [years] to life. But he was the young [man] who took me .... and introduced me to the game. My first drug package was from him.

PAGE 43... LINES 16, 17, 18 & 19.

Q: –how long did your relationship or your friendship, your business relationship with Mr. Jamison last?

A: Up until '91, until I got – until I got busted.

PAGE 45... LINES 8, 9, 10, 11, 12, 13, 14, 15, 16, 17, 22, 23, 24, & 25.

Q: Who is Dominican Pete?

A: Dominican Pete was someone who I met later on through a friend of Randolph Jamison who wanted two guys of African-American to – because he was Dominican, so he wanted two guys of African-American [descent] to work with him and become his bodyguards.

Q: And did you and Mr. Jamison in fact become Dominican Pete's (bodyguards)?

A: Yes.

131

Q: Okay. When you say that you worked as a bodyguard for him, would you describe your responsibilities?

A: I mean, my responsibility was to make sure --

PAGE 46... LINES 1, 2, 3, 4, 5, 6, 7, 8, 9 & 10.

...no one would take the drugs. My responsibility was to make sure when we went out that he was safe and just to watch his back when we was doing transactions.

Q: Okay. When you say transactions, what kind of transactions are we –

A: Drug transactions.

Q: And specifically what drug are we talking about?

A: Cocaine at this time.

Q: Okay. And are we talking about powder cocaine or crack cocaine?

A: Powder cocaine.

PAGE 47... LINES 16, 17, 18 & 19.

Q: Okay. And at that time, sir, how much was an eighth of a kilogram of powder cocaine worth?

A: Back then? It varied, it varied. Back then, we're talking '80, maybe around $3,000 maybe.

PAGE 48... LINES 1, 2, 3, 4, 5, 6, 7, 8, 9, 10, 11, 12, 13, 21, 22, 23, 24 & 25.

Q: Did you at some point become familiar with crack cocaine?

A: Yes.

Q: And when was that?

A: This was maybe around '82, '83.

Q: All right. And tell us how you got introduced to crack cocaine?

A: I had a gentleman approach me about this new drug, we called it, and it was crack at the time, and it was already rocked up, it wasn't powder. He gave it to me in rock form. So I was actually introduced to it that way.

Q: --Did you ever have occasion to sit with Pete's customer?

A: Well, I became a little closer to Pete after Randolph –Randy – got busted for robbery. He was my partner, he got busted, so I became a little closer to Pete once he found out that I was Hispanic, you know, I had Hispanic background and I was able to speak the language. He would –

PAGE 49... LINES 1, 2, 3, 4, 5, 6, 7, 21, 22, 23, 24 & 25.

...put me in the room with the customers, having them thinking that I was black and I didn't understand what they were saying, he would put me in there just in case they was talking about doing something to him or trying to beat him with the prices and all that. So he would put me in there as like a spy, figuring they could talk freely around me. So my role became a little more significant with him.

Q: Okay. At some point, did you break away or did your relationship with Pete come to an end?

A: Yes.

Q: Tell the ladies and gentlemen of the jury about that.

A: Well, it just got to a – it just got to a point –

PAGE 50... LINES 1 THRU 25.

...where I felt I wasn't really going nowhere no more with him, and I decided that I wanted to do my own thing, my own thing meaning I wanted to open up my own, you know, crack spots and all that.

Q: Okay. You indicated a few moments ago that at some point, someone had approached you with crack that was already rocked up I believe was the phrase you used?

A: Yes.

Q: Tell us where in time that happens with respect to your relationship with Pete.

A: Well, that actually happened after I broke away from Pete.

Q: Okay.

A: I broke away from Pete and I established two crack houses in Harlem, and then later on, the gentlemen that I was talking about came to me with an offer, because I had my own crack spot and he didn't have no place to really sell the drugs and all that, so he would –

Q: Tell us just for a moment how it was that you got around to establishing your two crack spots in Harlem.

A: From the money -- from the money and the drugs I was getting from Pete, I took that and just sort of like invested it into the streets and made my own drug and powdered up my own drugs and put it into the crack house.

Q: After you had established these two spots, you said –

PAGE 51... LINES 1 THRU 25.

...somebody approached you about selling crack?

A: Selling some drugs for them, yes.

Q: And tell us about that.

A: It was just they knew who I was, they knew what I was doing, they needed a place to get rid of their drugs, and we worked out a deal of what he would bring me and what would I give back, and it was like about 60/40. But again, the actual price, the 60/40, I was okay with it because I was doing my own – doing my own drugs anyway. It was more of just having him [as] a part of my team.

133

Q: At this point in time, sir, when you've got two of your own crack houses and this person approaches you and gives you crack that's already rocked up, how much money were you making?

A: I didn't have to give the money back then; it was all my money. So, I mean, I would probably go in the crack house with a 'ki' [kilo] or something, and at this time, I was probably making about maybe $5,000 a day. This was '83, '84, so this was good for then, and I was just starting off.

Q: What reputation, if any, did you have in the drug world in this time frame?

A: Well, just as – a lot of the older guys looked at me as a, you know, young and up-and-coming, you know, hustler and all that, and I had a good reputation at the time.

PAGE 52... LINES 1 THRU 14, 17, 18, 19, 20, 23, 24 & 25.

Q: Was there any reason that you stuck out?

A: Yeah. Well, first of all, I stuck out on the west side because I was from the east side and, you know, in your area, you know who's who, where they come from and all, and then I was, you know, like I said, I was from Spanish Harlem, so I spoke the language and I just stuck out.

Q: Did you have any kind of a reputation at this point?

A: Uh-huh. I mean, I had a reputation of being kind of, you know, wild and crazy, not wild like shoot-em-up, but wild like, you know, motorcycles, I was into motorcycles and just having fun and just being young and wild and that's it.

Q: Sir, did you become familiar with somebody named A.Z.?

A: Yes.

Q: Who was A.Z.?

A: A.Z. was someone who I approached also in the game about some drugs and all that, and later on, he became my boss.

Q: And did you – was there something of significance that you learned from A.Z.?

A: Yes. At the time, the crack houses that I had were –

PAGE 53... LINES 1 THRU 15.

...kind of like slowing down, so I knew I needed to branch off and try something new. So I heard about, you know, this guy named A.Z. and he was known, he was known uptown in Harlem for selling powder cocaine,

134

and at a basketball game, I approached him about doing some business and we talked and nothing came of the conversation at the time, and then maybe a few months later, we ran into each other again.

Q: And what ended up happening when you ran into each other?

A: We talked about some business, so he showed me his way of how he was getting money with the powder cocaine – he wasn't into crack; he was into powder cocaine. He was into putting powder cocaine into like these special bottles. They gave like an illusion that you was getting actually more than what was actually in the bottle.

PAGE 55... LINES 7, 8, 10, 11, 12, 13, 14 & 15.

Q: I see. I see. Once you established your connection with A.Z., how did the two of you do business together?

A: Well, A.Z., like I said, he had storefronts. You know, his main business was a storefront up in Harlem, [the Jukebox "game room and candy store" on 145th Street between Adam Clayton Powell Boulevard and Frederick Douglas Boulevard on the westbound side] and I approached him about opening up a storefront in my neighborhood, and so we did business and I did that, but it wasn't going as good for me at the time. You know, it was kind of slow.

PAGE 56... LINES 5 THRU 25.

Q: Okay. Sir, are you familiar with the term "crew"?

A: Yes.

Q: What is a crew?

A: A bunch of guys together hustling, getting money.

Q: Okay. Are you familiar with the term "strong" in relationship to the word "crew"?

A: Yes. I mean, they use it, yes.

Q: Would you tell the ladies and gentlemen what those two terms together –A: Well, "strong crew," I mean when you use the term, you know, "That crew is strong," you're talking about a bunch of guys, whatever they may be doing, who are about –I want to make sure – strong crew – guys that are not taking no mess, you know, a bunch of guys that's not taking no mess.

Q: Did this person A.Z. that we've been discussing, did he have a crew?

A: Yes, he did.

135

Q: Were they, and I use the word "strong" in quotes, was A.Z.'s crew strong?

A: No, actually, they weren't very strong. They was –

PAGE 57... LINES 1 THRU 25.
...just about getting money.

Q: And if you – what would they have had to do in order for you to be able to describe them as being strong?

A: Well, I mean, they would have to shoot their guns. I mean, you know, it was more of them – when a beef came up, they took care of it. You know, they didn't just let it go away, they took care of that situation.

Q: Okay. Did you have an opportunity to speak one day with A.Z. with respect to some problem he was experiencing?

A: Yes. One time I came to re-up, meaning I came to get some more drugs from A.Z., and at the time when I was coming to see him, he was in a little disarray because he had just got shot at by some other guys, and so he was looking to take care of that problem, but he didn't really have the guys he needed to go take care of that problem, so I volunteered my services.

Q: When you say that he didn't have the guys to take care of the problem, what do you mean?

A: Well, he didn't have the guys to go get the guns and, you know, come back and go take care of the situation, situation meaning the guys who shot at him.

Q: How was the situation to be taken care of?

A: Well, for his guys to go get guns and retaliate.

Q: Okay. You indicated that you volunteered your –

PAGE 58... LINES 1 THRU 25.
...services.

A: Yes.

Q: What does that mean?

A: Because I was still not really a part of his crew. I was getting drugs from him, but I was, you know, getting drugs from him, but I was, you know, I was still doing my own little crew. So I volunteered my services, meaning that I told him that, you know, whatever his problem is, you know, I'm a go home and get my guns and I'll be back.

Q: And did you, in fact, go home and get your guns?

136

A: Yes.

Q: And what happened when you went home and got your guns?

A: Well, I mean, I went home and got the guns and came back and me, him, and another individual went looking for the guys who shot at him.

Q: And what happened?

A: We found them and we shot them.

Q: Okay. And what happened?

A: Well, after that, after we shot them, no one died at the – no one died at this time, but we did get the guys who shot at him and left the scene and went back to – went back to his location and regrouped and talked about the situation, talked about the guys who didn't come back, you know, to deal with the situation.

PAGE 59... LINES 1 THRU 25.

Q: Your having volunteered and assisted A.Z. in the way that you've described –

A: Yes.

Q: How did that affect your relationship with A.Z.?

A: It actually made my bond with him stronger. He actually took me – he took me in after – he took me in. He made me a part of his crew after that.

Q: Why is it or how is it that that happened?

A: Well, he recognized – he recognized the strength, he recognized the loyalty that I was showing to him at the time.

Q: And how, if at all, did that compare with the strength and the loyalty shown to him by the other people who were part of his crew?

A: Not good.

Q: Not good? What do you mean?

A: Not good meaning that he didn't feel comfortable with them anymore because he felt that, you know, if he's getting this kind of money, when a situation comes up of people shooting or robbing or whatever, he needed to be able to depend on his crew to handle it and not have to go to an outside person.

Q: Okay. Sir, how much cocaine at this time after this incident where you've helped A.Z. out by going to get your guns and shooting at the people, how much cocaine are you –

137

PAGE 60... LINES 1, 5, 6, 7, 8, 9, 15 THRU 25.
...getting from A.Z. at this time period?

A: Once he made me a part of his organization, he showed me, you know, the way of bottling up the cocaine, the proper way of bottling up, the way he was doing it, and so I moved in position with him. I was probably getting about three keys, four keys at a time.

Q: Mr. Martinez, what time period are we talking about?

A: We're talking around '85, '85, '84.

Q: Okay. And at your peak in terms of dealing with A.Z., how much cocaine were you buying?

A: Well, actually A.Z., like I said, he had a storefront [The Jukebox] that was bringing him a lot of money, and at this time, he didn't want no more –he didn't want anything to do with the storefront anymore because it started creating a lot of problems for him as far as it was getting robbed, guys started coming in there sticking it up, because it wasn't no secure spot; it was just like over the counter, you know.

PAGES 61... LINES 1 THRU 25.

A: It was like a candy store. It was actually a candy store, but, you know, you would come in there and you would buy drugs also.

Q: You indicated that it had been robbed. Do you know did he know who was robbing him?

A: Yes. We found out some stick-up-kids started – we – some stick-up guys started coming into the – they robbed it like once or twice. And like I said, A.Z. wasn't a – he wasn't a very violent person and all that, so he didn't really want to deal with those problems, so he felt it was better for him to open up another spot and just pass that one on to someone in the crew.

Q: And what is it that A.Z. decided to do with respect to this particular spot that had been robbed?

A: Well, he called like a meeting with the different guys of his crew and offered it to like his brother and some guys he grew up with, but they didn't really want to take on the responsibility of dealing with those problems, so I was like one of the guys he asked since I was the last one to come into the crew, and when he asked me, I told him I'll take care of it, I'll take it.

Q: Meaning you'll take this particular store.

A: Yes. I'll take this storefront, yes.

Q: Okay.

A: Because it was a gold mine.

PAGE 62... LINES 8 THRU 25.

A: Well, first of all, I took care of the problem, the problem being the guys that was robbing the spot.

Q: And how is it that you took care of it?

A: I found out who – I found out who they were and then – found out who the guys were, the main guys, and then we – we had them murdered.

Q: Is it fair to say that you gave the order to have that done?

A: Yes.

Q: Once these individuals who had been robbing that spot were killed, what happened to – what effect did that have on the business at this particular storefront?

A: Actually it didn't have any effect. It didn't really slow anything down. Once that was taken care of, A.Z. took – A.Z. took the guys – some guys that were with me into the spot, into the storefront.

Q: And what time period are we in now where –

PAGE 63... LINES 3 THRU 13, 23, 24 & 25.

A: Around '86. This is around '86.

Q: And how much cocaine are you dealing or are you involved with at this point?

A: Well, you know, with A.Z. leaving the spot, it was still his kind of. You know, he just didn't – he passed it on to me, but I had to give him like $10,000 off of every key that I would get from him. So at this time, the spot, you know, on a good day, the spot was probably doing about three, four keys a day in bottles, $10 bottles.

Q: All right. And running seven days a week?

A: Seven days a week.

Q: In approximately a week's worth of time, how much money is it that you're making?

A: Oh, in profit -- profit in about a week, probably –

PAGE 64... LINES 1 THRU 11, 14, 15, 16 & 17.

...about $40,000. I would take out – I was probably paying about 15-, 16,000 for a key, so I would take out the – because, again, I put my own people in there, and so I covered all the expenses and all that. So once they paid me the 15- 16,000 for the key, then my 10,000, so they was giving me about 26 (thousand). Off a key, we was probably – off of one key, we was probably bag – bottling up about 45- (thousand), 50,000, and once I

139

took mine, then the rest was for them to split amongst them.

Q: Meaning the people who were working for you?

A: Yes.

Q: Okay. Sir, at some point, did you in this time period, in this 1986 – 1987 time period that we've been talking about, did you have an occasion to come to the Washington, D.C./Virginia area?

A: Yes. Around '86 – around '86, '87, they was giving a function Kings Dominion and we –

PAGE 65... LINES 8, 9, 10, 11, 12, 13, 14 & 15.

A: --we heard about the function, so we didn't really know what to expect, so we all jumped in our nice cars and made sure our New York plates was shiny and came on down to Virginia.

Q: Let me ask you, sir, you mentioned that you made sure that your New York plates were shiny. What significance do New York plates have?

A: It means a cocaine connect is coming, really.

140

Velma Porter: Letter to a Traitor

The following is a letter from Rich and Donnell's mother, Velma Porter, originally printed in Don Diva magazine– Issue #2, it was directed to Alberto "Alpo" Martinez, a drug dealer who became a government witness.

First let me start by saying that I am deeply saddened by the manner in which you portrayed my son, when in fact in your heart you knew what you said was untrue. It is easy to try and vilify the dead when the dead has no advocate to counter the claims against them. You were sadly mistaken though... as long as the breath of life remains in my mouth I will always be that advocate that my son's spirit cries out for in his shallow grave.

From the birth of the union between you and my beloved son, I knew that you would be the Judas, who would betray his name, love, friendship and honor. I can understand to some degree because you have always tried to emulate my son and walk in his shadows. You were feared but my son was loved. He was revered, while you were detested. I also understand because of your need to justify your own less than noble actions, you have chosen the narrow path of shifting animosity and disdain on others to dim the lights of some of your most atrocious crimes against the ones that loved you the most. "A coward dies a thousand times, a soldier dies but once."

Your spirit is trying to recover from the fact that you have snitched on the ones who have shown you a degree of love unparalleled. You admitted to snitching on your most prized confidant in D.C., Wayne Perry. That must have ripped his soul apart more than any sentence that could have ever been imposed on him. It is said that Wayne Perry was so hurt during his indictment he didn't even deny the accusations because he couldn't believe that the very man who he tried to keep alive, at all costs, was trying to kill him via a lengthy prison sentence. You also admitted to killing your friend Gary in a fashion unfit for the most profound of enemies. With friends like you who needs enemies.

You have set a dangerous precedent that should not be emulated in any regard. You have tried to convince the masses in the streets that snitching is cool and passé. You call it "Doing Po." I call it plain, ol' fashion "tellin'." Those that will compromise their manhood by giving you the time of day when you come home will only testify to their own weaknesses. You may have put fear in most, but real men will see you for who you really are; a no good, double-crossing parrot who tried to walk in my son's regal shadow and could never quite attain the grandeur that my son attained.

Your statements have made you an open target for criticism. You should have left the issue in the wind to blow away, but you decided to harness it like the bridle of a horse. The more you speak ill of a man that is not here to defend himself, the more you appear to be the envious, deceitful, amoral individual the world has known you to be all along. The sad part about this whole ordeal for me is the fact that I have loved you like a son and to some degree I still do. A mother can never stop loving a son, even when there is opposition and strife between her two sons. Richard was a man before his time. He was a movement that came from the ashes of the ghetto and transcended into something bigger than life itself. The protégé will always harbor hostilities towards his guide, because it is that guide that commands the attention without even trying. You will soon realize that you can never be Rich. Rich couldn't be Rich! The streets made and ordained him the prince of the streets. He was only conforming to the natural inclination of his nature. A Rich Porter only graces the pages of time once in a thousand years, so I doubt you or I will ever see the likes of a man, father, confidant, brother and philanthropist like Rich again.

While writing this letter Rich came to me in a moment of inspiration. He revealed to me that the reason you are vilifying him is because you needed a way to justify killing him for those 30 kilos. Of course you couldn't say, "I killed him for greed." You had to make the streets accept it with a seemingly legitimate claim or allegation. The streets don't lie and they see right through you. His spirit is at rest knowing that he loved you more than a friend could ever love another friend; he and I both. We accepted you as blood of my blood, flesh of my flesh. Can you live with yourself? I guess you can, you're just "Doing Po," right? When you practice deceit long enough you begin to believe it. The truth becomes lies and lies become the truth.

Your son will grow up knowing you through your words as being the biggest rat and disloyal friend that has ever walked the streets!

Thanks to you, people will snitch and call it "Doing Them". They will reason, "If Alpo did it than it must be alright to do." This couldn't be further from the truth. You have admitted to double crossing, double-dealing, treachery, trickery, deceit, disloyalty, envy and a host of other things and you think the streets will respect you for that? The streets are smarter than you think.

All in all, I have learned to see you for who you really are and not allow the hate to stop me from being me. Rich Porter will always live on. His name is untainted. AZ summed it up well when he said, "When you killed Rich, you not only killed Rich, you killed Harlem." Harlem and all the other 'Harlems' across America will never forgive you for that. The verdict is in... GUILTY!

The jurors are Michael Fray, Rich, Gary, Wayne Perry and countless others you have killed out of jealousy and snitched on out of pure desire to avoid pain and punishment. The irony is the very sentence you imposed on my son was the very thing you were afraid of the most (Death). That is why you snitched... to save your own wretched life; but in saving it—you lost it.

Velma Porter

Donnell & Richard Porter

REST IN PEACE

Peaceful Journey to Donnell, Richard and Ms. Velma Porter

We Are "The People"

In Gore Vidal's "Dreaming War" (2002) he quotes President Harry Truman's (1945-53) secretary of state, Dean Acheson as saying; "In the State Department we used to discuss how much time that mythical 'average American citizen' put in each day listening, reading, and arguing about the world outside his own country…It seemed to us that ten minutes a day would be a high average." Mr. Acheson, being the chief advisor to the President on all of America's business outside of our country, as well as being responsible for making sure that what the President ultimately decided (based on his advice) was done, was basically saying that WE THE PEOPLE (that's you and me) lacked the aptitude or the attention span (or both) to care about and/ or decipher the events going on in the world outside of our bubble. This was his idea in 1946 and he was not alone in his thinking. Here now in the beginning of the 21st Century, nearly 70 years later, thanks due largely to a nullified education system and the proliferation of drugs throughout our society, Mr. Acheson's rough estimate is probably more accurate than ever, and it would seem that his "ten minute" "high average" has greatly decreased. When you have lights/gas, cheaper food, designer clothes, platinum and diamond jewelry, SUV notes and exorbitant mortgages, and reality TV to occupy yourselves with, in an economic environment of less, less and lesser still, for the common-man and hustler alike, who has the time to worry about what *They* are doing over there? If you missed it, my point is WE THE PEOPLE are now officially (all of us) "NIGGERS." You've been unplugged.

Aaron Jones: THE JUNIOR BLACK MAFIA

Aaron Jones

He's been called the "Black John Gotti," not by his comrades or the people he did business with but by the people who were trying to crucify and execute him. There are a lot of young brothers and sisters out there who think that being called the "Black John Gotti" is some kind of honor or "prop." The reality is that this personification is what assisted in Aaron Jones receiving LIFE and DEATH from the United States of America.

He's alleged to be the founder of the "JBM" (Junior Black Mafia), an organization that has been made out to be one of the most feared black organized crime syndicates in Philadelphia history. Anybody and

145

everybody living in Philly were talking about Aaron and the JBM during the mid 80s and early 90s. If you weren't talking about them then you were not at all hip. Everyone had their own version of things and most made it up as they went along but everyone agreed, "They were not to be fucked with."

"The JBM had Philly on lock." According to the Philadelphia Crime Commission, Aaron Jones and his associates built the JBM into a violent multi-million-dollar drug organization that controlled all of Philadelphia between 1985 and 1991. According to the newspapers and other media: It was alleged that the JBM was comprised of 50 members and had up to 300 associates that were responsible for the sale of 100 to 300 kilos of cocaine generating between $10 and $30 million dollars a month.

The JBM's assets included plenty of money, mansions, luxury cars, furs, jewelry and weapons. The JBM was also linked to 33 legitimate businesses, such as auto detail shops, barbershops, and restaurants. It was rumored that the members of the JBM were young, well-connected, street-smart hustlers with a no-nonsense approach to their business. It wasn't until the guns began firing and the bodies began to drop that they began making newspaper headlines. The local gossips said the JBM was in business for 2 years, quietly amassing millions, before a local federal task force was formed to bring them down.

"Get Down or Lay Down"- simply put: join us or be killed was their motto according to police. This was used to headline many stories done on Aaron Jones and the JBM by the media and used by the prosecution to further substantiate their claim of unscrupulous violence on the behalf of the JBM.

Aaron Jones said to Don Diva: The motto "Get down or lay down" is the police motto coming from suckers on the streets. No one ever went around telling people that or giving this ultimatum. By 1989, the government associated 25 murders with the JBM. It was rumored that many of the alleged victims of the JBM were rival dealers and anyone who "played" with their money. The rumors about their violent tactics soared; if you skimmed off the top, if you tried to become independent, if you threatened their business in anyway, you were "dealt" with. The JBM had become so feared that survivors of alleged assassination attempts refused to testify against them in fear for their lives. An alleged JBM member was arrested for possession of a handgun while in the courtroom where a government witness was set to testify against Aaron Jones for allegedly shooting him.

146

The witness, who was confined to a wheelchair after being shot 10 times in the arm, hip, chest and face, recanted his testimony (for the time being). After a grand jury investigation, Aaron was re-arrested and the witness testified at the preliminary hearing with a sheriff's deputy standing between him and Jones to prevent eye contact. Now this really sounds like these brothers were ballin'–right? They were definitely puttin' their thing down, right?

The trouble with all this information is that it came from government and media sources–who often exaggerate facts to justify the exorbitant amounts of money the government often spends investigating and prosecuting individuals. Let's face it, it wouldn't look good for the media to write a story about a drug dealer who was moving 1 kilo every month that the government spent thousands of man hours and hundreds of thousands of dollars to investigate–now would it? And it would be politically damaging for the government to admit that they investigated a brother for years and was able to get nothing on him.

Now I am not trying to imply that there is absolutely no truth in what has been written about Aaron Jones and the JBM because I don't know! No one knows but Aaron Jones and his real comrades–but over the last few years it seems like everyone wants to write their story.

Don Diva contacted Aaron to set the record straight and give him an opportunity to tell his truth. While it seems everyone wants to tell stories of the evil streets and make confessions, Aaron being a true Don, was very hesitant.

Aaron Jones: I am very apprehensive about responding to your request…because you never know one's true intentions, [or] ulterior motives behind things…So many people try to come at you with games, only to exploit [me] for financial purposes.

****

There has been an explosion of books claiming to be about the "infamous" Aaron Jones and his comrades known as the J.B.M…all unauthorized and very inaccurate according to Jones.

Aaron Jones: I have nothing but contempt for the books written about me. These so called authors [are] trying to capture the psyche of my thing but all fall way short…you can't get information from none of these books about me because believe me they don't have a clue.

After overcoming his initial reluctance, Don Diva magazine became the first publication to interview Aaron, who is still on death row in a maximum-security prison, to get his sentiments on his case and the game. I visited Aaron on Death Row in February 2000, and although doing interviews in jail is nothing new to me, it was a new experience. When I spoke with the prison officials prior to going to see Aaron, they warned me that I had to go through a metal detector that was far more sensitive than those at the airport or in court.

This meant no under-wire bras, jeans with studs or belt buckles. Dressed appropriately, I entered State Correctional Institution (SCI) Greene– a prison deemed a "Supermax" due to the extensive security under which it is operated. I filled out my visiting form and presented my I.D. I was told to put all of my belongings in a rusty locker. The only thing I was allowed to bring into the visiting area was the key to that locker. I had no need for money since there are no vending machines or anything else for that matter in the visiting room. I really didn't see the point of all this since all of Aaron's visits are non-contact.

I would be visiting with Aaron through a Plexiglas window with two small screens on either side. I would barely be able to hear him let alone pass along any contraband. Once stripped of all of my belongs, I was brought down to the visiting area by a guard to wait for Aaron. As I waited for him, I tried to remember the points I wanted to discuss.

Aaron is only allowed a two-hour visit, once every week, so I knew I had to get as much information as I could. Even though the Plexiglas was going to be between my interview subject and me, I couldn't help being nervous. I just didn't know what to expect when I met him. I must admit that even though I know better than to believe everything I read in the media, his reputation had me a little shaken.

From the way he has been portrayed and the method in which he is being kept prisoner, I anticipated him being wheeled out like Hannibal Lecter. After 30 fretful minutes, Aaron was finally brought out. Without saying a word, his energy calmed me; he was not the monster people would have you believe. He had the peaceful vibe of a man who has come to terms with himself and his Higher Power.

Aaron Jones: I appreciate your honesty, you couldn't imagine what that means to a brother…I can tell when somebody is keeping it real with me…For years I remained in a passive mentality not wanting my voice to be heard because I know how cynical and pessimistic society is, especially when it comes to brothers like myself. People contact me to try and quote me one way or another.

Knowing full well how I am perceived, I felt it would be foolish on my part to say anything. Regardless of how I came off they would twist it around to make me look bad. I was not looked at as a man but as Public Enemy Number One, a monster because of all the saturation of propaganda.

****

Throughout Aaron's several court cases, he and his lawyer proclaimed racial discrimination and improprieties as well as his innocence in his capital murder case. Through hearsay, snitch testimony, street informants, rumors, exaggerations and out and out lies, Aaron says that he was personified to represent what ills society– drugs and violence. It got so bad that every murder case that was unresolved during this period of time was put on the JBM to further substantiate the J.B.M profile of drugs and violence. Stories were told and embellished upon to the point that the truth of events were no longer identifiable.

Aaron Jones: My federal (drug) case and murder case is nothing but word of mouth from a bunch of frogs (snitches) trying to find a way out. So who is the top prize? Me! There was no other evidence in either case, just hearsay evidence. I have no faith for justice in the judicial or should I say political system. I have come to terms with the lifestyle I chose years ago…My plight is a little different than most brothers, though all can make a claim of some racial injustice whether it is vindictive prosecutions, excessive prosecutions, disproportionate sentences or double jeopardy.

A lot of the way we are treated in these processes is a result of our own naiveté as a whole in our communities…I played no part in the capital murder…this brother will not be on bent knee trying to demonstrate a remorseful attitude to a system and to a society that never shows mercy itself and is built on tyranny and racial discrimination. I have a death sentence, sister, these people want to take me out under the premise that I was a Mafia boss. What's ironic about that is that not one white (Italian) so-called Mafia figure has ever been placed on the row here in Pennsylvania, if not anywhere else.

****

There is no doubt that Aaron is a true Don–not because he amassed millions, owned luxury cars, played the broads and lived "Ghetto Fabulous", but because he has proven himself to be a man of character and integrity. There are many that would argue this point because of his alleged crimes. However, the fact is Aaron made a decision many years ago, based on whatever he was going through at the time, to play the game and he played by the rules of the game until the very end. The prosecution relied heavily on the testimony of former JBM members. Under the Kingpin Statue 21 USC 848, Aaron was sentenced to mandatory life and was required to forfeit $6.2 million.

Aaron Jones: I've come to terms with my life and take responsibility for my actions and choices I made. I'm not going to blame the system, the environment...no one but myself... but I don't accept everything that's happened to me, especially this unjust death sentence.

****

Aaron is holding his head, dealing with his situation and making no excuses. He was indicted several times and never once did he cooperate with the government, even though his life was at stake.

Aaron Jones: As I sit on the row, to me it was never an option to take the stand on my comrades. That never even came across my mind as an after-thought, you feel me! I take solace in the fact that all the comrades I broke bread with remained true. That's why to this day all versions of our time have been diluted and fabricated...stories and lies from suckers who knew full well they had to step off when real brothers came on the set.

****

Being a victim of the snitch system, Aaron knew how the game worked. One of his associates, Frog Carson, told on him and Aaron's own brother in-law was an FBI agent that was key in putting him away. For most weak-minded individuals, who get into the game for all the glory with no guts, this would have been enough to flip. Not Aaron!

Aaron Jones: 'The game is to be sold, not told,' this is something [that] I heard a lot coming up. Truth be told, you had to have someone's blessing from the 'first' to be introduced to the game. There was a self-serving mentality that transcended down to later generations that bred a lot of those rats. In Philly I like to call them Frogs–they leap in bed with the feds. They conspire with them telling infinite lies and ad-libbing as they go along mixing up half-truths to make themselves sound believable.

****

While serving three different sentences, Aaron is now on death row in a maximum-security prison, where he will remain until his execution. Aaron's days and nights are very different from the lifestyle he was accustomed to on the street. Aaron is being held in the Restricted Housing Unit.

Aaron Jones: I am locked down 23 hours a day, Monday through Friday, and 24 hours a day on Saturday and Sunday. I get one hour of exercise in the yard during the week and I may sign up to go to the law library for a two-hour session once a week when it's my turn. I can have one two-hour visit and a 15-minute phone call every week.

****

Now for all you bad-asses out there, I want you to try to imagine being in a room no bigger than a walk-in closet. No television, no telephone, no radio, no clocks...nothing but a few books and some paper and a very small pen to write with. This is where you will eat, shit and sleep for the rest of your life. You will remain in this room for 23 hours everyday for the rest of your life with no other human contact. When someone does take the 8-hour drive to come visit you, it will be through a glass partition for two hours...no hugs, no kisses, no touching whatsoever. You'll go to sleep every night knowing you will never touch your wife, children, or parents ever again in your lifetime.

Most of you couldn't handle being alone without modern luxuries for a day, could you handle this? I walked out of that jail counting my blessings and appreciating my liberties.

Throughout my research for this article, Aaron reminded me that I could not get information about him and his comrades from the media or the various books that have been written. Aaron told me that everything that has ever been said or written about him is based on speculation and gossip, and the things that may have been true were embellished for drama and credibility.

Neither Aaron nor his real comrades have ever spoken a word about anything to anybody. All the stories that have circulated, all the testimony that has been given has come from third parties, snitches, wannabes, gossips, and liars. Know that the rumors that are being spread about you in the street today that make you feared, that keep your name ringing bells, whether they are true or not, they are painting a picture of you. They are being heard, compiled, filed, and you are being profiled. And if you are ever called upon to defend yourself before the government this information will be used against you in the courtroom and in the media to further assassinate your character. After time, rumors and speculation are, more often than not, accepted as truth and you can bet the people trying to persecute you are not going to try to figure out what the truth is or who's lying– as long as what they are hearing supports their depiction of you. Aaron has been in jail for over 22 years (as of the print of this book), every day he is in the fight for his life. He has come to terms with his situation and he doesn't fool himself.

Aaron Jones: Whatever happens happens, and whatever is going to be, is going to be. One thing for sure I will never give them the satisfaction to think I will crumble to this system looking for mercy so they can laugh in my face. I will never allow my circumstances to break my strong will as a man.

****

Aaron is a devout Sunni Muslim, who fully understands all that has happened in his life. Aaron tells us that where he is in life–physically and mentally–was preordained and it would be fruitless to entertain thoughts of "What if" "Should have" "Could have" and "Would have." His metamorphosis is complete.

Aaron Jones: In hindsight during my conversations and correspondences with Don Diva, I realized that I may have been taken out of context and misconstrued in a lot of areas. You see, I was addressing brothers that have already experienced the game and doing their time on certain topics they discussed in a previous publication not completely looking at the bigger spectrum…once again a brother loses sight of the bigger picture of things.

I shared some of my views of how I feel about my unjust sentence and the way I was prosecuted but in no way do I want to come-off as condoning that lifestyle. I've had plenty of discussions with younger brothers who come through, and what I usually get is that they are not trying to hear it. They are not listening to older brothers preaching to them about the streets. I said to myself, "Why even bother?" But then I realized that would be a defeated attitude I would be adapting to.

So for whoever is out there and wants to hear some harsh realities from someone they can identify with, I'm your man. Pay attention because what I am saying is on the real and may even be redundant to you but it's the truth. The streets are very alluring and seductive; they pull you in with all of the temporary desires it has to offer. The superficial and materialistic things like the fast paper, jewelry, all the slick rides; especially when you see a nigga pull up dressed fly with a dime piece on his hip, man you're like "that is going to be me in a minute."

The more you come up, the more them dime pieces are noticing you and coming at you in all directions.

So this is all you see, you're not trying to hear it, you want a piece of the pie. Before you even know it you're knee-deep in the game, you're short sighted with tunnel vision. All you see are the perks.

Unconsciously you know the risks at hand and what is at stake but you tune them out. You feel you can be slicker, smarter, do things a little bit differently than the last man did that you seen fall.

You're in denial and caught all up in the raptures of the streets. Your ultimate goal is to make a better life for you and your family, but on the way you begin to encounter more and more obstacles– things you didn't anticipate so you try to deal with them.

You're beginning to rationalize every move instead of seeing it for what it is. You rationalize and rationalize. Sometimes you may turn to whatever you use to get your buzz on to help you on the way. But younger brothers and sisters the inevitable will happen.

Like I said earlier they were all temporary desires and pleasures to begin with. There's no pension plan for players in the game. Yes, one or two may fall through the cracks but the hard truth is you will either come in or go under…that is the bottom line.

Now some of y'all may say "Man I'll take my chances coming into this lifestyle." Look at me. I am sitting on the row, ask me was it worth it. I'll tell you NO! The thing is, it's not just about you but how it will affect everyone around you who loves you, once things come falling down. Everybody has a plan, so don't fool yourself to think your plan is smarter than the next man's. Nothing is guaranteed in this game but death and prison.

The unexpected will come up and bite you in the middle of your plan. It's just a part of it– dealing with whatever, however, and whenever, so there are no delusions here. It won't last and when it comes time to pay the piper, nothing you may think you've accomplished is worth your life. So on the real, young brothers, choose another path and don't get caught up in the glitter. There is a lot of truth to that old cliché, "All that glitters is not gold" or "bling, bling," as ya'll may say now.

It is so easy to get pulled into the game/streets. You will begin to adapt the mentality of the game/streets, rationalizing, and living in denial of the harsh reality, which will inevitably come knocking. It is hard to change that mentality once you're in but just take heed to what I am saying to you now. Take a couple of steps back and look at the big picture...what's at stake...the destruction of your life and the lives of your loved ones who will be affected by it.

I'm out. One!

Aaron Jones–State Correctional Institute–Greene.

Interview by Tiffany Chiles

Edited By Cavario H.

FIRST DOWN, FIRST OUT

The story of Philadelphia's Junior Black Mafia has been rendered through many mediums, from newspapers and magazines to urban novels and movies, but none have truly done the journey justice. The crew of nearly 40 young soldiers first set precedence when they built an organization that generated tens of millions in illicit gains through their homegrown narcotics network. They maintained their alliance despite the federal government's ardent attempts to break their bond, through threats of lengthy prison sentences. Even the death penalty wasn't enough to counter the construct of their characters.

One of the youngest members of their mob, Derrick "Little Derrick" Williams hails from the Germantown section of Philadelphia, known as "Uptown" to those familiar with its history and infamy. He was released in March of 2005 and now shares the benefits of having survived the vicious streets of "Killadelphia" and nearly 16 years of incarceration.

The bold sections below are taken directly from the PSI (Pre-Sentencing Investigative report) documents that resulted from the late 80s, early 90s investigation of the infamous JBM crew. "Little Derrick" will navigate us through and between the lines of this foreboding document, affording us a greater understanding of the events mentioned herein.

155

UNITED STATES OF AMERICA

vs.

Derrick Williams

Education: Graduated from Cardinal Dougherty High School and in 1982 attended Temple University continuing education program from 1982 to 1983

Employment Record: From 1980 to 1989, Mr. Williams worked periodically for his father at Brett's Lounge, in Philadelphia. He ultimately worked as manager and earned approximately $300 to $400 per week. From October 1981, to January 1982, Mr. Williams worked for United Parcel Service during the Christmas holidays. He earned approximately $100 per week.

Dependents: None

Aliases: Little Derrick

Count One: Conspiracy to distribute cocaine, in violation of 21 U.S.C. € 846. 10 years to life, and a fine of $4,000,000.
Date of Arrest: January 13, 1989

Detainers: U.S. Marshal Service
Codefendants:

1. Bryan Thornton, a/k/a "Moochie"

2. Leonard Patterson, a/k/a "Basil"

3. Bernard Fields, a/k/a "Quadir," "Q"

4. James Price, a/k/a "Squeezie"

5. Sam Brown, a/k/a "Magic"

6. Kevin Bowman a/k/a "Black"

7. Reginald Reaves, a/k/a "Reggie"

8. Shawn Davis, a/k/a "SW1"

9. Christopher Laster, a/k/a "Dirty Black"

10. Joseph Cobb, a/k/a "Skip"

11. Anthony Long, a/k/a "T.L.," a/k/a "Tony"

12. Barry Richardson a/k/a "Earl"

13. Darrel Reaves

14. Michael Williams

15. Eric Pearson, a/k/a "Buttons"

16. Anthony Reid, a/k/a "Tone"

17. Ronald Mason, a/k/a "Rock"

18. William Perdue, a/k/a "Storm"

19. Larry Brown

20. David Baynham, a/k/a "Fat Dave"

21. Rodney Carson, a/k/a "Frog"

22. Earl Stewart, a/k/a "Unc," a/k/a "Mustafa"

156

On October 2, 1991, a federal grand jury sitting in the Eastern District of Pennsylvania, returned a 32-count Indictment, charging 26 individuals with various violations of Titles 18 and 21; and forfeiture, pursuant to 21 U.S.C. € :853. Derrick Williams who was the 17th individual named on that ill-fated indictment, was charged with conspiracy to distribute multi-kilogram quantities of cocaine, in violation of 21 U.S.C. € 846 (count one). During 1992, all defendants, with the exception of James Cole, pled guilty or were convicted of the charges and sentenced to lengthy prison terms. Mr. James Cole was a fugitive until May 1993. He was subsequently convicted and, on February 19, 1994, Mr. Cole was sentenced.

Cavario: How many actual members of the Junior Black Mafia were there?

Derrick Williams: There were about 10 more [members] but they were not on the indictment. Rodney Carson and Earl Stewart were indicted but they were not members of the JBM.

Cavario: Were you all arrested as a group?

Derrick Williams: Yes, because half of those that were indicted were already in jail so once the indictment was unsealed, all they had to do was come to the jail and serve us the notices. They may have only had to round up another 10 people from the street.

Cavario: Prior to the indictment, what sort of offenses were the members locked up for?

Derrick Williams: Mostly violent crimes; alleged murders, and attempted murders and so forth.

Cavario: How is it that out of 25 men no one cooperated with the feds?

Derrick Williams: I guess Aaron's ability to accurately determine character is at the base of that phenomenon, but when an individual determines that certain acts or behaviors are beneath them, that is the ultimate deciding factor. These men would not have cooperated with the government against their mortal enemies, instead they would meet that enemy on the field of battle –it's an honor thing. This was once the rule, now it's a rare exception.

Cavario: How and where was James Cole captured and how much prison time did he ultimately receive?

Derrick Williams: Allegedly he was captured on the highway in a traffic stop. He got life for an 848. You see, the connect told on him, he (James Cole) wasn't a part of us (JBM). He was our original supplier, he introduced the "connect" (Earl Stewart) to A.J. (Aaron Jones) after their separation. Years later, when the connect (Earl Stewart) got busted and started telling; he had to start from the 'Alpha' and that was James Cole–this is according to Earl Stewart. I never actually met James Cole.

[Mr. Williams was convicted on Count One of the Indictment and, on November 6, 1992, was sentenced to 223 months to run concurrently with the sentence he is serving in state prison. The court ordered that Williams be given credit for time served from June 1, 1989. The Sentencing Reform Act of 1984 is applicable in this case since the offense occurred between late 1985 and continued up to or about September 1991.]

Cavario: How is that you were given time served prior to being indicted in the JBM conspiracy?

Derrick Williams: Because they used my state case as a predicating act, which means that I committed a totally unrelated crime but they believe it was connected to a larger "conspiracy". They did this to try and bolster their claim that the JBM was a violent organization but by doing that they helped me. I didn't actually plead guilty to the federal indictment until November of 1992 but I received credit from June 1, 1989. My state time was actually 12 - 26 years, which I would have had to do 12 years of anyway. When they came to me with this plea, I took it because although I knew that I was going to have to do 85% of the time. I also knew that because they had established (for their own purposes) that my state charge was an act related to the federal case, they would have to run the terms simultaneously which meant that I would only be doing three more years for this huge federal criminal case than I was already going to be doing for the state anyway. Meanwhile, my comrades were getting thirty years and life for the same federal case.

The Offense Conduct

In late 1985, a violent drug trafficking organization began distributing cocaine and heroin in the Philadelphia area. Sometime in late 1986, this organization became known as the "JBM" sometimes referred to by various members of the organization as the "Junior Black Mafia." The JBM continued operating until September 1991 and was responsible for distributing in excess of 1000 kilograms of cocaine. The conspiracy is reflected in Count One of the Indictment.

Cavario: The government contends that the JBM had begun to operate as early as 1985, is this accurate?

Derrick Williams: I wasn't there at the beginning but you can't really cry about a year or two, [but] '87 would be more accurate.

In the early phases of the conspiracy, Aaron Jones and James Cole worked together as directors of the JBM. Initially, Cole functioned as the supplier of the cocaine, and Jones directed the distribution on the street. The cocaine was purchased by Cole in Florida, California, and elsewhere. It was then transported in automobiles to Philadelphia by members of the conspiracy. Earl Stewart was one of the JBM's main suppliers of cocaine. Reportedly, Stewart made deliveries of cocaine to the JBM in quantities as large as 230 kilograms. Jones would usually pay Stewart approximately $16,000 per kilogram ($3,680,000). These deliveries were generally requested by Jones, Cole, or Bryan Thornton, and were picked up by Bernard Fields and Shawn Davis (names number 1 and 8 on the indictment, respectively).

In approximately mid 1989, an apparent dispute occurred between Jones and Cole. Stewart began to deal exclusively with Jones and the other JBM members, excluding Cole. From at least this time on, Jones assumed complete control of the JBM. Jones continued to function as its leader except for when he was incarcerated– Bryan Thornton or Bernard Fields ran the JBM for Jones. During the time that Jones was in jail Stewart was informed by one of his Mexican suppliers that Jones and the JBM owed them approximately one million dollars. Reportedly, Stewart, the supplier, and Thornton met in Las Vegas to discuss the size of the debt. Thornton explained that the money was short and slow coming in due to the recent arrests of JBM members.

In late 1989, approximately one week after this meeting, Thornton paid Stewart $275,000 for previously delivered cocaine.

Cavario: Was this period of A.J.'s incarceration prior to the major JBM indictment?

Derrick Williams: Yeah, Aaron was in jail on another matter, I believe it was an aggravated assault. He got acquitted on that assault and then he got bailed out. But during the time he was in jail for the aggravated assault, he was charged with the stabbing of another inmate. Although the injury resulted in barely a puncture in the dude's arm, a big deal was made of it because it was an act of violence involving the alleged leader of a, purportedly, "violent criminal organization". He was out on bail so he was going to court from the street on that [inmate stabbing] charge. He showed up in court one day, was found guilty, and was immediately re-incarcerated... that was that, Aaron never saw the streets again.

When Jones was released from jail, Stewart informed him that he still owed the supplier one million dollars. At this point, the supplier was willing to settle the debt for $500,000. Jones proceeded to dismiss the debt, explaining to Stewart that he was going to forget about that money.

The JBM was divided into squads, which controlled cocaine distribution in various sections of Philadelphia; each squad was headed by a squad leader. These individuals supervised and directed other lower ranking members of the JBM. The squad leaders included, among others, Bryan Thornton and Kevin Bowman. Additional members who were identified as squad leaders are: Derrick Williams, Leonard Patterson, Reginald Reaves, Larry Brown, Eric Pearson, and Sam Brown. Each squad leader was responsible for distributing among the individual squad leaders by couriers. These couriers included Bernard Fields, Shawn Davis, James Price, Ronald Mason and David Baynham.

Another role that individuals had within the JBM was that of enforcer. Among those who acted as enforcers were Ronald Mason, Christopher Laster, Joseph Cobb, and William Perdue. As enforcers, these individuals were responsible for committing acts of violence for the purpose of controlling and expanding the drug business of the JBM. The JBM also used violence to promote internal discipline.

The JBM was an extremely violent organization; all members carried semi-automatic handguns and other firearms. Members of the JBM, on orders from Aaron Jones, participated in a number of murders and attempted murders. In order to protect themselves from injury by rival drug dealers, members would wear bulletproof vests and other types of body armor. A common phrase used by the JBM was "Get down or lay down," which meant, buy drugs from the JBM or get killed.

Cavario: Why was the JBM reported to be "an extremely violent organization"?

Derrick Williams: In order to kill King Kong you have to create King Kong [so] during that time, every violent crime that was committed was attributed to the Junior Black Mafia. I recollect reading articles in the newspapers where dudes that had been arrested for some of these violent crimes would actually make statements saying that they robbed an old

160

lady or shot someone because the JBM told them to do it because "they owed us money".

Cavario: Was the ill-famed "Get down or lay down" an actual slogan that was used by JBM members or was it more folklore that came about from certain practices that your group employed?

Derrick Williams: No, not at all. No one would go out using that jargon, there may have been overtones of that but as you know, the way the drug game works is: if you give people a fair price for a good product, "Get down, back down, lay down" doesn't even come into play.

In approximately 1989, there was a war between the JBM and the Craig Haynes group over control of the drug traffic in Philadelphia. In response to the shooting of several JBM members by individuals believed by the JBM to be associated with Craig Haynes, Aaron "AJ" Jones called a meeting of a number of JBM members. Jones stated that he had a source who would tell him when Haynes was at a particular location in South Philadelphia. He proceeded to order Laster and Perdue to go to 24th and Moore to kill Haynes. Laster and Perdue returned later and stated that Haynes had not been at 24th and Moore, but they had "slumped" somebody. The pair had in fact shot and killed an innocent bystander. This shooting occurred on July 11, 1989.

Cavario: When did you know that you had certainly passed the point of no return in terms of your criminal endeavors?

Derrick Williams: I guess I knew I was in it for the long run when the media kept talking about us– ast that point I knew I was going to have to ride it out.

Cavario: You were on the streets when the newspapers were doing stories about your team yet you continued to participate in this lifestyle--why?

Derrick Williams: Yeah, I fell in love with it. None of us had any real criminal records and we didn't know what it would be like when they came for us. We just enjoyed what the attention brought.

Additional murders or attempted murders that took place within the JBM were:

April 16, 1988 - Leonard Patterson shot and killed John Wesley Tate.

July 12, 1988 - Anthony Reid shot and killed Mark Lisby.

October 2, 1988 - Derrick Williams, along with another individual, attempted to murder Bobby Little.

161

[Court's account: On October 2, 1988, at approximately 12:31a.m., the defendant along with a codefendant drove up to the two complainants in a rust-colored Chevrolet. Mr. Williams got out of the car and fired his gun six times at complainant number 1 (this complainant worked for the JBM as a dealer and stole $8,000 from the JBM). Complainant number 2 was hit in the left leg while attempting to flee from the assault. The bullet shattered bones below complainant number 2's knee.]

Cavario: Who is Bobby Little?

Derrick Williams: He's the dude that I got 10-years for allegedly shooting but here's the kicker, he didn't even get shot; he was the actual target but the bullets missed him and hit his step-pop by accident. Subsequently, I was given two counts of aggravated assault: one for missing Bobby Little and one for hitting his stepfather. The judge said that he (Bobby Little) went through, "a traumatic experience" and sentenced me to 5 years for each offense– she ordered that they run consecutive which is absolute overkill. The altercation had absolutely nothing to do with drugs or a drug debt; it was a pride matter... that's all I'll say on that though.

Cavario: Did the judge in your state case know that you were part of the Junior Black Mafia?

Derrick Williams: There were all these cops in the courtroom so she knew I was somebody, plus they told her, "He's part of the Junior Black Mafia". My lawyer objected but once the bell is rung you can't un-ring it. These people were searching me right in front of the judge, I thought it was so cool [then] but what I didn't know was that they were prejudicing the judge against me. Two o'clock that afternoon I was on the street. Later that day I was in a jail cell... sweating. I didn't see the streets again for 15 years and 7 months. I was the very first one to be convicted as a JBM member and that's why I'm the first one to get out.

February 2, 1989 - Bernard Fields, Christopher Laster, Shawn Davis, Ronald Mason, Kevin Bowman, Joseph Cobb, William Purdue, and Derrick Allen shot and attempted to kill Terrence Ross, a.k.a. "Papers", an associate of John Craig Haynes.

February 15, 1989 - Ronald Mason shot and attempted to kill Allen "Paddles" Parker, a.k.a. Allen Green.

March 13, 1989 - Kevin Bowman and Anthony Reid shot and killed Neil Wilkinson and also attempted to murder Darryl Woods.

162

March 20, 1989 - Kevin Bowman, Christopher Laster, and Anthony Reid attempted to murder John Craig Haynes near City Hall in Philadelphia, Pennsylvania.

August 1990 -at the direction of Reginald Reaves and Sam Brown, Christopher Anderson and others attempted to murder Alphonso Caldwell, a.k.a. "Fony".

On many occasions, the JBM purchased multi-kilogram quantities of cocaine from various suppliers. A chronological record of the major cocaine shipments are as follows:

In May 1987, Bernard Fields and Dwight Sutton traveled to Florida and returned to Philadelphia with kilograms of cocaine. Once they returned to Philadelphia, they delivered this cocaine to Jones, Patterson, Bowman, Price, and Brown. This transaction was duplicated in June 1987, and again later that summer, when the same individuals returned from Florida with 10-kilogram and 50-kilogram shipments, respectively.

During the remaining months of 1987, various members of the JBM (including Cole, Fields, Sutton, and Baynham), picked up approximately 300 additional kilograms of cocaine from their supplier in Florida. These kilograms of cocaine were delivered to Jones, Patterson, Bowman, Price and Brown in Philadelphia, Pennsylvania.

In late 1987 or early 1988, Cole informed Earl Stewart that he was looking for a new large-scale drug supplier because his Florida source was drying up. Stewart began transporting multi-kilogram quantities of cocaine from a supplier in Los Angeles, California. Cole made an initial purchase of 20 kilograms of cocaine from Stewart (Count Five). This purchase was followed by numerous others. During the winter of 1987/1988, an additional 50 kilograms was purchased from Stewart (Count Eight).

Throughout 1988 and 1989, members of the JBM, including Jones, Fields, Brown, Thornton, Reaves, Richardson, and Davis attempted to persuade various Philadelphia drug dealers to begin purchasing their cocaine from the JBM. Specifically, from approximately mid 1988 through mid 1989, Darrell Jamison purchased approximately one kilogram of cocaine per week from the JBM. These deliveries were usually made by Fields or Shawn Davis.

It was further part of the conspiracy that in mid-to-late 1988, Cole purchased four kilograms of cocaine from Stewart on two separate occasions, for a total of eight kilograms of cocaine in Philadelphia, Pennsylvania.

On December 12, 1988, James Price was found to have in his possession approximately 14 kilograms of cocaine in Philadelphia, Pennsylvania.

Cavario: Was James Price busted with 14 kilos by the feds or local law enforcement?

Derrick Williams: Local law enforcement, they said that they were looking for a stolen truck and they noticed someone walking down the street with a large duffle bag, they stopped him and that's how they got him.

During the winter of 1988/1989, the JBM purchased approximately 100 kilograms of cocaine from Stewart. This cocaine, at the direction of Jones, was unloaded from Stewart's vehicle by Fields and Davis.

Sometime in mid-1989, Stewart sold an additional (undisclosed amount) kilograms of cocaine to the JBM. Once again, Stewart delivered this cocaine to Fields and Davis.

Sometime in late 1989, Stewart sold 230 kilograms of cocaine to the JBM.

Between the summer of 1990 and November or December 1990, James Cole made approximately four deliveries of cocaine, totaling approximately five and half kilograms of cocaine, to Sam Brown and Christopher Anderson.

On August 23, 1991, Fields purchased what he believed to be 20 kilograms of cocaine from Stewart. The 20 kilograms were, however, actually 10 kilograms of real cocaine and 10 kilograms of "sham" cocaine.

Cavario: Why would a legitimate connection sell his best customers 22 pounds (1 Kilo. = 2.2 pounds) of fake cocaine?

Derrick Williams: Unbeknownst to Bernard Fields, Stewart had already been busted in California for trying to buy something like 250 (kilos) from the feds. Stewart told them that he could get them the Junior Black Mafia in Philadelphia, the feds contacted law enforcement in Philadelphia and asked them if they knew about the Junior Black Mafia, then they arranged for Stewart to set up somebody from the JBM.

David Baynham testified at trial that he and Fields traveled to Florida in order to purchase cocaine for the JBM on at least four occasions. These trips occurred between Halloween of 1986 and February of 1987. Baynham testified that on each of the first three trips to Florida, he along

164

with Fields, would transport between 75 to 100 pounds of cocaine back to Philadelphia. He further testified that on the fourth trip, he and Bernard Fields transported approximately 100 pounds of cocaine back to Philadelphia. Baynham stated that he would receive between 5,000 and 7,000 dollars payment for each trip.

Derrick Williams was a squad leader for the Junior Black Mafia. He was responsible for the distribution and sale of cocaine in a specific area of Philadelphia. On October 2, 1988, he fired six shots at Bobby Little in an attempt to kill him for his alleged involvement in a drug rip-off. Mr. Little was not injured but an innocent bystander, Lorenzo Thompson, was injured when bullets shattered the bone below his left knee.

Cavario: After all that has transpired, do you have any regrets?

Derrick Williams: I remember I was talking to a girl in a beauty salon, and she asked me if I have any regrets and I told her that I did, she was surprised because you know that wasn't the standard answer. I told her that I regret not knowing that I could get a million dollars being a rapper or an actor, I told her that I regret having sold myself short. I was in college; I wish I would have finished.

Cavario: Do you think that you it would be worth your while to give the game another go today?

Derrick Williams: I don't believe that I could successfully sell drugs in 2006 because of the quality of dudes that are out here today and the way that they do things.

Cavario: If you were to try again, and you were to be busted again, have you learned enough about yourself to be able to accurately determine what you would do today?

Derrick Williams: Absolutely, I would never go against the code. Even though this time around, I'd know exactly what I was up against. I learned that it was unrealistic for me to look for, or expect, "justice" when I know that I was selling poison to people and I know that I was involved in shootings and so forth. I was not living a "just" existence and there is no way to get justice from wrongful actions. From the block that I lived on, I am the only one that went to jail. Today there are dudes from this generation that are definitely on their way, but from my time, I am the only one. When I went to court to get sentenced for my state case for the shooting, the judge actually gave me more time because she felt with my background, going to Catholic school all of my life [and] going to college, and also coming from a middle class background, there was no excuse for me choosing the life that I did. She said that I didn't deserve to be on the streets of Philadelphia. It was unheard of that a dude would get 10 years for shooting a dude in the leg in '89, that's murder time.

When I hear these dudes today talking about money and they talk like $250,000 is not a lot of money, I know that they've never seen real money. I challenge them to try walking down the street with money like that on their backs. When I went to jail I had $100,000, my man Mark had like $850,000 and he was only 24. Aaron had better than a million, I'm talking cash not assets or credit. There are doctors and lawyers who can't put their hands on cash like that, I'm saying being able to go and dig that kind of paper up out of the ground and really touch it. You could lay out the average person's whole lifetime, and in their whole life they will not have made a million dollars.

The "Black Mafia" mentality and where it all began

In or around 1963, Sam Christian and his associates came together in South Philadelphia to form the first "Black Mafia". They were extortionist, conspirators, killers, drug dealers, men-of-business and, in every sense of the word, Gangsters. Christian's crew operated out of Muslim Temple 12 on Philadelphia's South side.

When exactly the original Black Mafia was officiated is still in debate but the popular opinion, of the sophisticated sort, is the group formed its membership sometime in the mid-1960s. Its founder, Sam Christian, had come together with fellow founding members as the result of an arrest in April of 1968. Walter Hudgins, Roosevelt "Spooks" Fitzgerald and Sam Christian were all charged with assaulting police officers during a drug investigation by the Philadelphia Special Investigations Unit. Fitzgerald was also a Black Muslim convert known as Roosevelt Bey. Months after this meeting, the three men became the trio that would form the first African-American syndicate– The Original Black Mafia. Sam Christian was the leader. Sam was fiercely revered and he had an extensive and violent criminal history, which began in 1953 when he was just 14 years old. By 1974 he had converted to a Black Muslim. Sulieman Bey or Beyah was what became of Sam after pledging his allegiance to Allah.

Sam enveloped his Mafia family deep inside the stern walls of Islam, specifically Philadelphia's Temple 12. By 1968 the "B.M." roster read as such: Samuel "Sam" Christian, Jerome Barnes, Nathaniel Williams, Ronald Harvey, Robert "Nudie" Mims, Donald "Donnie" Day, Grady Dyches, Eugene "Bo" Baynes, Clyde "Apples" Ross, Charles "Black Charles" Toney, Robert "Bop Daddy" Fairbanks, Walter Hudgins, Richard "Pork Chops" James, and Roosevelt "Spooks" Fitzgerald who was 39, making him the oldest person in the group. All of these men were relatively young, but the youngest was Jerome Barnes, he was 23– Sam was six years his senior.

In September of 1968, the name "Black Mafia" was adapted. It was intended to be reminiscent of the Italian Mob and to evoke fear, and also to imply ruthlessness and violence.

Throughout the 1970s, the Black Mafia wrought havoc upon the citizens of Philadelphia; they robbed drug dealers or charged them a street-tax and murdered them when they didn't pay. They were brazen with their crimes, often leaving several witnesses– few ever dared to testify against them and the few that did didn't survive. Those that were courageous enough to bare witness against the "BM" met horrific deaths. But it wasn't necessary that you testify against the Black Mafia to bring death to your door. As is with the case of the family of Hamaas Abdul Khaalis, the Hanafi (Sunni) leader that dared to speak ill of Elijah Muhammad. Khaalis' young second wife, 26, and his eldest daughter, 22, his eldest son, 25, and his 10-year old son, were found bound, "hogtied," facing down, wrists and ankles tied together, and shot execution style. Three babies, one as young as nine days, were drowned, and after happening upon the gruesome scene while in progress, a family friend was also shot and killed.

Even card carrying members of the "BM" were not exempt from the group's animalistic retribution. While in prison, James Price, one of the 8 Mafia men responsible for the Khaalis massacre, was killed for cooperating with authorities in order to lighten his sentence. He was beaten, his testicles crushed, and a sharp metal object was shoved up his rectum. After cutting his body down as it hung from a ventilation grate, prison officials determined that strangulation with three tightly braided bootlaces was the ultimate cause of death. No one, it seemed, was out of the Black Mafia's reach. The powerful structure of the Black Mafia was finally dismantled in or around 1985 (on the street, anyway).

The name "Black Mafia" arose again in Philadelphia with Aaron Jones' "Junior Black Mafia", and there were tacit connections assumed between the two groups. Once he was released from prison in 1990, Black Mafia boss, Sam Christian, attempted to reach out to his organization's heir apparent, but the young guns were non-responsive. It was rumored that Aaron was "taught the way" by the old gangster but when asked about this supposed connection, my source commented that, "He was just a cool old dude and they locked him up for supposedly being involved with us but he wasn't though."

Sometimes groups who adapted the "Black Mafia" moniker are also known as "The Family" as in the case of Newark, New Jersey's Akbar Pray. But in Baltimore during the early to mid-nineties, there was a group of young thugs from the South Bronx's Sedgwick area. They were led by a sharp young man known on the streets by the name of "Boonie." They too were fly, fast, flashy and violent. Many deaths were attributed to this group of young men who were all barely in their twenties, none weighing more than 150 pounds. The primary soldiers were Rico, "Jack," Petey, Terry aka "Noodles," "Black Anthony," Dana, and "Twenty-Car Tye" who served as a lieutenant.

168

Their out-of-control behavior, extravagant cars, multiple gun fights and general hi-profile practices led to their ultimate destruction. Petey was shot multiple times on a dark west Baltimore street, he survived but never really functioned within the organization fully again. Dana was shot in the back of his head and he too survived although his eyesight began to fade. He was referred to as "Michael Myers" of Halloween fame after that shooting because of the way he walked away as though nothing had happened. The bullet was still in his head. Dana fell out of grace with the rest of his team, suspected of cooperating with authorities; it's unknown whether this was ever substantiated but the mere suspicion can drive an irremovable wedge between cohorts in crime. "Noodles" was stricken with diabetes and after losing a portion of one of his legs and then his eyesight, he passed away. He was barely thirty years old. Anthony ultimately fell victim to the poison he peddled and years after I'd left Baltimore I saw him roaming the University Avenue area of the South Bronx, strung out on crack cocaine.

Tye's car fetish and unreasonable need to be seen eventually led to his indictment and incarceration. He once had one of his vehicles, a BMW, featured in the New York car show at the Jacob Javits Convention Center in Manhattan, displaying its "hidden" compartments and "secret" gadgets. He is supposed to have turned witness against his former team as well. Boonie "The Boss" was sentenced to 25 years but gained substantial relief due to a successful appeal. After several years he was a free man once again.

Preacher's organization was also known as "The Family" and he was often referred to as "Pops" by his soldiers, and his girlfriend was called "Ma". The desire for family and the drive to rebel against the social and economic pressures of ghetto existence often combine to bring about the "Family" and "Mafia" mentality. The innate need that most human beings have to belong, to be protected and to flourish is the dark twin to nature's first law–survival!

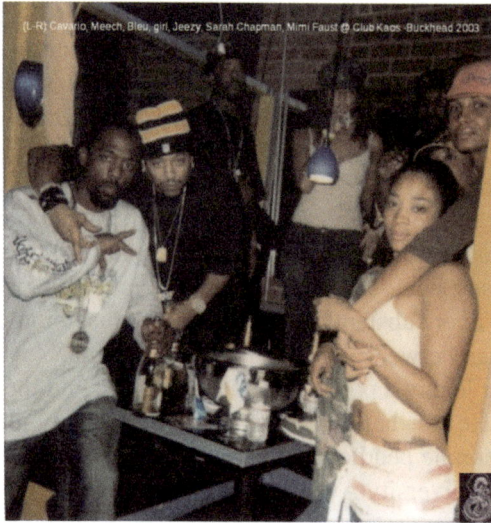

(L-R) Cavario, Meech, Bleu, girl, Jeezy, Sarah Chapman, Mimi Faust @ Club Kaos -Buckhead 2003

On October 20th of 2003 I was introduced to a man who had the most extraordinary collective of young men in his company, they were gathered from several cities around the country and ranged in age from early twenties to late thirties. They were huddled up in the VIP section of Chaos, back then a popular club in Atlanta's Buckhead. I was in the club with my homey Big Von, who I'd met in Daddy O's night club in Cancun, Mexico some four years earlier, "Yo, there's somebody that you gotta meet," Von announced over the music without making a real effort to raise his voice. I had no idea who V might be referring to but I knew that these people must be proper if he was so adamant that we make each other's acquaintances. I followed Big V across the club until we reached the velvet rope surrounding the VIP section. There were two big guys standing guard, but neither reacted as V lifted the clasp out of the post that supported the dividing line. He stepped forward and motioned for me to follow. We walked coolly over to one of the tables in the cul-de-sac and then V turned to me and said, "This is Meech, Meech this is Cavario, he has Don Diva." Meech smiled and said, "Wus'up homey?" Meech then glanced at Big V and slurred, "We got 'em." Then he put his arm around my shoulder and began introducing me to everyone around the table while V quietly slipped away before seeming to disappear –not an easy feat for a light-skinned guy standing 6 feet-7-inches tall. Meech introduced me to some brothers from Brooklyn, and some brothers from St. Louis and some brothers from Carson City, and Los Angeles, California then he continued with the Bronx, Atlanta and Florida. With each handshake I was addressed with a distinctly different urban dialect. That was the night that Meech invited me with open arms into his private section, his world, the world of B.M.F., the "Black Mafia Family."

"They thought they were making history, I thought they were repeating it."
–Cavario H.

"Let no man separate what we create, from every hood to Hollywood, coming to a ghetto near you. Death before dishonor. After us there will be no other...if it is– we got 'em!"
–The *Black Mafia Family* toast spoken before the commencement of each night's activities.

That night we drank, smoked and laughed like brothers, like genuine family and the above toast is how each evening that followed would commence. The energy was electric and it wasn't the obvious wealth circulating through the group. I mean, sure not having a monetary worry in the world can be intoxicating too but there was something more, this group had cohesiveness that in all my vast experience in the streets I had scarcely witnessed before. "...After us there will be no others".

When they shouted out last call I left Chaos with "The Family." It was only when we began filing out that I realized how many there were in our group. It was an overwhelming 40 deep but I would find that that was an average herd on an average night out. On special occasions that number could triple. One hundred twenty young black males moving in unison, marching as a single unit with a common accord –money, power and respect...but family was always first.

As we made our way out of Chaos that first night I observed the way that they seemed to watch over each other. I walked with them to the lot near the corner and they piled into several extremely expensive and exclusive vehicles, a Ferrari, the not yet released XLR, Cadillac's hard-top convertible, a few other not-so pricey whips with a lot of custom work, 24-inch rims, suede headliners, booming systems, souped-up engines, etc. I jumped into the Don Diva van and joined the convoy. We shot up Peachtree Street and headed north to Lenox Road, then over to Cheshire to Club 112. When we got to 112's parking lot, everybody parked and waited for everybody else to form up at the edge of the lot before walking to the club's door. To my surprise they were not greeted with open arms; the club's manager stopped them short, "No, no, no, not tonight!" Meech stood calmly and asked the guy what was the problem. "Y'all made mess in here last time and I don't care how much money y'all spend, I don't want y'all in here." I laid back ten or fifteen feet, observed and listened. It appeared that there was an altercation between the family and one of the other patrons, one of "the homies" turned to me and began explaining what had happened a few weeks earlier. "We was in here doin' our thug thizzle and this dude started gettin' stupid and bein' disrespectful. At first we ignored him but then the nigga got crazy so we slayed his ass in there, put him in a coma!" That beating earned the fam' infamy and a standing decree of "no entry" to 112. That decree remained in place until 112 was moved to Peachtree Street right across from Alex Gidewon's club Vision. (112 was eventually replaced by hi-rise condominiums, shops, a hotel, and restaurants, as was Vision.)

It was around 4 a.m. the Fam' was just getting wound up but the night came to an abrupt end due gaining no access to 112. Meech told me to come to "the crib" later that day; he gave me his number and told me to call when I was ready to come through. I was staying at a friend's place way out in the sticks because I had sold my house in Marietta a few months before but was back in the 'A' on magazine business. Around four o'clock that afternoon I hollered at Meech and he gave me directions to the crib. The house was a mini mansion off of Habersham, in a secreted little nook behind the Landmark Diner on Roswell Road. Aside from a few fold-up chairs and some flat screen TVs, the place was scantily furnished. All the rooms (there were about 6 or 7) had beds in them except for one, which had an air mattress. It was early so there were only a few cars in the driveway, a silver 745 BMW, a navy blue custom van on chrome rims and a Cadillac XLR convertible, that was slated to be released months from then but Meech was able to get one at about $30,000 over sticker. It was black on the outside and everything in its interior was wrapped in supple beige leather, except the headliner, which was suede. It sat on 22" inch wheels and sported a boomin' system. I didn't use the front door; I entered through a two-car garage and came into the house through the kitchen. This was the way that all entered the spot, which caused it to be christened "Club Kitchen," and believe me, the name was appropriate.

Former BMF headquarters called "Club Kitchen"

There were only a few of the homies in and then there were these two brown-skinned Hispanic gentlemen standing in the kitchen beside Meech. The smell of exotic and expensive marijuana permeated the air and I immediately located the source as soon as I stepped into the kitchen. There was Meech leaning against a black marble island/stove in the middle of the kitchen floor and there was a pound of green busted open next to him. Meech was rolling a blunt. I greeted him and shook his hand before being introduced to each of the gentlemen and shaking their hands too. We all got into a conversation about the magazine's content and who some of the individuals who had been previously featured were. Then Meech surprised me when he stated that he wanted to put his "movement" in the magazine. "What do you mean?" I asked. "I want us to be in the magazine as the first dudes to be in the mag' that live like that, ball-out and all that but we' not in jail, and we' not dead." My initial response was, "You're kidding, right?" As I began to laugh, certain that my host was just joking, he went on to explain his point and purpose for such a move.

"I ain't kiddin', I'm serious. I want 'em to know that we ain't robbin' nobody, we ain't bustin' no checks, we ain't fuckin' wit' no credit cards, and this ain't counterfeit money we out here spendin' every night in these clubs. This is real money, street money and we ain't in jail and we ain't dead. We the Mob and we here!"

I paused for a moment to process it. Then I responded, "And how long after you get in the 'hottest' magazine in America… and when I say 'hot' I mean law enforcement agencies from local to federal, follow our releases religiously, do you expect that you'll be maintaining that status?"

Meech's response was, "I ain't worried about it." I then looked directly into his eyes expecting to see insanity but all I saw was intent.

173

I turned to his Latino guests and asked, "¿Entiende" They responded in English, "Yea'." Their attitudes were just as cavalier as Meech's.

From that very day I lived and breathed with Meech and his mob, and we quickly grew close over the next few weeks, partying hard and bonding – right up to that fatal night. We hit every club in and around Atlanta, a minimum of two clubs each night of the week, and Meech bought out the champagne supply of every spot we entered. Even when it meant we'd all have to get two bottles a piece.

Each night surpassed the excess of the previous night's always over-the-top expenditures, and each night the group would swell. If we lost two guys by early morning, by the following evening we'd have four to replace them. If those four had moves to make in another city (it obviously wasn't all partying all the time, somebody had to be taking care of some business at some point), those four would be replaced by a new six.

How did that growth occur? Quite deliberately, actually. One night we were in Club Kitchen where everyone in the immediate circle would come together a few hours before we'd head out. I'd be out making magazine moves and I'd get a call from Meech, around 9 p.m. "C'mon home, homey, we about to get ready for the club." There would be so much eating, drinking, smoking and (for some) rollin' going on that we'd be virtually walking on clouds by the time we arrived at any club. Cats would be getting their hair braided or getting a shape-up while a new Bleu Davinci or Jeezy song provided amperage. It was like taking a cold shower before jumping into a pool of cool water. We were "there" before we even arrived.

This particular night, our caravan slid down Roswell Rd. toward the then thriving Buckhead Village, Atlanta's party center, which was ground zero for a veritable Mardi Gras every week from Thursday through Sat. We were definitely deep when we initially rolled out but by the time we reached the club's door, a spot called Shadow Bar (formerly Cobalt Lounge, the scene of the Ravens' Ray Lewis' double homicide incident), our numbers had increased exponentially.

After parking the cars, and literally taking up the entire parking lot, we soldiered like an invading army towards the club.

Meech spoke to the person in charge and told him, "We don't mind payin', we jus' don't wanna wait in nobody's line. We don't want nothin' free neither. Jus' tell us what you want for each man and count 'em as they come in." The guy knew who he was speaking with so he didn't hesitate to accommodate the crew's crushing numbers. Unlike most groupings of young males, that were generally a good deal smaller than ours, we were always quite orderly. We lined up and began to file in. The count was roughly 72 and the cost, as I recall, was $20 per head.

As the last man entered, the bagman, usually Brookyln boss "Illz" or "Pesci" as we sometimes called him, approached the club's manager and unzipped the large leather Louie satchel then paid the man, including a significant tip. There was always another bagman along but his bag was a lot heavier and a hell of lot more lethal. Neither bag was ever checked, and rarely were we for that matter.

Brooklyn BMF Boss
illz AKA "Pesci"

We went upstairs to the second level and made a beeline to the far right corner of the room, a vantage point that gave us a clear view of all comings and goings on that level. As we navigated a passageway to the VIP section (any section BMF was in instantly became the "VIP" area) we were greeted by an eager waitress who asked, "What'chall drankin'?" To which Meech responded, "How many bottles of champagne y'all got?" The young woman proceeded to name the various brands, "We got Cristal, we got Perrier Jouet, we got Dom, Krug, MOET Chandon…" Meech, ever the polite gangster, calmly interrupted, saying, "Bring us every bottle in the buildin' and a few bottles of Cuervo 1800." The girl looked like a deer momentarily caught in the path of an 18-wheeler. Then she composed herself and responded, "Uh, okay." But we were already on the move by the time she'd registered the command.

When we settled into our section, I did my usual scanning of the room. I was looking for who was looking at our group but I was also looking for who was watching our group (yes, there is a difference). I'd been going to clubs since the days of Disco and I always made it a point to make sure I knew who was around me. Reading the room is mandatory.
Once we settled in, and I was done registering the growing number of staring faces around us, I turned to Meech and asked, "Why do you keep buyin' every bottle of champagne everywhere we go, homey?" He smiled faintly and said, "That way anybody that come in the club and wanna ball, gotta come see us." I chewed on his reply for a few moments.

Meanwhile the waitress began streaming in the bottles. First, those who had arrived from the house, roughly 20 of us, were passed our own personal bottles. The other 30 or so bottles were placed on several circular tables around us. This was before the ostentatious practice of placing fireworks on the bottles for added fanfare began. That custom is a direct result of what the Fam' was doing during this period. People want that type of attention so badly that they're willing to break themselves to get it, so they certainly don't want anyone to miss it. But the "Mob" had no such concerns because for BMF ballin' was not a night out, it was a lifestyle.

While the waitress got us all set up, the homey Sekou, a tall light skinned dread-head brother who made sure that the party favors were always on deck, passed around the blunts. It wasn't too long before the air quality had been significantly upgraded. Although we shared blunts, everyone pretty much rolled their own. So at any given time there would be 20 or more blunts being passed around. No sooner did one leave your fingers was another being pushed into your face.

Once the last of the liquor arrived, the bottles of Cuervo were popped and poured. After everyone was properly supplied with a shot glass full of the tart tequila, Meech raised his glass and all of our glasses raised in unison around him. Then, all at once, a single voice with multiple origins spoke these words, "Let no man separate what we create, from every hood to Hollywood, coming to a ghetto near you. Death before dishonor. After us there will be no others, and if it is... we got 'em."

I was still silently mulling over Meech's champagne policy while the party left 2nd gear and sped toward 3rd (1st gear was well underway before we pulled away from the house). I was sitting on a couch beside Meech, on his right while Illz sat to his left. Bull and Bleu sat behind me on the back of the short couch with their feet planted in the seat. Big Cuzz was in close proximity, as was Rico. The rest of the immediate family members were milling around within a few feet of us. If anyone moved, to the bathroom, the bar, or anywhere in between, he was accompanied by a minimum of three others. An eye was kept on everyone, at all times.

Most everybody was wearing lots of heavy jewelry and pretty high when we were in club mode so there was no margin left open for an error to occur. No slippin'.

As I surveyed the club for the 'ump-teenth' time within that first hour, I caught the stares of a handful of brothers peering in our direction from the bar. They appeared to be staring but I could neither see nor sense any overt malice. I continued to grasp the neck of my Cristal Rosé, and take measured tokes on the blunt I was spending a few minutes with before the next rotation, as I observed the dudes circumnavigating the club's now considerably denser crowd. I noticed they couldn't seem to keep their eyes off our section.

Their body language wasn't aggressive in any way, but they seemed drawn to us. By the time they were within 10 feet of us, almost everyone had registered them. When the guy leading their stroll noticed they were being noticed, he quickly, but comfortably smiled. And when he was certain he was in earshot he spoke, "Hey man, we was tryin'a get off too but y'all got all the 'pagne."

At first he couldn't determine who might be leading this team of athletic jerzee donning dudes before him. But when Meech smiled, the dude undoubtedly felt the weight of 140 eyeballs lift off of him and his people. "Aye…" Meech motioned to his left, gesturing toward a table crammed with sweaty buckets that threatened to burst from the bottles and ice packed down into them. "Pass 'em a few'a those bottles, cuz."

The fella's face lit up with a mixture of delight and disbelief. Then Meech motioned for them to find a seat in our circle. "Damn man! Y'all doin' it for real! I like how this is lookin'," rhe dude said as he competed with the club's sound system. Then he asked, "Where y'all from?" Meech leaned in his direction and stated, "We from everywhere, Detroit, St. Louis, Chicago, Ohio, New York, L.A., all over…we a world wide mob." Again, Meechie smiled. His smile was contagious and we all seemed to become instantly infected. The dude and his boys looked around at all the wellness and then looked back at Meech and said, "Maaan! We need to connect or somethin' and see how me and my team can fit in."

Meech slid back into his position on the couch's back and spoke to Bull, "Yo, talk to 'em."

This was the secret of the BMF movement. In the America's corporate sector, they call it Merger & Acquisition. In the ghetto we call it blowin' up!

GHETTO THESIS

What is a Ghetto?

The quarter of a city inhabited by Jews.

That's the actual definition of the word according to Webster's Dictionary. But the meaning that the hood relates to would probably be the "area where, as a result of social or economic inequality, struggling people reside."

Thesis: a reasoned, formal argument written on a theme connected with the specialty of the writer.

The life that I've led makes the ghetto my "specialty" so, I write.

So many of my brothers and sisters in the struggle have sacrificed their lives and freedom for the glory and glitz of street life, many more are still willing to make that sacrifice but so few can really say why. I've sat still for some time and sought to understand what motivates us to leap into the abyss of death and destruction that is almost assured with street life. I'm not talking about the existential influences of hood and pop-culture, but more so the internal motives behind what is for some an uncontrollable urge to be ghetto famous– although we know that in the street this is the surest way to undo ourselves. If as many of us that claim to do it for the money actually did it for the money, law enforcement would really have to work instead of just relying on snitches or merely cruising the streets to observe the "Look at me, I'm fabulous" show happening on the avenues or in the parking lots of fast food joints and gas stations most weekends, all over the country.

Question: If you killed someone, would you run down the street with the bloody murder weapon, screaming, "I did it! I did it!" Of course you wouldn't. But what many so-called hustlers are doing in the street everyday is equal to just that. Why? Well to be honest, I really don't know... but I do have a theory.

I think the need for validation, the need to feel as though "you" have worth, is innate. I believe that too many of us were not given that validation during our developmental years. We were not taught to esteem ourselves from within, (as the term goes); the importance of being told that independent of all material things, we each have unequivocal worth, is too often overlooked or undervalued.

Too many of us were not hugged and did not often (if at all) hear the words "I love you", from someone whose love we needed; a mother, a father, a grandmother, or whomever our primary caregiver was. Without that innate need being nurtured, I suspect that there is a part of us that does not grow and remains in a perpetual state of need until we are given that validation or learn to provide it for ourselves. For many of us (and for many reasons) that latter option is the only one we'll ever have if we ever want to be well in the world.

The cover of Don Diva magazine's issue number 12 bore the picture of a headstone with the inscription "Every man desires wealth, respect and fame. What are you willing to pay for it?" This, I believe, is the common query that many young, poor people ponder–most without fore or aft thought... until their hole is dug.

Many of us have stumbled desperately through our lives trying to find, make or buy validation. I think the expression goes, "Looking for love in all the wrong places."

The overwhelming, judgment scrambling affects of hearing the hood call out our name, saying, "There he (or she) goes!" or "Damn, you that muthafucka'!" breathes life into the ghetto's aspiring legends, and it seems the high cannot be outpaced by mere reason... "These streets are surely gonna talk me to death... but I gotta shine, no matter the cost!"

Whatever you believe, I think it wise never to close your mind to the possibility that this too could be true. (Just in case).

I began to sell drugs at 13, which used to be considered a very young age prior to the crack era.

I was nurtured in as loving an environment as could exist in late 60s and early 70s in Harlem. The men in my life were hardened by the oppressive, disenfranchising, entitled-minded white culture that dominates the American social order to this day. As a result, smiles were a rarity unless experienced through their children's enjoyment of whatever comforts their desperate efforts could produce. It was unspoken but understood that a black boy was only truly ready for manhood in this world when he realized that there was really no reason to smile. Early on, my mother made the mistake of telling me that I was not made to be a hustler... she believed that I lacked the sufficient greed and larceny necessary to be successful at it. What she underestimated was my determination to be the best of the worst. What she overlooked was my intent to be respected by her as a real man. Most of all she missed the lesson that my developmental ecosystem was showing me: only he who hustles is a MAN.

I loved all my father figures and to this day I am bits and pieces of each of them –the hard, the cold, the desperate, the angry, the confused, the emotionally unavailable and the deadly. I emulated their swaggers, their command and delivery of words, which enabled them to lead men to…wherever. Also their rarely cracking death masks, their nihilistic doctrine of "I don't give a fuck!" –all that was them, is me... sometimes. Yet there's more. Through some twist of fate, some mistake in nature, I was taught self-love. Self-love is a direct contradiction to "I don't give a fuck!"

To balance the two is an act equal to the most skilled of jugglers, who balances and twirls dinner plates on the ends of pencil thin sticks. When I began to seek my true purpose in this world, I forced myself to take a long and difficult look at my life and the choices that I had made. I had always viewed myself as a man built for the most difficult times that life had to offer, the man that my "fathers" would respect. I never considered that the "most difficult" times that I would face would be in the confines of my 'oneness', and self imposed. When I lost everything that mattered to me, "hit rock bottom" as the saying goes, I wanted nothing more than to change, the questions were "how?" and "into what?"

Everything that I knew and had been exposed to, everything that was supposed to enable me to survive in this world began to seem useless to me. I had to go into myself… I chose to go into myself. I did not want to end up in prison, which at the time seemed almost inevitable, before I decided to seek a greater path. I simply did not want to end up penniless and destitute or alone without a mate to care for me and to receive care from me as I had seen happen to a few bona fide-bad-asses who I admired while growing up.

I always viewed typical behavior as unacceptable; when others were playing basketball, I was defying physics on my skateboard, and when they were playing stick-ball (ghetto baseball), I was riding one wheel for ten city blocks on my Apollo 5-speed bike, when they were trying to "be cool" on the block, I was skiing on Mt. Snow in Vermont. I'd do anything not to be like everybody else. But here I was some 13 years later, and I was just another drug dealing back boy, moving in no particular direction –just doing what I do.

It was at this point that I decided that in order to survive, I needed to do the untypical thing and seek my own depth without (or before) having to go to prison. It would be too typical to sit in a cell and write letters stating my intentions to be a more present father for my children and a better mate to my woman or confess over collect calls that I was going to change my life's direction when and if I ever got out. In light of the circumstances of incarceration, when one is deprived of all the trappings of the world, be it women or alcohol, drugs or cars, fame and oh yeah, money, it's not really a monumental endeavor toward redemption to say, "I've changed baby!"

Most anyone forced to face the consequences of their actions would seek salvation, if for nothing else, relief from grief, regret, guilt, sorrow, suffering, etc. So I came up with a plan, it was simple; I would stop me before they could stop me. I would bury myself in books and study before they could grab me, and confine me to a small space with limited stimuli and little else to do but read. I would pledge my fidelity to one woman and show her that I could be that man that she so often professed to need, want and desire (the thought of what she actually deserved, determined by where she was in her being at the time never really entered into the equation) but in respect to my union, my intention was to, before they could separate me from my woman, show her that I was all that she sought and greater.

My decision was not contingent upon her reciprocation (although it would've been preferable to what I got) but my motives were based more in me proving to myself that I was the man that I believed myself to be– built to withstand the hardest times life could invent. The most astounding realization was that many of the hardest times in my life were self-invented. The fact that I wasn't in jail and that I was making a very comfortable and reasonably quiet living did not ease my decision. I was in fact contented and a considerable bit more than able to adequately provide for my family, which in accordance to what I had been taught, was all that life was about. Subsequently, when I decided to manage change into to my life the only reason that I had was my faith in there being more to life. That may sound corny but I knew that my present course would never enable me to be a part of the "more"–so... I chose.

Close your eyes and imagine a huge room, brightly lit, it has no ceiling because the sky is the limit. This is the room I call "opportunity." In this room all things are possible, you can do absolutely anything, and there are no rules. You live in this room, (who wouldn't?) for most of your adolescent life on into adulthood. By the time you reach your late twenties, you're pretty much accustomed to the good-life. If, for whatever reason, this life becomes not-so-good to you and you begin to feel the need to get on a new path or maybe return to the original path that you were on (before the loss of innocence), you will have to go back through the room of opportunity –only, you may not recognize it then.

You see, throughout the years of good living, you hung pictures and collected trophies commemorating your conquests; the hearts you've broken, the lives you've contributed to the destruction of, the character sacrifices that you've made in the name of good living–they're all there. The once clean walls of the opportunity room, decorated with what you once considered all that validated and esteemed you, are now covered with vaguely familiar artifacts of your past. Why not just move on? Why come through the old room at all? Couldn't you just stop the behavior and live your life anew? I have to say, based on my own experiences, the answer is "No."

I found that the reason that one makes the decision to manage change into their life is most often because the old ways simply don't work for them anymore. When you've lost enough being the way you are change will find you. If life were as simple as changing your mind, to make everything alright, then there would probably be a lot more happy people in this world, but the truth is that when most of us change our minds, we tend not to face what has been left in the wake of our destructive behavior. We tend to believe that we can simply "move on." I found out that when we seek to be better, to get back on the righteous path, if you will, we are not likely to look at where we've been and as I've stated before, if you cannot acknowledge where you've been, you will most certainly find yourself there again.

As for me, upon returning to the room of opportunity, I found the walls to be very close, the space between them very narrow, and the accolades of an extraordinary super-nigga had all morphed into sharp, rusty razorblades, dripping with pain, sadness and dreams deferred. I was face to face with everything that I had ever done or neglected to do…it was the hardest of times and very much self invented.

You may ask why an individual seeking to be well would even go through such a place? I asked myself that same question over and over again, the answer that came to me each time was simple: on the other side was my salvation. For one to impose these conditions upon oneself is, in my mind, the defining characteristic of true humanity.

Nothing was promised to me by making the new choices that I did –I did not guarantee myself freedom, success in love or business, nor was I assured a place in "heaven" (if you believe in such). The only thing I was sure of was that if there is something greater, something worth living for, something that would make having given up the great room of opportunity worthwhile, then I would be ready to see it...because I had begun to manage change into my life, I would be *able* to see it.

How did I know it would pay off? I didn't, and because of the fact that I had never lived anywhere else but the room of opportunity I knew nothing about life outside of it, so when I left it (on my own and by choice) I lost everything that I knew through it, nearly sight itself. I stepped out of the great room into the infinite darkness... the only thing I had to guide me was my faith in the grace of divinity...the (God) in me. It was the closest to hell that I ever care to get, but I dealt with it, mostly because I felt challenged to. I stood and did not flinch (much) as all that I had known fell around me. I felt a great many things but fear was never one of them. What can I say? I'm a bad man. Well actually, the truth is, I'm merely a humble expression of the Universe that governs all things in the balance. I am today the man that my mother would be quite proud of.

I don't believe that the nature of a man can be changed but I do believe that the environment in which we are developed determines how our nature manifests action, just imagine what could have become of Michael Jordan had he not had the influence and guidance of his father. What if his relentless "attack and destroy" mentality had been nurtured in South Central Los Angeles?

One has to change one's environment in order to manifest change in one's life. If you cannot find the strength to change your environment, then when you've lost enough being the way you are, change will find you...you should welcome it.

Keith "PRISON KINGPIN" Gaffney

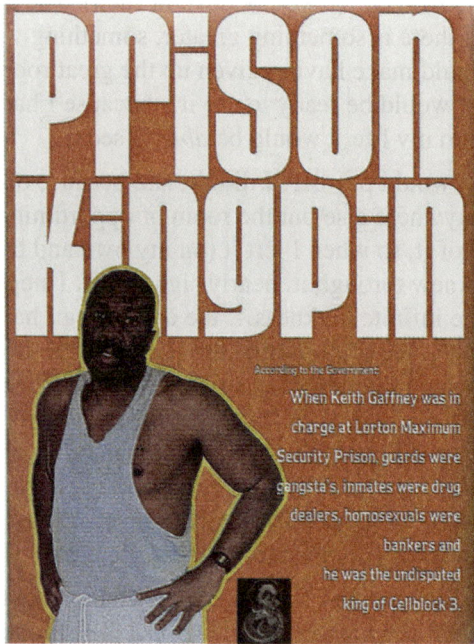

According to the Government:

When Keith Gaffney was in charge at Lorton Maximum Security Prison, guards were gangsta's, inmates were drug dealers, homosexuals were bankers and he was the undisputed king of Cellblock 3.

Keith Gaffney began serving his 36-year prison sentence in Lorton in 1973 for assault with intent to commit rape while armed, assault with intent to kill while armed, three counts of armed robbery, three counts of rape while armed, kidnapping and burglary–all stemming from the same offense. He was only 20 years old.

The government contends that Gaffney was a larger-than-life inmate inside of Lorton. Under his prison blues he wore a diamond and gold medallion of the Muslim star and crescent around his neck. His lieutenants held thousands of dollars of his money and when he wanted another inmate's jewelry he ordered that inmate beaten. When he wanted another inmate's job in the cellblock, prosecutors said that he ordered that inmate killed. When correctional officers needed cash they got it from Gaffney. When he wanted something from the officers, he got it.

According to testimony from inmate Gregory Smith, he (Smith) ran Gaffney's sex room that was called the "Hit Spot." When inmates came down to meet with their visitors they paid $1 a minute to have sex in a mop closet just outside of the visiting area. It was stocked with sheets, towels and a mattress. Although the maximum-security inmates were handcuffed when they met their visitors, Smith had a handcuff key supplied to him allegedly by Gaffney. He would unlock the inmates' handcuffs to allow them to move freely in the closet. To prove his allegations, Gregory Smith vomited up the key on the stand at Gaffney's trial. Smith had earlier wrapped the key in a condom and swallowed it.

How did Keith Gaffney get the key to the handcuff? This would be an easy task if the government's allegations of Gaffney having corrupt correctional officers on his payroll were true. According to trial testimony, it seems that there was nothing Gaffney could not do at Lorton Prison. According to the Assistant US Attorney, Thomas Hollenhorst, Gaffney was allowed to have sex with correctional officers, visitors, and inmates. The sex was only a small part of the power that Gaffney had at Lorton. Drugs in prison are a well-known fact and no matter how tight security is, drugs are always smuggled in. And according to testimony in three trials, Gaffney reigned over a heroin empire from 1989 through 1994 that flourished beyond anyone's comprehension.

Lorton Maximum Penn, Alexandria, VA.

Gaffney and his crew were housed in Lorton Maximum Security's Cellblock 3. This is where all the inmates on administrative segregation or those who are mentally challenged are housed. CB3 is the most violent block in the prison. The inmates there are serving the longest sentences, and in most cases have committed the most severe crimes and have the biggest problems getting along with other inmates.

Gregory Smith, an inmate who could not read or write, was doing time for murder and attempted armed robbery. Smith had known Gaffney since he was thirteen years old. They met in juvenile hall. When Gaffney and Smith got to CB3, Smith became Gaffney's right-hand man...until Gaffney put a $10,000 contract on his life. Fellow CB3 inmate Henry "Lil Man" James put an ice pick into Smith's neck, back and chest. Smith was flown to D.C. General Hospital and narrowly escaped death.

How did Gaffney and his inmate lieutenants operate a lucrative heroin business in a maximum-security prison? It all became clearer to prosecutors when Smith took the stand.

According to Smith, "Packages of heroin were sold through windows...we kept drugs seven days a week, 365 days a year." On a good day, usually the day after visiting day, when inmates are more likely to have money, "We made between $800 and $900 in one day. All that dealing is in nickel ($5) and dime ($10) bags, sometimes $20 bags, sometimes more. We cut drugs basically every day, as soon as we ran out," Smith told the court. "You have so much raw dope...you cut what you're going to cut, bag it up, and I passed it out, passed it through the door, [to] officers and whoever might need some."

Once new shipments went to Gaffney's testers and were 'cut' (mixed with other substances) it was time to "go to the table." The dope was cut and bagged daily at a rate of about 150 to 200 $5 bags an hour in Gaffney's cell with a curtain rigged over the bars. The inmates tore, folded and taped pieces of glossy magazine paper and used them as makeshift glassine bags to package three match head size doses of heroin. Nickel bags were grouped into piles of 54, and each pile went into green medicine bags that the D.C Department of Corrections used to give medicine to inmates. Gaffney and his crew then passed the bags off to runners who sold the dope.

THE TALE OF THE TAPE

Robert T. Green
Instead of working for the warden, Robert Green a correctional officer, was working for Inmate Keith Gaffney.

Henry James AKA Lil Man
According to testimony, Gaffney put out a $10,000 contract on Gregory Smith, and inmate Henry James put an icepick into his neck...

Gregory Smith
"I was in charge of the "Hit Spot"...the sex spot...If you give $20 you get 20 minutes in a mop closet with sheets, towels and mattress..."
-Gregory Smith"

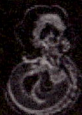

According to testimony, the dealer (runner) had to bring back money for 40 of the bags to Gaffney. The other 14 bags were for the dealer's to shoot, sell or exchange for favors- as long as he brought back $200 for the 40 bags of Gaffney's.

Gaffney allegedly used visitors and correctional officers to smuggle his drugs into Lorton. A Lorton Correction's Officer by the name of Robert Green smuggled in small balloons of raw heroin every other day- usually inside bags from fast food restaurants. Gaffney had visitors almost every visiting day, of which there were four each week. Gaffney mostly used women, who concealed his heroin inside their vagina or underwear. The inmates made sure it was Officer Green who strip-searched them on the way back to CB3. Green would tell them to "Bend over, squat, open your butt," and the drugs would be in their pocket the whole time.

The drugs came in tied-up in balloons with the end wrapped tightly over the heroin. Gaffney called the balloons "suitcases." Suitcases usually contained two to three teaspoons of heroin. One corrupt CO testified that he had brought in balloons an inch in diameter, tight and hard packed with powdered heroin inside. Once inside CB3, the raw heroin was poured into surgical gloves for storage. The gloves were tied tight, so in case of an emergency they could go up the inmate/smuggler's ass and the drugs would not be damaged. Smuggling the drug proceeds back out the jail to re-up (buy more drugs) was a little more tricky. Smith testified that they once used an ace bandage to tape $10,000 to Officer Green to take out.

Most of the money storage fell on inmate Tony Patterson. During trial, Patterson told the courtroom, "I'm considered a blatant homosexual...in jail." Patterson was the bank for a very specific reason: Hygiene. "Well, by being a homosexual, it might sound funny but I clean my rectum out like a woman actually cleans her vagina out. I'm not saying I had some disease; I made a [douche] and always had homemade devices, which would be a shampoo bottle or something like that. But later on, as I lived at maximum security, I had an opportunity to obtain a Massengill from the commissary."

Patterson often stored in his ass, more than a half-ounce of heroin, as well as sizable amounts of cash which he first folded in half and then wrapped in a piece of plastic he tore from a trash-can liner. He usually held 99 to 1,000 dollars per day in his asshole safety deposit box. "On visiting day it would be much more," Patterson testified. Sometimes he had three visits a week from Mona Lisa Gaffney, Keith's sister, who took the cash and gave Patterson balloons to take back to the cellblock. Mona Lisa was one of Gaffney's most reliable smugglers, according to trial testimony.

Tony Patterson became the super snitch. Patterson testified for prosecutors at all three trials– Officer Green's, Keith Gaffney's and Mona Lisa Gaffney's –in exchange for not being indicted as a co-conspirator, which could have been his third felony conviction and his third strike. His testimony paid off, as he is on the street today. At the same time Gaffney had Officer Green working for him, an old friend named Walter Harris showed up at Lorton Max; Gaffney and Harris started hanging together immediately. Gaffney had known Harris since their teen years in D.C. juvenile facilities. A heroin addict for well over 25 years, Harris, who was 47 years old at this time, had been behind bars for most of his life.

By 1990, Gaffney's enterprise was really "smoking" and Officer Green was benefiting tremendously. He wanted to show Gaffney his appreciation for taking care of him and allegedly brought a female correctional officer wearing civilian clothes to Gaffney's cell. It is also alleged that Green sneaked Gaffney his institutional file from the front office, including a document listing his charges and sentences. Once Gaffney had the file he began some creative editing in order to get moved from maximum security to Lorton's medium security facility. Using an institutions typewriter, Gaffney retyped parts of it, leaving off some of his convictions and changing consecutive prison sentences to concurrent ones...thus shortening his sentence from 36 years to life to 24-to-life.

Gaffney was found not guilty of tampering with this file at his trial. However, almost six months after he allegedly had the file, he and many of his crew including Walter Harris were moved to Lorton Medium Security.

According to Tony Patterson, Gaffney told him to try and get transferred to the medium facility too. How Patterson managed to get transferred to Medium is a mystery. But under direct questioning by Gaffney's attorney, Patterson said he'd done a favor for the sergeant of the CB3 day shift. "Yes, I sucked [his] dick," he said. In exchange the sergeant walked Patterson's paperwork up to administration and he was transferred to Medium.

Life in Medium was sweet and very lucrative for Gaffney. He added additional correctional officers to his payroll and his drug trade continued to prosper. Gaffney often had more money than he could get rid of.

According to testimony, he had his family members as well as Correctional Officers such as Sheila Harris, (Walter Harris' wife), taking money out of the prison. On one visiting day Gaffney underwent a routine search before going out to see his visitor. The officer saw that Gaffney had money three inches thick flapped over his belt and because the officer was on Gaffney's payroll, he was allowed to pass through. This same officer testified to receiving $100 each time that he smuggled money or drugs for Gaffney.

In Medium, Gaffney also continued to have sex with women and at his trial, prosecutors presented a snapshot of Gaffney naked. There was a second photograph of Gaffney posing with a woman. The woman was a correctional officer in Medium.

One night in June of 1992, there was too much money for Patterson to hold, so Gaffney took it to his buddy Walter Harris to hold. Harris put it down his underwear and went to sleep. Harris claimed that he hadn't gotten a hit of heroin that day so he got sick that night. He began trembling and sweating in his sleep and this caused the money roll to fall out. The next day when Gaffney came to collect, Harris did not have the money. Gaffney flipped and then threaten Harris' life. Harris was shook and he realized that his life was definitely in danger. He eventually "found"

189

the money under his bed and returned it but he was scared for his life –he told Gaffney he wanted out.

Harris went to the Captain, told on Gaffney and had himself placed in protective custody. Gaffney sent Officer Green to Harris with big bags of Heroin to bribe him into not talking but Harris refused. He was shook clean, he gave up heroin in fear for his life. Gaffney sent Harris a note saying, "I think I know how my man John Gotti felt after his right-hand man, Sammy the Bull, turned on him." Shortly after Harris snitched, corrections authorities took their first steps in trying to catch and prosecute Gaffney. They sent in Emergency Response Team Officers to raid their dorm and put an end to Gaffney and Patterson's business.

Patterson got caught with some weed and 19 small packets of synthetic heroin. While the officers were seizing this stuff, Patterson reached into his underwear and put two full heroin suitcases and $510 in his ass. The officers knew what he did and he knew they knew. The officers were ordered to do a body cavity search. Patterson stopped them by claiming that by law they needed a search warrant to do that.

So instead, the officers locked him up in a control cell to wait out the drugs. They put him on suicide watch for 24 hours and observed him through a window around the clock. They would stare at him through the window until his bowels could hold no more and he passed the heroin.

Patterson then stripped and started burning everything in the cell, including his clothes. He even flooded the cell by stopping up the toilet. His ploy worked and he was taken back to Maximum. Patterson made a phone call, and hours later he testified that in an amazing measure of Gaffney's power, he got a visit from Mona Lisa in an empty office in "control," where he passed her the money and the drugs to take out of the prison. The evidence was gone so the Department of Corrections could not indict Gaffney and Patterson at that time.

After the raid at Medium, the conspiracy ran for roughly another two years, with Gaffney back in Maximum. When Gaffney was finally indicted in January 1995, he was less concerned about the testimony of fellow inmates and dirty cops than what one of his girlfriends might tell the FBI. Patrice "Peaches" Oden allegedly knew it all. Peaches was a high school friend of Gaffney's daughter. She began visiting Gaffney in 1990 when she was about 15, according to her testimony before the grand jury. Peaches testified that Gaffney had her make three-way calls to his drug suppliers.

Twice, Peaches testified that Gaffney tried to arrange to have sex with her and failed. On one of those occasions, while she was visiting him, they waited for a signal from a correctional officer and they ran out of the visiting room into a nearby mop closet that presumably went for a $1 a minute. According to her testimony, Peaches refused to have sex with him and he got upset. Peaches testified that Gaffney had a terrible temper and when she wasn't home to receive his calls he threatened her. "Once, he told me that it wouldn't be nice for him to get upset with me...I would just be standing at the bus stop somewhere or coming out of the house...and someone would walk up to me and slash my face from ear to mouth..."

Prosecutors granted her immunity from prosecution for her offenses in exchange for her testimony against Gaffney. But Peaches was more afraid of Gaffney than the prosecutor. When Gaffney's trial date came, Peaches ignored her subpoena and was nowhere to be found.

Even with Peaches out of the picture, it didn't look good for Keith and Mona Lisa Gaffney. Both took the stand in their defenses and denied any wrongdoing stating that all testimony against them were lies.

However, a slew of felonious inmates and corrupt guards told a dramatic tale to the contrary. There is no exact accounting of how much dope and money the drug ring moved but estimates seem consistent with 12 to 15 kilos and $250,000 per year. All within' the walls of Lorton prison.

The Gaffney's defense attorney tried hard to show that except for the weed and synthetic heroin, no drugs were found by the FBI or the D.C. DOC (Department of Corrections). They also told the jury that no money was ever found and that both Mona Lisa and Gaffney's mother still lived in the projects.

The jury found Gaffney guilty under the Kingpin Statute for running a Continuing Criminal Enterprise (C.C.E.). Gaffney is serving his Life sentence without the possibility of parole in the worst prison in America...ADX Florence. He, like most of the notorious inmates in the ADX, spends 23 hours a day on lock down with little to no human contact. For well over a year, Don Diva has been corresponding with Keith Gaffney, who has become a devout Sunni-Muslim and has changed his name to Khalif Mujahid.

Throughout all our correspondence with Brother Khalif he has maintained that a racist prison system and a FBI agent who was obsessed with him framed him. Like most inmates at the ADX, Gaffney's mail is heavily scrutinized and his phone calls and visits are almost non-existent. Because of the notorious reputation that Don Diva Magazine has for revealing unpopular truths as well as the disdain that the Bureau of Prisons has for Don Diva Magazine because we have become a vehicle for the voices of inmates and the streets, many of Brother Khalif's letters were held back by the facility. Therefore, it has been a painstaking task to get Brother Khalif's side of this Hollywood-like tale of racism, jailhouse snitches and "fake" drug conspiracies.

"Sister Tiffany, they aren't putting any shade or cover on it now, because they are making it very obvious now that they hate your magazine and are trying to stop me from doing this interview. They are trying to push all of my buttons to push me over the edge and really make me blow. I am so irate but you know sister I will not let them get the best of me."

"I am from Washington D.C. and came from a neighborhood named Congress Heights on Condon Terrace, which was often called the "most dangerous street in Southeast D.C." I've had a long tenure in the D.C. prison system and the Federal Prison System, since I grew up in prison. I've acquired a so-called jailhouse reputation as a leader, according to prison officials and the U.S. government."

"I've been boxing since I was 12-years old, during the 1970s I became the champion of the middleweight division in the D.C. system and in 1981, I became the first prisoner to turn professional in the system as a lightweight. So my reputation in prison really came from being a fighter and a strong convict, which in turn made me stand out amongst fellow-convicts and most definitely prison officials."

"I am self-educated but during my trials and tribulations, prison officials have always singled me out as a leader, because of my standing on my principles, beliefs and my unwavering faith. I refuse to compromise who I am in the struggle to gain freedom. I have done most of my time in the D.C. system but also have been in and out of the federal system during some of the 1970s, 1980s and since 1994 when the U.S. government sent me to USP Marion, in Illinois. The FBI agent that was assigned to work at the D.C. Department of Corrections beginning in 1992 had become obsessed with me after hearing about me and learning about my prison life from officials and jailhouse snitches–whom I absolutely despise."

"The more this agent's obsession grew for me [the more] it turned to hatred, because he could not fathom how I had so much respect, love and loyalty from prison officials, prisoners and people on the street."

192

Thus because this FBI agent was also assigned to the Drug Task Force, he began to manufacture a case against me to keep me from going on the street because my prison time was getting short." "I was devastated about being back in Marion in 1994 and in 1995. This FBI Agent had me indicted in Alexandria, VA on a 10-count indictment for running a CCE–a multi-million dollar drug ring for heroin in D.C. prison system. I was convicted in May 1995 after only 5 days of trial of 5 of the 10 counts. I was only convicted because my trial attorney, a well-respected D.C. Lawyer named Mark Rochon, sold me out and did what he could to make sure the government won a conviction. He didn't call any of my witnesses and even tried to talk me into taking a plea to LIFE in prison even though he knew this alleged drug ring never existed. The government had no drugs, and no drug money to present at my trial.

This FBI agent and the racist, right winged conservative court in Alexandria, VA used mandatory drug laws to take my life by fabricating a fake Kingpin case." "They didn't have one person come to testify at my trial from the street that they brought me drugs, not one official who worked in the prison testified that a drug ring existed other than convicted officials who came to testify against me to get a sentence reduction. These two officials were convicted for taking drugs to FBI informers in other prisons that had nothing to do with me, and this all happened years before my indictment and trial. They used me as a get out of jail free card."

"I should never have been charged with 846 C.C.E. There were no proceeds from drug money, no property, business or drugs, money, cars, homes and no one came to court to testify that they worked for me and had money or profit that was made from working for me nor was there anything seized by the government. The government had 3 inmates come testify that they worked for me, but was paid a shot of heroin, but was paid no money, and had nothing to show from working for me." "I was never tied to any drug organization on the street and no one on the street that I know was ever arrested for having drugs. It's very important to know that other than these two convicted officers that lied on me for sentence reductions, the government's only witnesses were inmates, who were known jailhouse informers. The government claimed that this alleged multimillion-dollar drug ring ran for 4-1/2 years. What prison has millions of dollars in it that inmates have and allows the drug ring to go on for years?"

"My sister Mona Lisa Gaffney, who has been my strongest supporter since I've been incarcerated, was devastated and enraged after sitting in that courtroom at my trial and listening to how the government was outright lying on me and had actually coached their informers to lie on me and mention her and my mother during their testimony."

"Mona Lisa started a non-profit committee and joined other community activist to try to expose this racist FBI agent and make our entire family, friends, community and people who knew me aware of the viciousness and wickedness of this agent. The Alexandria, VA court system and this attorney, Mark Rochon who she seen sell me out and made sure he didn't fight hard enough to win my case." "The day of my sentencing, Mona Lisa, my family, some friends and other community activists marched and protested my conviction in front of the courthouse.

This infuriated this FBI agent and the U.S. Attorney's office, because they saw that Mona Lisa was organizing a strong group and my support system was getting stronger. This FBI agent and the U.S. attorney's office decided to go after Mona Lisa to get her out of the way. They wired her telephone and listened as she learned every day how to fight the system, [they] learned her itinerary to her rallies and meetings she attended."

"The panic set in when in 1996 this FBI agent and the US Attorney learned that Mona Lisa had gotten a young sister, who used to come see me in D.C. prison, to go to a lawyer and sign an affidavit, and make a video confession that this FBI agent tricked her to lie on me at the grand jury and that the US attorney threatened to lock her up and take her daughter if she wouldn't lie on me in court. This Woman, Patrice "Peaches" Oden-Jackson, would not show up to testify against me at trial, and called my attorney two days before trial and told him they tricked her and she wasn't going to show up to lie on me."

"After learning that Mona Lisa had the smoking gun to get me back in court, and evidence to prove that this FBI agent committed perjury by lying at my trial, he hurried and arrested peaches and told her if she goes through with the affidavit and video he would get her 30 years for conspiracy. Then he had her go to another grand jury to lie and say Mona Lisa threatened her for being a government witness."

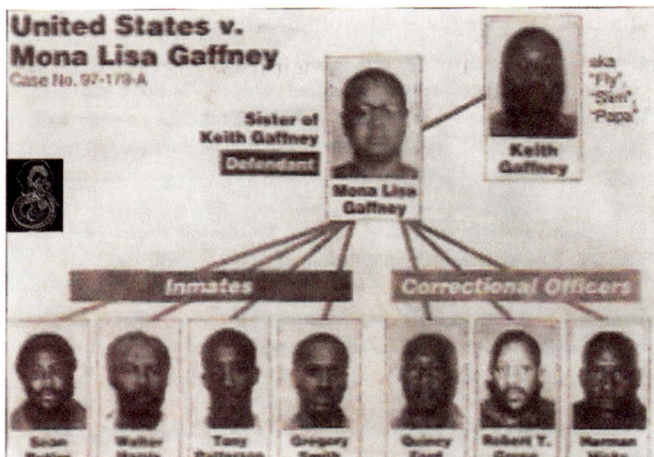

United States v.
Mona Lisa Gaffney
Case No. 97-179-A

Sister of
Keith Gaffney
Defendant

Mona Lisa
Gaffney

Keith
Gaffney

aka
'Fly',
'Slen',
'Papa'

Inmates   Correctional Officers

Sean Butler | Walter Harris | Tony Patterson | Gregory Smith | Quincy Ford | Robert Y. Green | Norman Hicks

"In April 1997 this same FBI Agent, Daniel Sparks, arrested Mona Lisa in her home. Three racist people in Alexandria, VA indicted her with a D.C. Correctional Officer whom she didn't even know on a 7-count indictment. This is racism on a whole new level. They alleged that Mona Lisa distributed heroin to an officer named Robert Green, who was arrested in 1996 and agreed to be a government informer and lie on Mona Lisa and testify against her and other people he arrested for a sentence reduction."

"If Mona Lisa was distributing drugs and bribing officers, why wasn't she indicted and tried with me?

How come the things she was indicted on were not mentioned in my indictment? It is important to note that Mona Lisa's indictment said that she was giving this officer Robert Green drugs and getting money from him even after I left Lorton. So who were the drugs going to? And how could I be giving Officer Green money to give Mona Lisa during the dates her indictment says when I was in Marion Illinois at the time?"

"They appointed a white attorney to represent Mona Lisa who tried to convince her to accept a plea to 3 years in prison and become a government informer or else FBI agent Daniel Sparks and the US Attorney were going to arrest our mother next. I told Mona Lisa to have her attorney subpoena me to testify for her because I could help her attorney prove that her indictment was fabricated."

"I was never called back to help Mona Lisa at her trial and an all white jury found her guilty and the judge gave her 17-1/2 years in prison for nothing. This is a now 51-year-old woman who has never broken the law in her life. She is now in prison just for supporting her brother."

Mona Lisa Gaffney in Federal Prison serving 17-1/2 years on drug conspiracy charges.

"Mona Lisa lived in the projects and was on public assistance when she was arrested. My mother's health just deteriorated after they arrested Mona Lisa and gave me Life for a fake Kingpin case. My mother passed December 21, 2000 because I feel like she gave up after those devils took Mona Lisa. My mother had lived in public housing for over 40 years until her death, so where is and what happened to these millions that these people claimed I made? This money never existed!"

"I would like to point out that this is the most conservative court system in the US. The reason that the US wants to try people in Alexandria, VA is because the Eastern District Court has the highest conviction rate in the country and the appeals court is the worst circuit in the country."

"It is important that our people in society know that this is how treacherous, and vicious our so-called US government does people who are poor and have no voice or the strong support system that is needed to defend yourself against false allegations."

"My mother died grieving for her children. My sister, Mona Lisa is now 51 years old and is sitting in a federal prison with a rack of time for nothing."

"I would like to acknowledge all of my brothers and friends from New York, Chicago, Atlanta, New Orleans, Cleveland, Kansas City, St. Louis, Detroit, Oakland and Philly. My Brothers Murad and Shahid Muhammad who will forever be my life long friends. It is important that I let my brothers and friends know that I am now a Sunni-Muslim and I no longer answer to my old nickname "Fly" because I am on another path now."

"My brothers and sisters, what these people did to Mona Lisa and me, they do to our people everyday. We must learn the system and realize that the people in congress, senate and in the court system are mostly right wing racists, who used to be involved in racial groups and organizations. But since they can't lynch us anymore, they want to put us away for life so we can all die in jails and keep our people from growing in the population. All you rappers, entertainers and athletes, be smart and enjoy life –stop beefing over small stuff and petty jealousy. Much respect to Mike Tyson, Roy Jones Jr., Mark "Top Sharp" Johnson, Allen Iverson, Alonzo Mourning, Nas and all the fighters and rappers and basketball players that are conscious!

Peace and Love, Brother Khalif.

Brother Khalif (Keith Gaffney) sent Don Diva a box of documents to prove the existence of the Committee for Justice for Keith E. Gaffney-Bey that was formed by his sister. Included was documentation to prove the existence of many fundraisers given by Mona Lisa for her brother indicating her dedication to clearing her Brother's name–long before she was indicted as a co-conspirator. In addition, throughout the FBI's investigation during the early 90s, Brother Khalif provided us with letters that he had attorneys write on his behalf to prison officials protesting the conditions in which he was being held. He also provided proof that he has lab reports in his possession where the FBI and agent Dan Sparks sent Peaches' money ($225) to a laboratory to see if Brother Khalif's fingerprints were on the money. Thus indicating that Brother Khalif's bouts with racial injustice began long before his indictment and sentencing.

Original article written by Tiffany Chiles

Edited re-release by Cavario H.

The Latin King Nation "AMOR DEY REY"

King Louie

"Amor Dey Rey" means "King Love", and that is the call and creed of the Latin King Nation; a collective brother and sisterhood of people of many different Latin descents. In the Latin King and Queen Nation you are not just Dominican or Puerto Rican or Cuban, etc –you are Latino… you are royalty. This is the basis of the Latin King doctrine. The Latin Kings were originally founded in Chicago, in the early 1940s. The national organization currently has chapters in several states including Illinois, Connecticut, Wisconsin, Florida, Massachusetts and New York. Upon entry into the Latin Kings, members take a name of their choosing, preceded by the honorific "King." Members typically wear a necklace of yellow and black beads; the number and pattern of the beads signify the rank of the wearer. The Latin Kings' emblem is a five-point crown. The five points on the Latin Kings' crown represent Love, Respect, Sacrifice, Honor and Obedience–some members also have tattoos of the crown.

The leaders for every chapter of the Latin Kings are called "Supreme Crowns" or "Supremes" –there are five Supreme Crowns. Certain Supreme Crowns carry titles that relate to their duties and responsibilities within the Latin King Nation, such as "Prince," "Warlord," "Treasurer" and "Crown Advisor." The Fifth Crown is the lowest rank of the five. The First Supreme Crown is the highest ranking and that position can only be held by one man– in this instance, that man is the infamous "King Blood" of the New York chapter.

Before he was King Blood he was just Luis Felipe. He grew up on the streets of Maria de Jesus, one of Havana, Cuba's poorest slums. Luis never knew his father, and his mother was a prostitute. Poverty and hopelessness were all that he knew as the Cuban revolution was on its last legs and the country was in turmoil. Luis Felipe says he dropped out of school in 1973 at the age of 11 and tells a story of one morning in Cuba, when he was making his way home and suddenly he felt the barrel of a gun against the back of his head. He dodged, ran behind a car, pulled out a .38 Caliber revolver and fired several shots that hit the gun holder's arm. Before he had a chance to run away, the police arrested him and charged him with attempted homicide. The young Felipe was given 10 years in a Cuban prison.

By the next year, Cuba was in a state of desperation and seemed overtaken with lawlessness. That's when Castro opened his prisons and freed what he called "the undesirables." Many of our readers would be familiar with this true-life event through the movie Scarface. Like the character Tony Montana, Luis Felipe became one of the "lucky" ones, setting off across the Straits of Florida in makeshift boats made of car tire inner tubes and old wooden furniture. More than 100 refugees traveled together, their fate in nature's indifferent hands. Felipe remembers seeing sharks slicing the water's surface just before they rammed the raft next to him, and an old man was thrown overboard. The sharks ripped the old man apart, filling the water with deep-blood-red clouds. "I felt like a prisoner of the sea," Felipe said.

Felipe landed in Miami two days later, traveled to Key West, then to Puerto Rico, and eventually wound up in Chicago. There he reapplied his street skills, dealing cocaine and heroin and developing a reputation for ruthlessness. At age 14, he joined a renegade faction called the "Pee-Wee Kings." "I shot people, I killed people... I have been shot and stabbed myself."

It was this behavior that led to Luis' incarceration in 1986, during which the bullying of Latinos by Five Percenters caused him to start the New York chapter of the Latin Kings in Collins Correctional Facility in Helmuth, NY (30 miles south of Buffalo). They became unified so they would "not get fucked with," –Luis was serving time for the murder of his girlfriend whom he had shot in the head.

King Blood, who was also known as "Inka" and to some of his closest comrades as "Pops", wrote a 42-page manifesto stating the goals and history of the Latin Kings along with lessons and rules of conduct. In it he stated that the organization was about preserving and enriching Latino culture and providing economic and social support to the Latino community and that a failure to adhere to the manifesto may lead to disciplinary actions. The punishments included: suspension from the L. K.s, a B.O.S. (beating on sight) or a T.O.S. (termination/assassination on sight).

The other "Crowns" under King Blood were Jose Gabriel aka "King Teardrop" the second Supreme Crown or Prince, and Jose Melendez aka "King Epic" the third Supreme Crown or Warlord.

The Latin King's New York chapter grew substantially in the New York prison system and that included women's facilities as well–the females were referred to as the Latin Queens. The leader of the Latin Queens was Zulma Andina aka "Queen Zulma" or "Luna," the women were as dedicated as the men were in their effort to uphold the Latin Nation, actively demonstrating this by way of B.O.S.s' and T.O.S.s'.

By 1991 the Latin Kings began to become more organized, they were having monthly meetings with all the boroughs of New York City. Borough leaders were chosen to run each chapter and make sure its members followed the bylaws of the "Family." King Blood declared the Latin Kings a cultural organization. There were more than 3,000 Latin Kings at Rikers Island Prison alone, with another 4,000 on the streets of New York, not to mention the Latin Queens and the youth corps, the Pee-Wee Kings. Ironically, it was this same year that things began to crumble.

While in New York's prison system, King Blood had an incident with prison security, which claimed that he was sending orders in the mail to have someone killed. Due to this, Blood was placed on mail watch and copies of all of his outgoing and incoming mail were made. The prison security said that they noticed violent letters of murders coming from behind the wall and eventually the FBI was called in to investigate. They began to monitor the writers and recipients of King Blood's letters who were all Latin Kings or Queens. The FBI kept close eyes on the entire chapter from 1992 to 1994 and contended that King Blood continued to send orders of what they refer to as T.O.S.s' and B.O.S.s'.

When King Blood chiseled out the Latin Kings 11 commandments (stressing loyalty and secrecy, while forbidding drug use, lusting after other King's women, and homosexuality), he made it clear that compliance would be strictly enforced. According to correspondence seized by federal prosecutors, the punishment was severe in the extreme. Remember: breaking the rules could result in B.O.S. or T.O.S.

The F.B.I. made discoveries of robberies, arsons, kidnappings, and gruesome murders, which they claim were mostly documented in King Blood's own letters. If this is the case, then the government allowed the shots to be mailed out and lives were taken under the government's watchful eye in hopes of bringing down more Latin Kings along with King Blood.

In June 1994, U.S. Attorney Mary Jo White handed down an 80-count indictment naming King Blood, Queen Zulma and 36 other Latin Kings with crimes ranging from racketeering and drug trafficking to eight murders–including those of seven Kings–all during a six-month period. The government's evidence was 20,000 pages of letters from King Blood and other Latin Kings and Queens. She labeled the Kings a rigid, hierarchical organization that beheaded, burned or beat wayward members, and maimed and killed outsiders. While she admitted that she stated goals of the organization were "very worthy", she also said, "We don't see evidence of the positive projects they talk about in their literature."

Latin Kings

The following events of murders, attempted murders and assaults were alleged by the government:

In 1993, King Blood ordered the murders of Ismael Rios aka "King Jr." and Ronnie Gonzalez aka "King Ronnie" after they refused to follow the orders of, and aligned themselves in competition against, Gabriel aka "King Teardrop"– the then "Supreme Crown of the Five Boroughs." The orders were carried out in January 1994, after Blood deceived Rios and Gonzalez into believing that their dispute with him was at an end. The Kings gunned down Rios, who died and attempted to kill Gonzalez who ran away and escaped unharmed.

In May of 1993, King Blood began to view fellow Latin King Rafael Gonzalez aka "King Mousey" as a threat to his leadership and therefore enlisted friend and subordinate leader, William Cartegena aka "King Lil-Man" to kill him. When Cartegena proved unsuccessful at killing

201

Gonzalez, Blood enlisted 3 other Kings to commit the murder. Those three Kings then drafted five other Kings to carry out the order. The five Kings went to where Gonzalez was supposed to be and then shot and killed Gonzalez's brother-in-law Victor Kirshman. Gonzalez was seriously wounded from shots fired at him but the shooters were not successful in killing him.

Unhappy with Cartegena (King Lil-Man) because of his failure to kill Rafael Gonzalez and also because it was believed that he had stolen money from the King's treasury, King Blood directed Jose Gabriel (King Teardrop) to strip Cartegena of his power and to kill him as well as his girlfriend Margie Carderon aka "Queen Margie" because Blood believed she knew too much about the organization's criminal activities. In a letter King Blood wrote about Lil-Man to King Blaze, "I believe that he deserved to muerte [dead] but I don't want…King Tutie to take this mission, he's the First Crown, and he's doing a great job, so have the security team to take care of this." In September 1993, Cartegena was choked to death by several Kings who thereafter chopped off his head and cut off his hands to remove his Latin King tattoo.

His body was then burned in a bathtub. Lil-Man's head and hands were never found. Later the same month, Kings were selected to murder Queen Margie but failed when they attempted to shoot and kill her. They then decided to burn down the apartment building where she lived. Although Margie escaped the fire, two of her neighbors suffered severe burns.

Pedro Rosario aka "Pete Rock" was an inmate at Rikers Island and considered an enemy of the Latin Kings because he had slashed several of their members who were incarcerated with him. In early February 1994, Blood gave the "green light" to the LKs' at Rikers to assassinate "Pete Rock." Afterwards Pete Rock was severely slashed in an attempt on his life. The Kings leader at Rikers, Jose Cruz aka "King Blaze" issued an order taking the green light off of Rosario. King Blood overruled the order and wrote in a letter that Rosario must be terminated because he had attacked Kings, and whoever tries to challenge the Nation in any kind of way, must feel the "Almighty's wrath." It is unclear whether or not the order was ever actually carried out.

Queen Zulma ordered a B.O.S. on Annette Martinez for merely falsely claiming to be a high-ranking leader of the Latin Queens. For her "dissension," which was considered tantamount to treason, a group of

Queens and Kings, including Zulma carried out the order on May 7, 1994 causing serious injury to Martinez.

Queen Zulma (Top)

In spite of those events occurring, King Blood denied being the cause of lives being lost, and said that the Federal Government was responsible. Explaining that the government just sat back and let people get killed and that if someone wrote him a letter saying, 'Hey bro, this guy messed up, we think he's supposed to get killed,' and the government saw it, they were supposed to arrest that person for conspiracy to commit murder instead of copying the letters and waiting for a response from him (King Blood).

He also stated that nowhere in their bylaws do they talk about T.O.S. or B.O.S. and that those letters could mean anything, including "Tons of Shit." Blood goes on to say that because they (government) knew how many people followed and admired him, they created all the negative publicity to make a big case so he wouldn't get out of prison.

Twenty-four of the 36 charged on the indictment became "sit-down men." They sat down and spoke with the government about their charges and pleaded for lesser sentences in exchange for their testimonies and cooperation. The weakest links of the defendants on the indictment included King Teardrop, King Green Eyes and King Epic–formally the top men.

Jose Melendez aka King Epic, who was clearly one of the most violent members, ordering and carrying out terminations, gave detailed information to prosecutors regarding past criminal activities as well as uncharged activities that he knew were, at the time, still occurring. He admitted to eight murders and he offered to act as an informer.

This cooperation with the government backfired on Epic when they reneged on their deal because (they claimed) he lied repeatedly about his involvement in various crimes. Epic argued in a hearing to appeal the prosecutor's denial of a reduced sentence, "I believe no cooperating witness in the whole Latin Kings case gave them more information than I did," –loosely translated, "I'm the biggest Rat you got!"

In a desperate effort to convince the prosecutors to give him a deal, after denying him one, Epic set up an elaborate plot to frame King Blaze for what would look like an attempt on King Blood's life. Epic knew that charges were brought up on King Blood within the "Family" (Even the Godfather can be charged, if it's perceived that he violated law) for probation and a fine.

King Blaze

So he led authorities to the paperwork and the 8-inch 'shank' (a crude homemade knife), which he himself placed on the recreation room roof in the prison. Blood knew there was never going to be an attempt on his life because he knew his relationship with King Blaze would never call for that.

Another informant, Sammy Serrano, got 33 months instead of 75 years to life, in exchange for his cooperation and served that time in Auburn State Prison in New York.

In October 1996, Queen Zulma received 18 years in prison after pleading guilty to being involved in the assault on Annette Martinez and conspiring to kill Islander Navarez.

While King Blood was on trial in 1996, Latin Kings from all over came to support him, in and out of the courtroom. They were saluting him and chanting "Amor Dey Rey." He received a life sentence in solitary confinement (no human contact ever again) in Florence ADX, super-maximum security prison, a place often referred to as "Hell on Earth" by its inmates.

The voice you will be hearing in your head as you read the next few paragraphs will be that of Roberto L. Santos aka "King M.O." He is the head of the Brooklyn based Latin Kings:

"From 1992 to 1994 bodies dropped all over…[as well, there were] Arsons, robberies, kidnappings, attempted murders, guns, heroin and crack distribution in the Bronx, Brooklyn Staten Island, Manhattan, Buffalo and other places. The F.B.I. and Marshals raided the houses of the Kings all over the metropolitan region and charged us with racketeering, RICO law, murder, kidnappings, armed robberies, assaults and other acts of violence, arson, narcotics, trafficking guns, using the postal service to inform each other of the affairs of the enterprise, and to communicate criminal plans, including T.O.S., traveling in and use of facilities in interstate commerce in aid of the racketeering activities, it goes on and on…"

King M.O.

"We were also charged with and convicted for narcotics trafficking from January 1, 1993 to summer 1994 and the shit goes on and on. I was charged with three bodies and two kilos of heroin. One of the three bodies was broken down to manslaughter. I blew trial with the state and got 44 years. Luis Felipe aka King Blood received 45 years in solitary confinement plus natural life after trial. Michael Mueleon aka "Toast to the King Mike" received 100 years to life in the State, everybody else who kept it real took pleas of 25 to life and 10-15 to life. The Rats are home now, somewhere telling on someone else, but God don't like ugly. This is the price one pays when you're in the game–all bad things come to an end."

King Blood now sits for 23 hours a day in an 8-feet/8-inch by 12-feet/3-inch cell with a concrete desk, stool and bed that are permanently fixed to the floor. His only window to the world is a twelve-inch, black and white television. A Judge Martin said extreme measures were warranted because Mr. Felipe had manipulated his prison privileges in the past, by ordering three murders from his cell.

What is a gang? According to law enforcement/government organizations, gangs are groups of individuals that come together to conspire and commit criminal (or at least) anti-social acts. I think that most private citizens would agree with this definition. But here's another question: Can a group of individuals that initially came together with the apparent intent or purpose of criminal activity change their agenda and direction at any point? Many private citizens believe that with the right leadership and sincere dedication they (the gang) can become positive. But it appears most (not all) in law enforcement and in government do not believe that such a turn-around is possible.

This is the same government that was built on bloody revolutions and civil wars not that many generations ago (not so many that we should forget anyway). Revolutions fought by "gangs" revolting against the unfair, one-sided conditions imposed upon them by the colonization of this country by the British. So in fact, the people who relentlessly pursue and prosecute these street organizations that have been popping up in our ghettos, hoods and barrios since at least the early 1900s, are aware (presumably) of what can happen to the reigning power structure when "gangs" become organizations and organizations become socio-political machines for the common people.

Simply put it spells R-E-V-O-L-U-T-I-O-N. "They" tell you, that you should fear gangs because of the violence that gangs tend to impose on their communities. Of course the gangs that bring destruction and degradation to their respective communities shouldn't be tolerated but what the government really fears is any organization that seeks to govern itself and operate independent of their orchestrated confusion, even if that organization operates within the parameters of their laws–gangs simply can't be tolerated if they begin to show any progressive signs of organization.

Much of the violence that was committed by the LK&QN involved, almost exclusively, its own members or other like organizations. That's not to excuse the Latin Kings' actions but to illustrate that like American revolutionaries of the past, they (LK&QN) had rules and regulations, and like in the history of this government, if "you" opposed this nation or swore your allegiance to this "Nation" and then betrayed that "sworn allegiance" you were punished. Also, as in this government's history (past and present) there were those who were corrupt and they abused power and responsibility as well–to this day the United States seeks to execute traitors.

These days, the LK&QN is struggling to portray itself as a legitimate organization, working to better the conditions of Hispanic Americans and for the most part, trying to live by the rules laid down by their founder. "Amor Dey Rey" means "King Love".

Article by Cavario H.
Researched by Cavario H. and Tiffany Chiles

"Cease chasing the bait, and seek the source." –Cavario H.

MY BROTHER'S KEEPER?

This is the story of three brothers. Their names have been spared simply because they're not significant in this instance. They were related, not by the blood in their veins, but by the blood on the streets. These brothers didn't have the same primary caregivers, but they did share the same birth parents; their mother was pain and their father was desperation.

They had been separated from one another long before they were even conceived, but as fate and social design would have it, they found each other in the midst of adolescence, just as they were approaching adulthood. The "Bros'" were from the same hood so they were constantly running into one another at house parties, playground basketball games and other hood events. Before long they hooked up, and began getting high, hanging-out and running through chicks together, they were like Three the Hard-way. They were inseparable, almost indistinguishable; one was rarely ever seen without the other two.

It was the mid 80s, and almost every car was "kitted-out" with after-market, aerodynamic ground effects, and blasting a boomin' system, bumpin' Big Daddy Kane or Eric B. & Rakim. Getting paid in full was the theme of the era, it's all young brothers and sisters in the hood were concerned with. Young, over-developed and sexually promiscuous Puerto Rican and Black girls (we called them Similac babies) were running wild and fucking everything that moved, as long as it moved on four wheels and could afford dinner and a movie. The boys were big and awkward, bigger than their older brothers in most cases, and most of their fathers were locked-up or cracked-out or dead by now. They had premature growth on their faces and their voices were that of a full-grown man although they were only fifteen and sixteen years old. The girl's asses were bulbous and protruding and resembled perfect spheres of flesh, when squeezed into skin-tight Gloria Vanderbilt jeans. They had attitudes that made the boys hate them enough to slap them down and at the same time want to impress them, even if it was at the risk of their freedom or lives. Nobody cared about basketball contracts or rap contracts– that shit was for nerds. A real bitch wanted a real nigga– a hustlin' nigga.

One of the Bros' had a homeboy in Washington Heights who claimed that he could get them all the cocaine they could handle, and with that, they decided that it was time to get paid.

They hit the block and pumped-up, the product was top notch, La Reyna is what their connection called it–it means the "The Queen". It wasn't long before they had "cheese" lines a block long. The Queen ruled the streets because she sniffed better, cooked quicker and rocked'up bigger and harder than any other blow on the block. The Bros' paper was rolling in, the blunts were rolling up, and the cognac was rolling back. The Bros' were getting higher than a 747, and they went 'up' just as frequently.

Now, it wasn't as though they weren't smoking and drinking together before they were hustlin' together, but now they could afford to do it from sun up til' sun down. They had the best "trees," the best liquids, and oh, yes, the best pussy. Time passed, quickly, and things seemed to happen fast. The first two years flew by, laced with party after party, fast money, fast "hoes," fast cars and expensive clothes.

On occasion, jealousy brought beef, beef brought bodies and of course, the bodies brought the bulls. The narcotics and homicide squads were more than just a little familiar with the Bros'. The Bros' viewed the occasional hit as an option that had to sometimes be exercised. You're only as strong as your most recent conflict indicates.

One night, after one of the big "Baller" basketball games at Rucker Park in Harlem, the three of them were rolling up the Ave', back to back, in black-on-black Mercedes Benzes, when they noticed a van following them; they made a couple of quick moves and then they split up. One hit the Deegan expressway heading south, while the others went across town to their respective "safe houses," probably their mother's or girlfriend's places. Apparently, their pursuers knew about these safe houses because they were waiting for the Bros'. when they arrived at their destinations.

After the obvious confusion, things calmed down. The Bros' were arrested and taken to lower Manhattan. They were each fingerprinted, then taken to another building and put into separate rooms. One was put into a room in which the color could only be described as a "friendly" blue– every inch of it, from floor to ceiling, a soft blue. Meanwhile the other Bro's room was completely red– blood red.

They both sat up for the remainder of the night, preparing, and waiting. They knew that someone would come to ask them a bunch of questions, but hours passed before they even saw another human being. Early the next morning, just before dawn, the doors of their rooms opened, almost simultaneously, and the smell of coffee permeated their small spaces, accompanied by eggs, toast and sausage. Right away, the Bros' knew what was poppin'; but the weed and liquor had worn off, so they didn't hesitate to dig in.

209

The brother in the blue room was cool and his breakfast was hot, his coffee was sweet and decaf and his visitor was polite. He could see the sun shining into his room through a window, with an air conditioner in it, situated high above his head. His server came, served and left.

At the exact same time, the brother in the red room was also being served, but his server stood quietly and stone faced by the door.

When the bro' was just about to place the first fork full of food into his mouth, the whole plate was knocked onto the floor. His server's only words were, "Eat shit!" then, "Blam!" The door slammed shut. Needless to say, the bro' was dazed and confused. Then he noticed the coffee, undisturbed on a small wooden stool, just inside the door. The coffee was strong and he needed something in his system– he was feeling none too well by now.

The 20-ounce cup was filled to capacity with strong, black, unsweetened coffee and plenty of caffeine; and it probably tasted the way one might imagine liquid shit would taste, but the bro' didn't hesitate to drink it.

An hour and a half later, the Bro' in the "friendly" blue room was resting comfortably on the cot his hosts had provided him. Meanwhile, the Bro' in the red room was pacing back and forth, nervously; even if he could sleep he wouldn't be able to do it on the wooden chair which was the only piece of furniture in his room. Besides, he was trying to figure out what the hell was going on. He started to wonder what time it was, but he had no window and they had taken all of his jewelry which included his Franck Mueller timepiece, so he couldn't even guess how long he had been a captive.

A few more hours passed and the Bro' in the blue room got his second visit, and considering the circumstances, he felt better than he had in a long time; he felt he was ready for anything.

The person that entered the room was a fine sister that looked to be about 24 years young, 5'5, 124 pounds and sporting a black pants suit, nicely filled out, with her tight, 34-D, 22, 36 frame– honey was bad.

The brother sat up and immediately started fixing his clothes and wiping his mouth; wearing heavily shaded glasses to shield her eyes from the bright blue walls, the sister walked directly toward him with a big, friendly smile on her face and extended her hand.

In it was a huge peppermint ball; he grabbed the peppermint and slammed it on the concrete floor then popped some of the larger pieces into his mouth. Bro' knew what the deal was, but he was a player and no broad was gonna put him in a 'trick-bag'.

At the same time, bro' in the other room was getting a visit; his visitor was not at all attractive or friendly but he did have a smile on his face. The visitor was a 6'5, 300-pound plus, sunburned, white man, sporting a military haircut and tattoos that said, "Red, White & Blue... the only colors that matter!"

Meanwhile, bro' in the blue room was chillin', as the sister introduced herself, "Hello, my name is Renee," she said. The Bro' extended his hand and gave Renee a smile that said, "You already know my name." At this point neither of the Bros' knew exactly what their respective circumstances were all about. They figured maybe their names had been ringing on the streets a bit more than usual so "the people" wanted to let them know that they knew who the Bros' were. But as the day wore on, the questions became more specific, and then out came the photographs.

When bro' in the red room saw the photos before him, he became visibly agitated– not to mention the 20 ounces of coffee that was working on his brain as well as his bladder.
The pictures were "After Shots"–photos that are taken after someone's been shot– blood, guts, brains and all.

Meanwhile in the blue room, Renee and the Bro' were establishing a rapport, and casually discussing the graphic nature of the deaths depicted in the photos before them.

The questions being asked in both rooms were nearly identical, but Bro' in the red room was a lot less comfortable.

The Bros' denied knowing anything about everything they were questioned about and the hours passed like days, but their hosts weren't totally insensitive; they eventually offered the Bros' a bathroom break.

Bro' in the red room was ready to explode so he didn't hesitate to accept the invitation, although the invite included hand and feet shackles.
Homeboy in the blue room was not only becoming weary of his bright accommodations but he too could use some relief. The doors to their rooms opened almost simultaneously, and when the Bros' saw one another, it was as though they were seeing each other for the first time.

If one had to judge by the look on his face, Bro' from the red room had an expression that might have led one to believe that he was scared nearly to his death. Granted, he hadn't eaten in at least ten hours and he had 20 ounces of liquid caffeine flowing through his bloodstream and attacking his central nervous system and now he was looking at his homey, just 5 feet away from him, and apparently quite rested and obviously well fed. He could see his Bro' making small talk with a beautiful female cop and he also noticed that he wasn't wearing any cuffs or shackles. The red room Bro's eyes widened and his face filled with confusion.

The Bro' from the blue room stared at his comrade and couldn't help but notice that he was sweaty and visibly shaken, this sight upset his entire mood. Now he suddenly had a greater urgency to use the bathroom, and as he stepped into the small restroom and the heavy door slammed behind him, the face of his Bro' was all he could see in his mind. On the other side of the wall, in another small bathroom, the bro' from the red room was trying desperately to use the bathroom, but his shackles were interfering with his movement, and his mind was distracted as he tried to figure out why his partner in crime was apparently so relaxed under the circumstances.

He began to wonder, "Did he make a deal? Did they 'flip' him?" All sorts of shit was racing through his mind. At the same time, Bro' in the other bathroom was buggin', asking himself, "Why did that cat look so scared?" And wondering how great was the possibility of his cohort rollin' over on him. The "people" had them fucked up for sure; they had planted the seeds of dissension, and the tree of deceit was quickly taking root. If the Bros' soil had been truly solid it would have been improbable, if not impossible, that those seeds could sprout.

When they were taken from the bathroom, they were intentionally kept from seeing one another, so that the last images they had of each other would stick in their heads. But the bullshit that was rockin' their minds at this point didn't just start, their foundation was weak from day one– let's go back a few years.

When the Bros' first met, they were always at a party or some other hood function, and they were always smoked-up or drunk. You see, what brought them together were their common interests, the weed, the booze and the broads. The truth be told, these dudes had never been in one another's presence while sober. My street niggas know what I'm talking about. They know about comin' in 3 or 4 o'clock in the morning puffin' a blunt after having had a few 40-ounces of beer, a couple of fifths of liquor and/or several blunts throughout the course of the day.

They know about putting the blunt their puffin' out, and placing the half that's leftover in an ashtray for the next day. Then that following afternoon, when they awake, while their head is still reeling from the previous night; before their feet touch the floor, even before their eyes open, they feel for the ashtray on the night-stand beside their bed and they grab that leftover blunt and smoke it, so they begin their day.

As the day wears on, and that blunt begins to wear off, nothing is what they think it is, or what they want it to be and reality begins to creep in. At that point, frustration drives them to their next blunt or the next beer. As the day wears on and that blunt and beer wear off, someone suggests a liquor run, "Go get that Remy, yo!" They're looking to replenish themselves with cognac courage. They think, all day, that they're keepin' it real, when they lounge on the block and politic with their niggas while hollering at the bitches that stroll through the hood.

Back to present day:

In the instant the Bros' were returned to their respective rooms, reality hits; and in what was probably their first sober moment in years, they realized they didn't really know one another at all.

There was no one in either of the rooms when they were taken back, so they both just sat and stressed a while. Later Bro' in the blue room got another visit, and this time it wasn't "fine-ass" Renee, it was the agent from the red room.

He didn't bring any peppermints; but he was carrying a folder, which he told the Bro' contained a statement against him made by his Bro'.

At first he just stared blankly at this big cat standing in front of him, giving him the worst news he's heard since his dog died. The Bro' knew that the feds ate black males for breakfast, lunch and dinner and the agent glared back at him as though he was next on the menu.

When the Bro' got over the initial shock of the agent's size, he started denouncing his association with the Bro' in the red room, which was exactly what "the people" expected; in fact that is what they were trying to achieve– division. He was not allowed to read what was in the folder but the Bro' in the blue room wasn't about to play himself out-of-pocket by countering the claims that the agent was telling him were being made against him. All he would say was that he and the other Bro' were hangout buddies. The image of his Bro', on the other side of the thick cinder block wall, sweaty, and shook was still fresh in his mind.

Meanwhile in the red room, Renee was making her introduction, and she brought with her a burger and some fries. As the Bro' scoffed it down, she began to tell him (in her own words of course) all that his homey had shared with her. When the Bro' saw Renee, in all her glory, he knew there was a strong possibility of his homey having bragged about the shit they had done in his effort to impress her because that was his thing. He was always the first cat to the bar, buying up all the champagne while wearing every piece of jewelry he owned or could borrow from Jacob the Jeweler, even though the other two Bros' would tell him to keep a lower profile. He was out of control. He was what some call, a "shiny" nigga and every article of clothing that a shiny nigga buys, every car he cops, and every move he makes is solely to impress anyone who will pay attention to him. And as far as he's concerned, everyone is paying attention.

A cat like that doesn't know himself; he has never taken the time to think about what it is he needs or likes for himself.

He has allowed himself to be so influenced by things outside of himself that he has become detached from his true self; he is then making decisions for a "being" who is a stranger–even to himself. He is powerless in his own reality, and he is no-ones' brother.

By the time Renee was done, Bro' in the red room was exhausted from stress. The only comfort he or the other Bro' had was the belief that the third Bro' was still free; and when they were asked about him, Bro' in the red room would only say, "I don't really know that cat, we jus' hang out buddies." Believe it or not, by the time the Bros' lawyers found them, they hadn't done too much damage to their case. The fact that the Bros' didn't spill their guts wasn't so much about them being "stand up" guys, as it was about the fear that they had of having to explain how they could know anything without knowing everything.

They were each sure that the other had sold them out, but when their lawyers received the affidavits on their respective clients, the charges were serious but the name at the bottom of the sworn statements was neither of their clients.

When the lawyers asked the Bros' if they recognized the name, they each claimed they had never heard of the person before that moment. A couple of months passed, and because of the nature of the charges against them they were not given ransoms, (oops!) I mean bails. The Bros' didn't communicate the entire time and when their trial began they were, to their surprise, on the same side of the table.

Their confusion was replaced with horror when they saw the third bro' walk in and sit on the prosecutor's side. It seems that their "Brother" had been stopped in his car earlier that year with a gang'a coke and a dirty pistol, he never told the other Bros' about it, and after three hours in custody, he made a deal.

Now I could go into a play-by-play of the court drama, but by now you've read enough to know it went badly for Bros' 1 and 2, and they did not live happily ever after.

The third Bro' laid low for a few months after the trial, then he was right back in the limelight, "ballin'" and shot "callin'." He's out there now, you probably know him, "He be wit'cha mans and 'em."

"You think it's a game, and yes, it is...just not the one you think." – Cavario H.

Beginning of the end...

We hit the strip club Strokers on the east side of Atlanta. We descended on the joint about 25 strong. We'd gotten our night started in the usual fashion, blunts, bottles, and (for those that partook) beans.

Meech wanted to bring a monsoon to the room but there was about $7,000 in singles in the entire establishment, I knew this because when we walked in, and he made the usual order of "Every bottle in the building," he also requested some singles to begin the evening's rain ritual. It took over twenty minutes for someone to return with the singles and that was after DJ Funky announced to the dancers that they needed to stop dancing (as though there were no other patrons standing there) and bring all of the singles they had to the back immediately.

Nearly a half hour later a very tall, very dark complected security cat came lumbering toward us as we stood in front of Strokers relatively tiny stage, picking targets, and eye-fucking the voluptuous frames of the naked females before us. The big black dude stopped in front of Meech and stood like a statue slightly off balance. He was leaning back a bit because his NBA length arms were operating as backboards for the banded bills that someone had stacked from his palms to his shoulders. He stopped and stooped, then Meech began pulling stacks from the top and tossing them behind him. Each man took an arbitrary amount and passed the rest along. This process continued till the last man's hands were filled, and then all 'hail' broke loose.

For the next fifteen minutes, the chicks on stage battled the barrage of bills being flung at them from every which-a-way. They tried to stay focused on their routines; look sexy, be seductive, throw it back, now make it bounce, left cheek, now the right. But as the money began to accumulate quickly around their feet it became increasingly more difficult for them to kick their legs up and drop suddenly into a crotch-crushing split because the bills were piling up from the floor so rapidly. At the same time, they were being hit, literally, from ever direction with thick wads from way back. Some of the homies were reeling their arms so far behind their heads before releasing a fist full of fast $1's that you could've mistaken them for major league pitchers.

In a matter of minutes the dancers were literally shin deep in dollars. Imagine trying to run through a fresh pile of fall leaves raked together over well over a foot high, and for a length of five or six feet... while you're wearing six inch glass heels.

It was an all out assault, with DJ Funky rockin' and the chicks rippin' and several of the homies rollin'. Then suddenly everything stopped.

"Yo! We need more singles!" The DJ had to halt all the action once again and the girls had to usher the cash to the back again. This time all of the singles were taken from the bar as well.

Once again we waited for the singles to be tallied and recycled back to us. The black giant returned once more and we went at it again.

We ran through their 'pagne and paper in record time, and Meech was over it. "Yo, we outta here, homey. They can't keep up. They only got like $7,000 ones in the whole building." He said in his always ever calm, evenly pitched tone.

So we were off but we took the talent with us. We trooped out to the parking lot and after quickly counting every head, everybody jumped in something with wheels, it didn't matter if you arrived in it, if it was in the caravan and there was an empty seat then it was yours if you wanted it.

Word was left for the ladies that we'd be heading over to the Swissotel (now the JW Marriott) in Buckhead some 30 minutes away (if you obeyed the speed limit, which almost no one in Atlanta does) and that they were invited to join us for more fun and more funds. I needn't tell you that they damn near beat us there.

It was about 3:30 in the morning and not a creature was stirring in Buckhead. But there was a valet line from the hotel's lobby entrance all the way out onto the street and half way up the block. Once again, it was on! Meech covered everybody's parking, over 40 vehicles, then we went upstairs to the Presidential suite to hit Cali' Kush, drink Cuervo, and Hennessy and yes, more champagne. Fifteen strippers rolled in and went straight to the bedroom where Meech gave 'em game, "Now listen here, you ladies are our guests and we appreciate you comin' through and fuckin' wit' us. We here to have fun and y'all here to make some money so here you go." He handed each girl a thousand dollars before continuing, "Y'all can go out there and do y'all thing. You can dance for my boys and they gon' tip you. Anything else is up to you. Ain't nobody gon' touch you if you don't want, ain't nobody gon' disrespect you."

They left the room butt naked and smiling. The music started playing and the dollars started raining from everywhere. There were homies from all over the country in the lavish room; the Lou, New York, Atlanta, Ohio, L.A., Chicago, everywhere! Some of us had just met that day, some of us knew each other already but we were all as one. In the morning we ordered a breakfast that would gag Henry the VIII. Club Kitchen and another swanky hide-away were just blocks away but niggas was too tired to drive so some went to another room, others crashed on the furniture. Later that night, we did it all again, over $50,000 cash dropped in one night. That was Mafia life.

"They were infected before they were informed and so they were destined to die in the dark." –Cavario H.

That Fatal Night...

J-Bo & Big Meech

On the afternoon of November 12, 2003, around 4 o'clock I awoke (barely), my mind was sort of foggy because we hadn't too long come in from another all-nighter... a tripleheader, in fact.

"Yo, homey, come check this out." I was barely awake when Meech ushered me into the garage at 'Club Kitchen'. We'd been on a world wind 21-day tour of the town and by now the days were melded together into to one long, crazy, fun-filled party bonanza. I rubbed my eyes in an attempt to make them focus, as I watched my step through the doorway leading from the kitchen into the garage. When my eyes were finally able to focus I found myself before a beautiful white convertible Ferrari. Its black roof was reclined and its bright blood red leather innards were revealed. The supple lamb was wrapped tightly around every inch of the vehicle's viscera, and two flawlessly white lines raced around the headrests and did donuts on the door panels, then skipped across the steering wheel before jumping onto the dashboard and descending down, by way of the leather laden shifter to the plush ruby mats. It was art on 4 wheels with white five star rims.

218

"Whoa, bro'! This is beautiful. I don't know whether to drive it or fuck it!" We laughed and then he told me the story of how he came to be in possession of the car.

"I got it from an auction, there was this older white dude biddin' against me for it. He was standing there lookin' at me like, 'this saggy pants nigga ain't got no money'. I'm standing there with my braids all fuzzy and shit, bein' cool. He bidded then I bidded, then he bidded again, and I bid one mo' time... he stopped biddin' after that." We were standing side by side admiring the results of this battle, but then Meech turned to face me and said, "Cuz, I'm tellin' you it felt so good to outbid that white man, bruh." Then Meech flashed the most satisfied smile one is ever likely to witness, let alone possess.

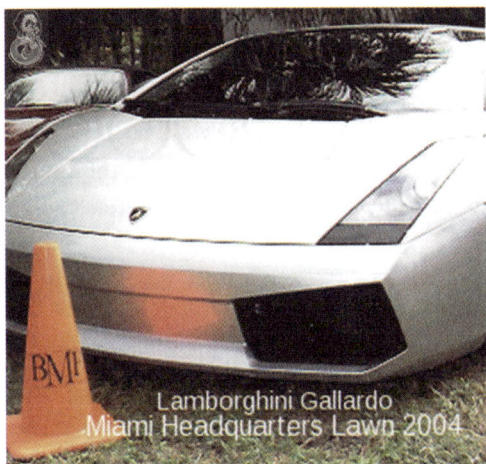

Lamborghini Gallardo
Miami Headquarters Lawn 2004

This is what it was all about, at its essence, Meech's drive was closely related to getting revenge on poverty. He, like many, always knew that he was worth more than the conditions that his fate had placed him in as a child. But others didn't seem to know,

Meech knew that by the way "they" looked at him. So when he arrived, there was no way he wasn't going to show 'em his true form. I realized then and there that all the hyperbolic behavior and over the top fan fare was about the quickest route to his rightful place. For him to have been able to outbid a white American male, the personification of his and his brethren's oppression, it was a moment of absolute freedom. It was the

Part of Big Meech's luxury car collection -Miami 2004

kind of smile that you would have to wrench away from someone. They can't be taken, but they can be replaced.

"What we gon' do t'night?" Meech asked as we stood admiring a few more seconds before turning to walk back into the kitchen. "I think we should chill the fuck out," I said sluggishly. "Niggas is tired, fam'," I continued. "Niggas is lookin' crazy!" I laughed. Just then Bull walked downstairs and made his way toward the pantry. "Look at cuzzo's eyes, they all dark and shit… (laughing harder) niggas is breakin' out and shit." Bull made a low groaning sound behind me. I turned back to Meech and finished, "Fa'real tho', bro'. We've been out for the past 21 days straight. Niggas need some rest." Meech agreed, "You right, homey. Okay, we gon' chill t'night." I was sort of surprised because he usually had an argument for me when I tried to introduce caution. For Meech there was really never anything to worry about. Always calm, and always in control.

"Cool. I gotta go meet T.I. at Patchwerk, then we goin' to Magic City. I'll bring some chicks back with me." Meech nodded his head and we walked in different directions.

Later that night I met Tip at Patchwerk studios. After we chopped it up for few, me, Tip and Tiny headed over to Magic City. It was one of those infamous Wednesday nights.

When we walked in, the first thing I noticed were some extended Family in the center section making a monetary mess. I threw them some recognition and they reciprocated. We made our way to the far wall, where the DJ Booth was. T.I. stood to my right against the wall and talked while Tiny enjoyed a dance.

To my immediate right, stood Anthony Jones also known as "Wolf", he used to be Puff's (Diddy) bodyguard and friend. He stood stoic and stared across the floor intently at the fam' affiliates in the center of the room put it up in the air.

After a few minutes he rushed out the door. A few minutes later, Tip introduced me to DJ Toomp (I call him Atlanta's Kool Herc) and we got into a deep cipher. We left Magic City about an hour or so later and headed to T.I.'s studio, which at the time stood on Walker, a nook in downtown Atlanta.

He played some music and told me of his plans, which he has continued to exceed. I took a photo of him, he has a Glock sitting on an MPC, a most prophetic and honest image.

220

I headed back to Club Kitchen around 4 a.m. but I stopped at the Landmark Diner on Roswell Road. Club Kitchen is right around the corner from it, hidden in a cul-de-sac sort of like the Bat Cave.

As I sat at the counter placing my order, I glanced at the televisions above me. "Two men are dead here in Buckhead Village tonight. There are bullet holes everywhere." As I watched the screens with the police lights flashing and cops milling about looking bewildered, I thought to myself, "I'm glad my family didn't come out, they would'a definitely blamed BMF for some shit like that."

By now BMF had become the big bad wolf on the streets of Atlanta. Anytime anything happened anywhere in the Atlanta area, it was blamed on BMF. On a couple of occasions BMF wasn't even in Atlanta. Once we were all in New York, probably getting thrown out of the W Hotel in Times Square because the whole floor wreaked of pungent Cali bud. I tried to get Meech on the phone to see if anybody wanted something from the diner but when he didn't pick up, I called Ill Pesci and then Bull. No one picked up, and judging by the way dudes were looking when I left hours before, I didn't have a problem believing they were knocked out or laid-up in the crib.

I watched the news until my food came then I hopped back into the Don Diva conversion van and hit the corner off of Habersham. When I pulled up and saw no signs of life at the house I just figured they'd gone around the corner to the other house where Meech had all of his black vehicles parked. We stayed there for a few days a week or so before. When we did, I'd ride with Meech in the black convertible Cadillac XLR or the black Porsche Cayenne Turbo (neither of these cars would be available for months.)

I was on my last leg by now and couldn't drive any further, I just ate my veggie burger and set the bed out in the back of the van, I put on some music and slipped off into a deep sleep.

My phone started ringing about 9am and when I saw the people, like my homey Big D from Queens calling at that hour, I knew something had happened and I had a strong guess what it was.

"Yo, you a'ight out there? I heard what happened last night." I was still groggy but the rush of blood to my head woke me up instantly. "Yeah, I'm good, homey. What'chu heard?" I wanted verification of what I already knew. "Ya boys got into with that kid's man. I heard him and his man didn't make it tho'."

221

I dropped my head into my hand, "Damn!"

After assuring my comrade that I was good, I hung up and called J-Bo who wasn't too long off the road to St. Louis. He'd hung with us for a few days and was preparing to leave the house earlier that evening. I was surprised he picked up after the 9-hour drive, but he did.

"Yo, I think you need to head back here, bruh. There was a problem last night." J-Bo was still ride weary, "Yo, word? What happened?"

I gave him the abridged version as I understood it at that point. "Damn, I need to come back there, huh?" J-Bo responded rhetorically.

"It looks like it. Call the rapper, you know he was wit' Zippo."

"A'ight, cuz."

When J-Bo hung up, I tried the same numbers except for "Dude's". I didn't know then that he'd been arrested for double homicide but I figured he wouldn't be answering any phones either.

A few minutes later a car pulls up and it's a younger homey, nerdy kind'a kid but loved and respected in the Family. "Yo, help me clean this house up." As we walked into the house he explained what had happened –the gist of it anyway. "They was at Chaos and the kid came in buggin'. It calmed down but he came back so the club put him out. When 'Dude' and 'em came out he started bussin'. 'Dude' got hit in the ass and Bull caught one in the foot." I stopped him and asked if they were alright. "Yeah, they went to the hospital and when they found out who 'Dude' was, they kept him."

I finally spoke to Bleu early that afternoon. He reiterated the story I'd heard from the little homey and then asked, "What should I do, homey?" I said, "Lay low and see what you hear, what you see but don't be seen or heard. You need to find out what's goin' on. They definitely did a graphite test on him so they know he didn't kill nobody. But they arrested him anyway. Chill on the goin' out and keep your ear to the ground."

I was scheduled to leave for New York that same day for the 1st official Don Diva party at MAARS 2112 in Times Square.

The Family was to be my surprise honored guests. But plans had changed drastically.

Oddly, Meech and I had spoken one morning while chilling on the staircase in Club Kitchen. He told me that his wife had called and told him that his son Little Meech woke up crying for him in the middle of the night.

"He never did that before, homey." I said simply, "Go home, bro'. These streets ain't goin' nowhere, these young brothers will be alright without you for a few days." Meech said he would think about it. As I hit the road heading for New York that afternoon, I thought about the past three weeks and the past 24 hours and I knew that wherever Meech was at that moment, he was thinking about it.

Big Meech circa 2013

Come home soon, Family: Ill Pesci, J-Bo, & "Big Blunt". Shit ain't the same without y'all. Welcome Home, Rico.

"The difference between age and experience is a matter of time." –
Cavario H.

223

Out of Print

Contrary to what many on the streets today believe, there was once a 'code of ethics' –a 'manner of operation' within the game of drug dealing aka "hustlin'." It was an unwritten, often implied by action rather than by words, "book" of rules and regulations. But in the years subsequent to the '70s, the book was stolen, lost, hidden or simply thrown away, and in thinking back, that event seemed to correlate with the inception of nerds into the game.

I mean the guys who came from straight families and middle-American-minded homes and then (once cheap crack made a connect out of everybody) decided that selling drugs and making money at the risk of life and limb would be fun. At the inevitable point when the nerds came face-to-face with the worst-case scenarios the life had to offer, they decided since they were never of the "thing" anyway, they need not adhere to its doctrine. That's when the book got completely defiled.

The nerds were/are the dudes that sat quietly during the reign of the stand-up hustler, or stone cold killer or grand-gangster (I call this group the "Pros") and studied his every mood and move. The nerds are natural studiers, mimics if you will, they watched Pros pop bottles, scoop broads and lean like Gs' while driving elegant automobiles and they said to themselves, "I want to be like that cat." But the streets are a cold and uncaring place for one to make one's living and before long, death comes of it.

After while the nerds came to realize that they could never be part of the glorious game so they sought other avenues, and while the nerds were developing these avenues, the Pros were burning-out, dying off and going to prison. The world was changing around the pros but too many (not all, just some) did not evolve with the changes. Technology and new rules were implemented and not long afterwards the pro was all but extinct. His old ways did not work with the new world, the world where information moved at the speed of light.

Before the pro knew it, the profit had been taken out of everything he touched but when one becomes accustomed to living a certain way, it's difficult to find change – "bend with the wind or break" they say–and many pros could not bend. Meanwhile, the nerds were building empires and developing industries, they began to command wealth and assumed the swagger the pros once possessed. They had found new games to play, some even made-up games of their own and quickly applied all that they had studied.

Now this is where human nature, fate and divine-design come together to create the greatest drama the underworld has ever known; the nerds (not all, just some) began to assume the roles of the pros as the pros sat by (some in prison, some on the street) and watched their women, clothes and cash change masters. Now, the nerds pop bottles and splash the Ave with a dash of gangster's class and Gs' just freeze in bewilderment, wondering where it all went.

The pros survived so long at the top of the food chain because they were resourceful, and although they had lost their advantage, they hadn't lost their gift for sighting a come-up. The pros on the street began to communicate with the pros in the joints and explain to them the flip-flop that had gone down. Time and motive are a deadly combination when set before a street-nigga– the pros in the joint hollered back to the pros on the bricks and instructed them to keep them up on every mover that moved and every shaker that shook. The '80s and then the '90s shot by and by the beginning of the 21st century some ol' pros were returning to the streets, their minds were set on 'get-back'.

"We gon' get-back our broads, our bottles and most importantly our blocks"–that didn't happen.

Twenty years is a long time to be out of the loop and the rate of revolutions-per-minute was staggering to the average ol' pro. He couldn't catch-up no matter what type of pressure or play he applied. "You can't rob these new-niggas' stashes, 'cause they keep their paper in the bank... you can't kidnap'em 'cause they believe in calling the police." The ol' pro began to realize that he was the master of a game that no longer existed.

The nerds, despite their successes, were still unfulfilled. They began to feel that they had to prove to the ol' pros as well as to the people they had convinced that the walk and talk was their own, that they really were what they appeared to be.

They opened their doors to the ol' pros and in a final effort to get the last pieces to the puzzle the nerds entered into illegal enterprise with the pros' and for a short time it seemed the game was back!

Like most things, it was good until it went bad... when the government began snatching bodies off of the street in the mid-nineties, the nerds reverted back to their true natures, "I'm not the one that you want... this

225

isn't really my life... I wasn't raised this way... I made a mistake and I want another chance".

The pros found themselves locked up or locked out once again.

You see, the nerds saw only the exterior of the game, they saw only the flash and pizzazz of it– the intricate, unspoken foundation could not be observed from their standpoint, off in the corner, shrouded in shadow. They never knew what made it all work, so when they inherited the board, the game lost it's soul and purpose, it became simply something to do.

The "book" was awash with tears of regret and the blood of sacrifice... sacrifice of friends, family and camaraderie. Nerds had undone in the space of 10 to 12 years what it took 80-plus-years to establish.

Don't get me wrong, there were violators before the '80s but for the most part the 'thing' withstood. But after the inception of the new breed, what I call "nerd-kind", more commonly known as "new jack hustlers", the rules went out of the window, the streets went out of control and the book itself went... Out of Print.

The Birth, Life and Death of a Recidivist: A short essay

This piece is based on observations that I wrote notes on while in an adult detention center (City Jail) in Georgia.

Amazingly enough I had never spent any significant time in a cell despite my many arrests: from earliest adolescence, through to my first few years of adulthood. I don't attribute this fact to anything other than good people who happened to be cops, an occasional good lawyer and most often plain ol' good fortune.

Up until this time, the longest I had been held in custody was for a weekend in a Bronx precinct. The only lesson that I walked away with from that particular experience was how to make a McDonald's hamburger last 6 hours.

The time (and I use the term "time" loosely, it was actually 18 days) that I spent in Cobb County's Adult Detention Center afforded me a lifetime of information. I was there just long enough to know that I never wanted to go to jail again, my head simply wasn't that hard– I got it the first time!

Recidivism: a tendency to relapse into a previous condition, especially criminal behavior.

I found myself in the county lock up for a second time because the bail bondsman, after nearly a year, decided he no longer wanted to be responsible for my bail of $33,000, and he wasn't required to return my $5000 bond fee– nor did he offer to.

So after having a good meal, and a good night's sleep in my own bed, I put on the most comfortable drawstring linen slacks I had and I put on a slipover Italian silk shirt, and a pair of Ferragamo slip-on loafers (the point is– no strings or belts equals a little dignity in the holding pen) and then I went and met with the bondsman's investigator who said he "only needed to verify some information" –after a year? Yeah, sure buddy!

After the initial arrest a year before, I sat for 3 or 4 days, which in Cobb County (where I've heard cops from other counties say *they* were hesitant to drive through) is a relatively quick departure from their swift and unrelenting grasp. They believe in keeping their beds filled.

Why was I there in the first place? Well let's just say that in C.O.B.B. you can "Count On Being Busted" for something if you're there long enough... I will say that it wasn't violence related.

What made the 18 days and nights that I spent there so important for me to write about it was not so much what I personally experienced there but what experiences were shared with me while I was there and the lessons that I got from them.

That is what I'm going to share with you now.

September 22, 1999/ 1:05am

I've been in here since Wednesday, September 16 and I have watched, listened to and spoken with just about every man in here–some young and some old.

I've heard some unsettling stories as to how many of them came to be in this giant room full of bunk beds. The place is like a concrete and glass fish bowl for people. There's a room just like it directly across from us and apparently one on either side as well. The guard's tower is dead center of us all and they can see everything that any of us do, and I do mean everything, the lights never go off, thus I won't be straining my eyes to write this diary. (Smile)

Some of the stories that I've been told are so far-fetched that I'm hard pressed to believe them. I've reached a point (some time ago) in my personal evolution where I recognize every situation as a lesson, even if I don't recognize what it is that I'm supposed to be learning. I accept that every experience I survive is a gift from which I grow–so as much as I speak, I listen. Less even.

Sometimes I scan my surroundings, as though I'm going to see something that no one else can (or will.) At "lockdown" I lie quietly on the two mats I have on the floor (courtesy of the County) and I look at the faces around me, black and white, from boys to men, and I sometime catch them staring blankly into the high (about 3 stories) ceiling. Then I think to myself, "What are they thinking about?"

One might guess the most obvious at first– they're thinking about going home. But when I think back to the conversations that I've had with some of them I don't really recollect anyone mentioning going home more than once in most cases, and at most twice in others.

As I watch their eyes, I think I know what they're doing… I think they're going back in time trying to imagine what their lives would be like if they had made different decisions, not just the one that led them here–now, but all of the decisions before that led to this moment in their lives.

228

The decisions that led them to points in their existences that left them with less, and lesser still, favorable options from which to choose. I feel most believe that their past decisions have gotten them to a place where no good decisions are available. They lay there on the floor or in the bunk with their forearm resting across their foreheads and they barely blink. They seem to be more concerned about being out, than they are about getting out. Not knowing what poor or "bad" decision they'll make next or how long it will be before they end up in a situation like this again.

They are worried and frustrated and scared and angry.

Worried about what this system will do to them–Frustrated because they allowed themselves to be subject to it–Scared that they can't do anything to prevent themselves from falling victim to it again–Angry they've been idled long enough to think about it all.

But in spite of these circumstances everyone has been getting along pretty well, supporting one another and basically respecting each other's space (most of the time).

People who would probably not even acknowledge one another on the street are sitting down elbow-to-elbow, eating together and confiding in each other. They are seeking understanding and, for the most part, finding it.

I guess when men find themselves in a common struggle, prejudice and disregard succumbs to the inherent need for brotherhood.

In this small makeshift community there's little room for judgment. At some point everyone will have turned to someone and said, "Do you need?" or "Can I use?"

It's a humbling observation to experience.

My imagination runs and I think about the possibilities, "What if we left this place and remembered the things we had learned about ourselves and the different types of men around us?"

What if we applied the theory of "Maybe, although he's older or wealthy or Latino or white or even a 'junkie', maybe he knows what it feels like to be worried, frustrated, scared and angry."

No one likes to feel alone, yet we all, at some point, feel so.

At some point in time we have all experienced the feeling of disconnection from everything and everyone. We think there's no one who could possibly understand us. This is probably the most frustrating and deeply frightening thing a human being can go through. I imagine the frustration and fear that results from, what I call lonely to the core, can make a man so angry that he might want to destroy himself from the inside out. I also imagine an overwhelming sense of no self-worth and futility in being. I guess what I'm describing is death walking and willing to kill anything or anyone in its path.

But I'm willing to bet that when, through circumstances, individuals in this state are idle long enough to recognize they are really not alone at all, that in fact they're one of an unimaginable number of human beings in a common struggle, they then wish to let death rest and life live.

Without one another, we are without *Grace of Divinity*, we must accept that we are all just b.i.t.s. & p.i.e.c.e.s. (Brothers In The Struggle & People In Every Circumstance Except Safety)

September 24, 1999/ 1:22am

I'm not really sleepy right now and it's probably because I slept for a few hours this afternoon. There's an older guy that sleeps on a mat on the floor near the wall about 3 feet away from me. He's 52 years of age but in speaking to him I'm reminded more of a younger man.

He spoke about his mother earlier; how beautiful she is and how youthful and caring she is. His eyes filled with pride as he told me how well she could dress and cook and it isn't difficult to tell that he draws his strength and sense of self-worth as well as his security from this wonderful woman. It's as though he were an infant, so dependent upon his mom.

Our conversation was initiated when I asked him what he was doing in here (aside from the obvious) and he responded with the innocence of a child and said, "Learning from my mistakes."

I sat quietly and listened to him speak about his children, especially his 11-years-young daughter whom he adores.

He talked about how he's going to "get it together" when he gets out "this time." He said, "I ain't comin' back here no more," after every few sentences.

When I first looked at him and felt compelled to ask him what he was in there for, I thought that I was supposed to talk to him, you know, deliver some information to him. But not long after we began to speak did I realize that I was supposed to listen and to acknowledge him.

After understanding that, I sat quietly and listened while he assessed the wealth in his life. We spoke for at least an hour before he decided to call it a night, at which point I immediately began to write and try to put the moment into perspective.

I've come into contact with so many people and so much information since I've been here that I've had to be very still to find and focus on the lesson in this experience. As I write, I begin to think I had better keep my mind's eye open and concentrated on the overall situation and not just where I am and when it will end. I don't want to lull myself into the thinking that I'm surrounded by trees and they're blocking my view of the path, only to later realize it was the forest I was being shown in the first place.

We all seem to have the same idea that our being in this place is intended to teach us something about ourselves, and I'm thinking that this thinking is correct. But I suspect that we know but don't want to acknowledge what we know, which is—we did something or neglected to do something at some point, and that is where the form of the lesson was determined— the lessons necessary for us to achieve total realization and acceptance of self.

I believe that is the ultimate reason for being. Too often we exercise the power of free will or choice, destructively. As a result, the form of our lessons tends to be the most time consuming and difficult.

September 28, 1999/12:25am

I've just laid down for the night and a thought flashed in my head, I am thinking back to a conversation that I overheard earlier this afternoon, it was between a brotha' 43 years of age and another brotha' approximately 27-years-young; the younger bro' had just returned from court and he said that he was offered a 20-year sentence on which he would have to do 10 years before he could even be considered for release.

He didn't kill anyone or commit armed robbery, his situation involved drugs –not tons, not even pounds but grams. Grams of cooked cocaine, which he "assisted" in the sale of, had put him in the position to have to accept 10 years in prison or risk being sentenced to life in the event that he took it to trial and a jury pronounced him guilty.

The older brotha' was sharing a story about a similar experience he had when he was younger. He too was threatened with life incarceration if he didn't accept the state's offer of "20, do 10" but he decided not to accept it. He sat for a few months, preparing to fight for his life. He was brought

231

back to court and he was given another offer: 10 do 5. He refused this offer as well.

He went back to his cell and waited a couple of months more.

When he was brought back to court the third time, the state made him an offer of take 5 do 1, he did not hesitate to refuse and was immediately returned to his cell.

After sitting for two more months he was offered the "deal": sign an admission of guilt and he would be released immediately with "time served" (he had sat for 7 months).

Its amazing how negotiable justice is and how powerful patience can be. Anyway, the young bro' listened to the story but when it was done, he was still apprehensive about testing the patience of the court. The young brotha' was at a major impasse, a "live or life" situation. I thought to myself how unprepared and unconditioned he was for making such decisions. I also thought that to be incarcerated and separated from one's family, one's support base, must compound the dilemma tremendously. I wondered what life experience could possibly ready one's mind and spirit for a decision like this? How much education was necessary to make an "educated" decision in an instance such as this one?
Life is a series of decisions and the quality of one's existence is determined by how well he makes them.

Now the original thought that prompted me to pen was as an individual considers selling narcotics (by the way, my being here has nothing to do with drugs either), he is making a major life altering decision– I mean real deal life/death stuff. Taking into account that the majority of the people making that decision for the first time are in the age range of 13, 14, 15, 16 and 17-years-young, I would say it's safe to assume they are not thinking of that decision [to sell drugs] as a major, life altering decision. The care and consideration that should be involved are just not present.

As I thought further, I figured as time passes and the involvement becomes deeper, the decisions become more serious with more regularity and even though they are more life affecting, I still doubt they are sufficient grounding to prepare one for the decision this young man was faced with– between death and dying, life and living.

If you find it difficult to determine the differences between these things, then you will probably find yourself choosing among them at some point in time.

Do you think you're ready?

October 3, 1999/1:33pm

I've been in this room referred to as a "Pod" for nearly 18 full cycles, I have come into contact with so many different types of people that I'm experiencing information overload. There's so much I need to put on paper but I don't know where to start.

When I first began these writings I mentioned coming into contact with and speaking to men of all ages, backgrounds and lifestyles. I wrote about the common struggle that they now share under their present circumstances but as I have continued to interact with them I have begun to see other commonalities among them.

They all seem to sense that there is something "wrong" and they all seem to believe the "wrong" exists outside of themselves, out of their control.

I've heard many stories of poor decision-making and irresponsible behavior and they (mostly) end with the same line; "I'm gon' stop lettin'… (drugs and or alcohol, women or friends) make me do this, that or the other, because I ain't comin' back here again!"

It seems they're all tossing their fates to the wind.

Don't misunderstand me, I don't believe any one of us is beyond making a poor decision but we are all (most of us anyway) equally capable of learning from our falls, but in order to do so I believe that we must first accept complete, total and full responsibility for them.

For instance one man (white male, approximately 36 years of age) told me about the particular circumstances that led to his being here now.

"Jimbo" basically told me that a situation that led to a situation led to his being here.

Jim's girlfriend is a "crack smoker" (his words) and to support her habit she got involved with a pimp and she began to prostitute herself. Naturally, she and Jim went through a lot of confrontation and conflict about this decision, which eventually led to her running away from Jim.

She got deeper involved with the pimp and became pregnant.
When the baby was born, Jim was there, at the hospital, at her side.
When the doctors became aware of the cocaine addiction, they immediately contacted Child Welfare authorities and then informed the parents–which they understood Jim to be the father because he had signed

233

the birth certificate–that they shouldn't try to take the baby until Child Welfare representatives arrived and got a chance to speak to them.

Jim immediately took command of the situation and told his girlfriend to get dressed as he wrapped the child up so they could leave.

Subsequently the police were called and Jim was arrested for kidnapping and child endangerment.

While he was in jail on this charge, he had an associate take his truck and the money that he had on him. During the time it took him to get out, his associate had given his money ($300 dollars) to another guy for a cable T.V. component that he told Jim was worth $600 dollars.

When Jim got out on bail on the kidnapping and endangerment charges, he immediately proceeded to look for his girlfriend whom he found with the pimp.

He tried to persuade her to leave with him but she refused, they got into an argument and then a fight. The police were called and when they checked Jim's truck they found the cable T.V. component and somehow discovered it was stolen.

Apparently Jim's associate hadn't spent the $300 the way he claimed he had.

Jim was promptly re-arrested for grand larceny because the component was worth over $500 dollars (at least his associate didn't lie about that).

Jim was now facing 20 years on Georgia's stripe suit wearing, ball and chain dragging, big hammer swinging, prison gang, because grand larceny is a felony and Jim is a repeat offender.

I don't know what eventually happened to Jimbo because I got the hell outta there the next day when somebody finally put up $500,000 in property for the $6,000 in cash that I was waving around.

I do remember something else that Jimbo said though...
"I'm here for the here and after and if you ain't here after what I'm here after, you'll be here after I'm gone."

Amen Jimbo... A-men!

234